EXPLORING INNER SPACE

Exploring Inner Space

Scientists and Religious Experience

by

DAVID HAY

MOWBRAY
LONDON & OXFORD

Copyright © David Hay, 1982, 1987

This revised edition published in 1987
by A. R. Mowbray & Co. Ltd.,
Saint Thomas House, Becket Street, Oxford, OX1 1SJ

First published 1982
by Penguin Books Ltd,
Harmondsworth, Middlesex.

Typeset by Hi Tech Typesetters Ltd, Oxford
Printed and bound in Great Britain
by Billing & Sons Limited, Worcester.

British Library Cataloguing in Publication Data

Hay, David, 1935–
    Exploring inner space: scientists and
    religious experience.——Rev. ed.
    1. Experience (Religion)
    I. Title
    291.4'2   BL53

ISBN 0–26–467120–1

In Memory of Sir Alister Hardy, F.R.S.

Contents

Preface to the Second Edition

This book is about a puzzle.

On the one hand, stretching as far back as it is possible to find written records, the human species has left widespread evidence of its awareness of a sacred presence in the world. Several archaeologists go further: they say there are material remains indicating that the same awareness extended deep into palaeolithic times.

In Europe until recently, it was commonly assumed that this presence still pervaded reality. I can remember as a boy at school reading some passing remarks by the Victorian savant John Ruskin.[1] He was commenting on the unattractiveness of the hidden parts of nature compared with what is open to view – untidy tangles of roots and squirming animals perhaps, as opposed to the more orderly and pleasing display of life above ground. Since God didn't intend man to gaze on subterranean things, thought Ruskin, there was no necessity to make them attractive. Within Western culture, this view of the creator as a kind of gardener, intimately concerned with the aesthetic sensibilities of his creation, was interwoven with a belief that the sacred gardener's presence could be directly experienced by those who had the grace and sensitivity to become aware of it.

On the other hand, although I too was brought up within the same tradition, even as a schoolboy I found such notions laughably eccentric. No doubt this was partly due to the fact that, as a science specialist, I was in touch with modern European scepticism. For those who follow that line of reasoning, the supposition that people have been in contact with a sacred presence is more than mere eccentricity, it is downright mistaken, and disappears as they become emancipated from their ignorance. However, once we grant that it *is* a mistake, it must rank as one of the most monumental blunders of all time, having in all probability been with us for over 95 per cent of human history and forming a central assumption of every great civilization. Such errors call for explanation.

Personally, I'm now inclined to doubt the 'monumental error' theory. My purpose is therefore to present in a readable way the story of how some of our recent forebears became convinced of this view, and why scientific research over the past few years is making their opinions seem less certain.

Part One, 'Religion Becomes a Puzzle', opens with a chapter illustrating the pervasiveness of religion in time and space. I go on to discuss some brilliant and original forerunners of contemporary science who criticized and explained away not only religion but, more especially, religious experience.* In parallel with the growing criticism, there was a massive loss of confidence in the European religious institutions.

Chapters Five, Six and Seven form Part Two, in which I explain what I mean by the experiential dimension of religion (for this second edition, I have written a new chapter on how our understanding of the term has been influenced by the religious history of New England). I note that behind a crumbling institutional facade there may continue to lie the hidden realm of personal religious experience.

Part Three, 'Modern Explorations', tries to answer that question. After an admirable start under the leadership of the New England psychologists William James, G. Stanley Hall and E. D. Starbuck at the turn of the century, the scientific study of religious experience took on a fresh lease of life in the mid and late 1960s. Research over the last fifteen years or so has revealed that such experience is much more widespread in

* It could be argued that I make too much of the opinions of great historical figures like Marx and Freud. Several of their ideas, it may be said, have been greatly modified or discarded. But it is through the vigour and novelty of their views as first expressed that the mood of society changed and religion steadily became less plausible to many people. It is this mood that I want to illustrate. In any case, the fate of ideas is never uniform; while scholars are aware that revisions have been made, there are always those who object to revisionism.

British and North American populations than was thought likely. Even in the five years since the first edition of this book was published, there has been a considerable increase in information, which I have summarized in the revized version of Part Three. We now know quite a lot about the content of these experiences, how people make sense of them, and what their social and personal consequences are. I believe that the sort of new material which is presented here shows the inadequacies of some earlier theories of religious experience, and I discuss an alternative explanation.

No doubt the latest flowering of research is in part due to the development of sophisticated methods of investigating intimate experience. But I suspect that one of the latent reasons for curiosity is the growth of popular interest in the possibility of justifying religious belief on experiential grounds. That would certainly be an issue for many of the new religious movements springing up in the industrial West. I doubt if the findings reported in this book, taken in isolation, could be used to 'prove' the correctness of religious interpretations of reality. On the other hand, I do think they press upon us the need to be more flexible when we try to understand people's awareness of the sacred, and more sceptical of the many attempts to explain it away.

In 1969 the late Sir Alister Hardy, formerly professor of zoology and comparative anatomy at Oxford University, began to advocate the use of modern social surveying techniques to explore the nature and frequency of reports of religious experience in Great Britain. I had independently become interested in the same possibility and this led me to cooperate in the work of the Religious Experience Research Unit which Sir Alister set up in Manchester College, Oxford (now renamed the Alister Hardy Research Centre).

I owe a considerable debt of gratitude both to him and to his successor as director, Edward Robinson. Through their agency I was able to employ, as my research assistant, Ann Morisy, an invaluable and delightful co-worker. The result of our many heated debates is that Ann's ideas appear in the book inextricably mixed up with my own. Since taking over as director of AHRC I have had the privilege of sharing ideas with my research colleagues there, especially Geoffrey Ahern, Michael Jackson and David Lewis.

While on the subject of research, I must also express my thanks to Andy Greeley, Bill McCready and Norman Bradburn who, in the late 70s, were colleagues at the National Opinion Research Center at the University of Chicago. They gave generous hospitality, advice and permission to use some of their research instruments. More recently I also have much cause for gratitude to George Gallup Jr. and Gordon Heald of the Gallup Organisation. Ted Wragg, Jim Eggleston and Philip Gammage, successively in charge of my department at Nottingham University, have been generous with encouragement and facilities.

In writing a book of this kind, which strays across many academic boundaries, I have inevitably leaned on the expertise of colleagues. My good friend Denis Rice of Leicester University read the whole text and suggested many improvements and alterations. The following people read and gave me advice on one or more chapters: Alan Aldridge, Eileen Barker, Chris Binns, Bernard Brady, Douglas Davies, Peter Davies, Jimmy Dunn, Alan Gauld, Bob Gosling, John Guest, Bernard Hamilton, Mike King, Richard King, Ken Levine, Miller Mair, Peter Moore, David Morton, Brian Quinn, Jill Robson, John Shotter, Douglas Tallack, Michael Watts and Glyn Yeoman. All remaining mistakes or inaccuracies are of course my responsibility.

My final thanks go to Hilda Ratcliffe for typing the original manuscript so beautifully, to May Orton for preparing the typescript for the new edition and to my wife Jane for her understanding and affection while this book was being hatched in a closed room by her hermit husband.

DAVID HAY
Alister Hardy Research Centre
Manchester College, Oxford, 1987

Part One

Religion Becomes a Puzzle

1

The Religious Animal

'In the beginning all is religious.'

ÉMILE DURKHEIM[1]

Recognitions

An ordinary man, standing by the coast, saw something strange and difficult to describe: 'a mountain range or small mountain floating in the midst of the water, and moving here and there without touching the shore'.

In this way the Aztec chronicler Tezozomoc[2] recalls the extraordinary moment when one of his people first saw the ships of Cortes anchored off the Mexican coast in 1519. Two cultures, so far as we know created by peoples utterly isolated throughout history and in all probability since palaeolithic times,[3] were about to confront each other. Hardly less strange, you may think, than a meeting between modern man and a deputation from outer space.

But the biological necessities of the species are such that, even though they were total strangers, the two groups would be able to recognize in each other the kind of behaviour necessary for human beings to survive. The Spaniards, after all, had to eat, and there must have been a moment of relief amidst the anxiety of the Indians when they saw some people climbing down from the ships (which they now called 'towers', perhaps because it was becoming more possible to make judgements of scale), getting into a small boat and starting to fish, some with lines, others with a net. The emperor Moctezuma's emissary, who saw them later, though noting their unnaturally pale skin, describes the colours of their jackets casually enough, comparing them at times unfavourably with the local fashion.

3

On their heads, some of them wore large round hats 'like small *comales* (flat dishes for baking tortillas) which must have been sunshades'.[4] So there were categories of ordinary experience, such as ways of keeping your head out of the sun, for which their languages had more or less equivalent symbols. Though they had never seen horses, the Indians were able to make a usable analogy, describing them as a species of huge deer, but without horns. They could even give a vivid description of something as totally novel as cannon fire: 'A thing like a ball of stone comes out of its entrails: it comes out shooting sparks and raining fire. The smoke that comes out with it has a pestilent odour, like that of rotten mud.'[5]

But the two peoples were not out of touch even in matters apparently of the highest level of abstraction, such as religion. Of course the differences between Aztec and Spanish religion were obvious. Bernal Diaz, who served as a soldier in the conquest of Mexico, describes with military directness his horror at what he saw in the Aztec capital of Tenochtitlan.[6] Standing with Cortes on the heights of the main temple in the city, he was shown the sights by Moctezuma: dreadful shrines with walls and floors so caked with blood from the endless round of human sacrifice that they were black and stinking; priests, their waist-long hair tangled and clotted with blood from their gory duties. Later, when he saw the building where the bodies of victims were butchered and cooked for ritual cannibalism, he knew he was visiting Hell.

Some have said that Spanish and Aztec religion were mutually recognizable in their common bloodthirstiness (it was only a generation since Torquemada had presided over the Spanish Inquisition). This is an easy jibe. Cortes was able to draw other, more substantial comparisons, which would make sense to a European, in his second dispatch to the King of Spain:

> This great city contains many mosques, or houses for idols, situated in the different precincts. The principal ones house the priests of the religious orders. All these priests dress in black and never cut or comb their hair from the time they enter the religious order to the time they leave it. The sons of all the principal families are

placed in these religious orders at the age of seven or eight years and remain till they are ready for marriage . . . The masonry inside the chapels where they keep their idols are carved with figures and the woodwork is all wrought with designs of monsters and other shapes.

Cortes agreed with Diaz – the Aztec religion was the worship of devils:

> I overturned the idols in which these people believed the most and rolled them down the stairs. Then I had those chapels cleansed, for they were full of blood from the sacrifices; and I set up images of Our Lady and other saints in them. This disturbed Montezuma and the natives a good deal, and they told me not to do it. They said that if it became known, the people would rise against me, as they believed that these idols gave them all their temporal goods.[7]

However repellent their rituals, the Aztecs shared with the Spaniards a belief in their dependence on a supernatural power or powers. Cortes knew where to set up the images of the saints.

There have been many theories which attempt to explain the bloodiness of the Aztec religion. Laurette Séjourné[8] saw it as a more or less cynical corruption of the earlier Toltec religion, manipulated to suit the military ambitions of the Aztecs. She claims that it was in their search for victims for the gods that they did indeed subdue an empire in Mesoamerica. More recently, Michael Harner[9] has interpreted the ritual cannibalism of the Aztecs as a mechanism for ensuring that there was a supply of animal protein in their diets. Central America was short of animal species suitable for domestication. Therefore human meat was the only large-scale source.

Whatever the reason, Séjourné speaks of the underlying religious philosophy as being more humane. The central figure was Quetzalcoatl, whose image is to be found everywhere in Aztec artefacts. It was believed that he had created men and had taught them agriculture, the crafts and science. His ministers were required to be 'virtuous, humble and peace loving, and considerate, and prudent, and not frivolous but grave and austere, and jealous of custom and loving and merciful and compassionate and a friend of all'.[10]

It was these same men who, in Tenochtitlan, presided over the torture and sacrifice of vast numbers of their wretched fellow humans. In Séjourné's view, this discrepancy precipitated a social crisis, attended by reports of supernatural phenomena of a type not unknown in European history. It so happened that in Aztec lore there were predictions of a second coming of Quetzalcoatl, from the east, at about the time of the Spanish arrival. During the ten years prior to that, there had been a gloomy procession of signs and omens: fiery signals in the sky; a strange bird caught by fishermen with a mirror on its head in which Moctezuma saw a frightening vision of the future; monstrous deformed beings in the streets of the capital. When Cortes landed, Moctezuma was terrified, certain that it was Quetzalcoatl. The Franciscan Bernardino de Sahagún reports Moctezuma's feelings: 'This is what he felt in his heart: He has appeared! He will come here, to the place of his throne and canopy, for that is what he promised when he departed!'[11]

In the material sense at least, Moctezuma's worst fears were realized. With a ferocity that betrayed the deeper traditions of their own religion,[12] the Spaniards utterly destroyed the Aztec civilization. Later, an Aztec poet expressed his grief in religious terms reminiscent of the Psalms:

Nothing but flowers and songs of sorrow
Are left in Mexico and Tlatelolco,
Where once we saw warriors and wise men.

We know it is true
that we must perish,
for we are mortal men.
You the giver of life,
you have ordained it.

We wander here and there
in our desolate poverty.
We are mortal men.
We have seen bloodshed and pain
Where once we saw beauty and valour.

We are crushed to the ground;
we lie in ruins.
There is nothing but grief and suffering
in Mexico and Tlatelolco,
Where once we saw beauty and valour.

Have you grown weary of your servants?
Are you angry with your servants,
O Giver of Life?[13]

Blindness

However much the motives of the sixteenth-century
Spaniards were corrupted by greed for gold, they had a
fierce certainty that religion mattered. By the second half of
the nineteenth century a considerable number of Europeans, particularly in the north, were far less certain. The
reason for the decline in the power of the church in modern
Europe forms one of the central themes in the sociology of
religion and I do not propose to go into that now.[14] One of
the results of this decline, however, was that religious belief,
which had once been accepted almost without question, became a problem. Several anthropologists began to see
religion primarily as a social phenomenon, invented by men
for their own purposes.[15] Since modern society was usually
thought to have evolved through a series of stages from
primitive beginnings deep in the past, presumably religion
had evolved with it. If that were so, perhaps there might
still exist in unexplored parts of the world tribes whose
social life was so primitive that they had no religion.

The Victorian anthropologist Sir Edward Tylor put it
this way:

Ethnographers, if looking for a theory of development
to explain civilization, and regarding its successive stages
as arising from one another, would receive with peculiar
interest accounts of tribes devoid of all religion. Here,
they would naturally say, are men who have no religion
because their fathers had none, men who represent a
prae-religious condition of the human race, out of which
in the course of time, religious conditions have arisen . . .[16]

The descriptions of strange peoples brought back by nineteenth century missionaries and explorers often supported this view. One of the most famous of these was Samuel Baker. In sturdy Victorian fashion he attempted, with his wife, to trek to the undiscovered source of the Nile. He discovered and named Lake Albert, after the Prince Consort, claimed it as one of the sources of the Nile, and was knighted for his trouble. He saw himself as the forerunner of enlightenment: 'The explorer is the precursor of the colonist; and the colonist is the human instrument by which the great work must be constructed – the greatest and most difficult of all undertakings – the civilization of the world.'[17]

It is within that imperialist context that we have to place Baker's interpretation of what he experienced in the Nile Basin. Addressing the Ethnological Society of London in July 1866, he spoke of the White Nile as a place 'where man is represented by so abject and low a type that the mind repels the idea that he is of our Adamite race'. Later he goes on:

> The most Northern tribes of the White Nile are the Dinkas, Shilooks, Nuehr, Kytch, Bohr, Aliab and Shir . . . Without any exception they are without a belief in a Supreme Being, neither have they any form of worship or idolatry; nor is the darkness of their minds enlightened by even a ray of superstition. The mind is as stagnant as the morass which forms its puny world . . . The men are perfectly naked, apparently not knowing they are so . . . [18]

Sir Samuel was a man of action, not an intellectual,[19] and he was not primarily concerned with explaining the origins of religion. Indeed, he was a very conventional believer, and had a hunch about the people of the White Nile which he thought might help to sort out some troubling discrepancies with the biblical account of creation. These tribesmen didn't look like Europeans; they had no religion; they didn't know they were naked; they lived thousands of feet above the ocean on a plateau which, as far as he knew, had never been submerged. 'Are these races the result of that historical creation when God said "Let us make man in our own image"? Or are they descendants of a family as ancient or of greater antiquity than those whose arrow heads of flint, excavated from the drift are the testimony of prehistoric man?'[20] If these strange people had no knowledge of God, perhaps they weren't part of the creation story described in Genesis, but belonged to a world which had existed long before 4004 B.C., the computed date of Adam's creation. Should that be so, at least it would reduce the problem of explaining how, in less than 6,000 years, 'the human race that commenced with a unit has entirely lost its individuality, and has divided into numerous and distinct types or families, differing in language, colour and in physical conformation'.[21]

We may wonder how Baker was so sure that these people had no religion. From his writings it appears that two main experiences influenced him. Firstly, he found much of the behaviour of the people he met morally repellent, something he felt would be remedied by the introduction of Christianity. Secondly, he hardly ever saw or heard people doing any of the things which he could recognize as religious by the standards of his own Christian culture.

He describes one apparent exception to this, which he observed during a stay with the Lotuko tribe. When someone died, it was the practice to bury them initially in a shallow grave. After a few weeks, when the body was sufficiently decomposed, it was exhumed, and the bones were cleaned, put in an earthenware jar and carried to a cemetery near the town. The Lotuko did not seem to regard the place as sacred, though, because 'signs of nuisances were present, even upon the bones, that in civilized countries would have been regarded as an insult'.[22] Nevertheless, it occurred to him that this custom might have its roots in a belief in the resurrection of the body. Accordingly he talked about religion with one of the Lotuko chiefs, a man called Commoro. The discussion was somewhat stilted since it had to take place via two interpreters, first from Lotuko into Bari, then Bari into Arabic, in which Baker had some facility.

In fact he could make no progress in unravelling any religious meaning and the metaphors he used seemed to cut no ice with Commoro. When he asked whether the experience of wandering in dreams might suggest the existence of a spirit, Commoro was unconvinced. (Sir Edward Tylor, sitting in Oxford, was soon to say that this kind of experience was one of the major origins of religious belief.) On another tack, Baker took a grain of corn, put it in the ground and, emulating St Paul, said, 'That represents you when you die. That grain will decay, but from it will rise the plant that will produce a reappearance of the original form.' Baker records Commoro's reply as one worthy of a Victorian rationalist: 'Exactly so; that I understand. But the original grain does *not* rise again; it rots like the dead man and is ended; the fruit produced is not the same grain that we buried, but the *production* of that grain: so it is with man – I die, and decay, and am ended; but my children grow up like the fruit of the grain. Some men have no children, and some grains perish without fruit; then all are ended.'[23]

At this point Sir Samuel retired, baffled. 'It was extraordinary to find so much clearness of perception combined with such complete obtuseness to anything ideal.'

Baker's first suspicion was fairly near the truth: the exhumation and re-burial of bones does have a religious meaning for the Lotuko. They believe in a 'Supreme Being', Naijok, who is associated particularly with the dead.[24] Nowadays the first books on African religion that anthropology students are likely to meet are on the sophisticated belief systems of the Nuer[25] and Dinka[26] tribes – eloquent evidence of how severely misled Sir Samuel was about the tribes of the northern White Nile. At the time he made his original claims, Sir Edward Tylor commented that they were already out of date, and 'one of the rasher denials of the universality of religion' current in his day. He went on to say: 'Even with much time and care and knowledge of language, it is not always easy to elicit from savages the details of their theology. They try to hide from the prying and contemptuous foreigner their worship of gods who seem to shrink, like their worshippers, before the White man and his mightier deity.'[27]

Baker was, and remains, a vivid and interesting writer, but he was a man of his time, certain of his superiority and contemptuous of most of the peoples he saw. The resulting coarseness of perception was shared by many of his explorer/missionary contemporaries. More recent anthropological practice normally involves learning the language and participating in the everyday lives of the people one is trying to understand. It is very remote from the casual interchange

Baker had with Commoro. The transference of religious metaphors across four languages and cultures is more or less guaranteed to obscure subtleties of belief. Increasing sensitivity in field work shows that religion is a well-nigh universal phenomenon, occurring in some form in practically every culture.[28]

The remote past

Time has tended to support the view of Tylor, who, writing in 1871 on the possibility of the existence of tribes without religion, said, 'The theoretical niche is ready and convenient, the actual statue to fill it is not forthcoming.'[29] Consequently the search for the beginnings of religion shifts to the remote past. But there are difficulties about this. The blindness which Baker and others suffered from becomes much more of a problem in the study of prehistory. Archaeologists often find stone tools from palaeolithic times and work out what they were used for or how they were manufactured. By examining rubbish heaps with minute care they can give fairly accurate accounts of what the people ate. Sometimes, from the detailed patterns found on exposed floors, experienced archaeologists can make highly informed guesses about the way ancient societies were organized. But what about the religion of those remote times?

The religious artefacts of people as close to us as the West Highland Scots of the beginning of the nineteenth century are few and far between. Yet we know, because folklorists managed to collect them in time,[30] that the oral traditions of those Gaelic people were suffused with prayers and religious poems. They celebrated the most trivial of everyday activities, from making a bed, milking a cow, sweeping the house or baking, to covering a peat fire for the night. The intention behind their public acts and the meanings they associated with the physical objects were revealed only because it was possible to talk to them. It could therefore be that nothing at all remains on a prehistoric site which can be interpreted as a 're-ligious object' in spite of the fact that the people living there may have invoked the help of a perceived spiritual presence even for such an everyday task as collecting a handful of berries. We can never know, but speculation is sometimes supported by archaeological finds which can plausibly be interpreted as indicating a religious intention.

The most moving example of such a find in recent years took place in 1960 in the Shanidar cave in Northern Iraq. Kurdish tribesmen were still living in the cave when the American archaeologist Ralph Solecki began the search for human remains in 1951. By 1960 he had reached layers which had been occupied by Neanderthal man and he and his companions had managed to uncover several skeletons. One of them, labelled Shanidar IV, was found in a grave about 23 feet down from the surface of the modern cave floor, at a level dated 60,000 years ago. As a matter of routine, soil samples from the grave were sent for analysis to the Paris laboratory of Mme Arlette Leroi-Gourhan, an expert in fossil pollen analysis. At first disappointed with the contents of the samples sent from Shanidar, Mme Leroi-Gourhan dropped the idea of a large-scale study.[31] But in 1968 she finally examined the samples from Shanidar IV and was amazed at her discovery:

> She found under her microscope pollen and flower fragments from at least eight species of flowers. These flowers represented mainly small, brightly coloured wild flowers. She recognized relatives of the grape hyacinth, bachelor's button, hollyhock and a yellow flowering groundsel. Mme Leroi-Gourhan thinks that the flowers were probably woven into the branches of a pine-like shrub, evidence of which was also found in the soils . . . [She] deduced that no accident could have deposited such remains deep in the cave. Neither birds nor animals could have carried flowers in such a manner in the first place, and in the second, they could not have deposited them with a burial. Finally, one species of flower, the hollyhock, a very large pretty flower, grows in separate, individual stands. Therefore she concluded that someone in the last Ice Age had ranged the mountainside in the mournful task of collecting flowers.[32]

Solecki noticed during his stays at Shanidar that similar flowers still grow there today – they were often picked by his Kurdish workmen to wear in their sashes and turbans. It is difficult to dismiss the conviction that at that Neanderthal funeral 60,000 years ago there was a religious tenderness for the departed person which would be perfectly recognizable to modern man.

The very fact that Neanderthal graves have been discovered frequently and over a very wide area is usually taken to imply a belief in survival after death, as is the practice of dusting the dead with ochre, presumably to restore colour to the pallid corpse. What these customs imply is, of course, open to very diverse interpretations. The same is true of the evidence for the religious nature of a palaeolithic cult associated with the cave bear.[33]

In 1917, Emil Bächler, curator of the museum in St Gall in Switzerland, began excavating the Drachenloch, a cave nearly 8,000 feet up in the eastern Swiss Alps. He had been given the clue which started his search by a local schoolteacher, who had found teeth and bones belonging to the extinct cave bear in the Drachenloch. The cave, which is 230 feet long, contained evidence of human habitation throughout palaeolithic times, and from the very large number of bones found there it is clear that the people had lived by bear hunting. Towards the back of the cave, beyond the living quarters, Bächler found a large stone chest, covered by a heavy slab. Inside it were seven skulls of cave bears, in every case with the snouts pointing to the entrance. Further back he found other skulls, apparently arranged in a pattern in niches in the cave wall. Since then, similar finds have been made in other caves throughout the Alpine region of Europe, and also in more low-lying country, the most complex probably being at Regourdou in southern France. Several scholars have contended that these are the remains of a magico-religious[34] cult.

One of the reasons for this opinion is that ceremonies connected with bears continued to exist into modern times amongst a number of hunting tribes living in the northern parts of Europe, Asia and America.[35] Johannes Scheffer wrote a history of Lapland in 1673[36] which quotes eye-witness accounts of the bear ceremonial as seen by travellers. More recently still, a film was made in 1931 by N. G. Munro of one of the last examples of the cult among the Ainu people of northern Japan.[37] In all these cases, great emphasis is put on respect for the bear and regret that it has been killed. After the meat has been eaten, care is taken to maintain the bones intact and to place them in a chosen sacred spot, as seems to have been the case among the Neanderthals. The purpose is to ensure, either by magic or by entreating some divine power, that stocks of bears will be maintained in the future. Johannes Maringer[38] has inferred that the modern ceremonies were a magico-religious survival from the last interglacial period 'into our own times, even though the historical link remains obscure'.

Conclusions of this type can never be more than speculative, and the evidence for the palaeolithic bear cult has been dismissed as inadequate by some scholars.[39] Nevertheless, it is important to take account of our enforced blindness in these matters. Evidence is accumulating from several directions which makes it seem more than likely that religious awareness made its impact on the culture of *Homo sapiens* from very early on in his history.[40]

There is a large amount of evidence similar to that given in this chapter which suggests that religion is a universal phenomenon amongst the human species. Objects which almost certainly have a religious significance have been left behind even by the Neanderthals, long since extinct and belonging to a separate subspecies of man. Similarly, in spite of the theoretical hopes of some of the Victorians, it has not proved possible to identify with any confidence a primitive tribe which has no religion. Thus, in the contrasting dimensions of space and time, religion seems to be present wherever we look carefully.[41] (This is not meant to imply that *all* people have always been religious; in every human community, I would assert, people understand what the religious dimension of life is, but of course the attention they give to it may vary greatly.)

By examining the moment when Spaniards and Aztecs introduced themselves to each other for the first time, it was possible to see that, even amongst different ethnic groups which had never before come in contact, there was a commonly recognized category of life which we label 'religion'. Of course it is more complicated than that. Although Cortes identified Aztec religion easily enough, Sir Samuel Baker missed it completely in the upper Nile region. But perhaps the reason Cortes knew what he was looking at lay in the fact that Spanish and Aztec societies in the sixteenth century had reached a similar level of social and technological complexity. Large stone-built cities, the economic and technical resources necessary to sustain them and a complicated social hierarchy to administer them were common to both cultures, as was a written language. It was easy to pick out the huge temples in Tenochtitlan and to identify the priests with their long black robes, reminiscent of those of Dominican friars. It was relatively easy for people like Bernardino de Sahagún to translate the pre-conquest codices they managed to save from the flames. Beyond that, the work of understanding Aztec belief involved exploring its hidden aspects, the oral traditions and interpretations of reality collected by Sahagún and other early missionaries.

In a very simple economy like those that Baker encountered on the Nile, there *could* only be a very few external objects which at once proclaimed themselves as religious. Sir Samuel used public behaviour as another criterion for identifying religion, and nearly got at the truth when he saw the burial customs of the Lotuko. But in most cases he was put off by what he saw as the sorry state of public morality amongst the Nilotic tribes. To his eye they were so often cruel, untrustworthy, thieving, lying and ungrateful that they just couldn't be religious. These problems are, of course, species-wide, but as is evident from the exploits of the Spaniards and Aztecs it is erroneous to conclude from such behaviour that religion is lacking. Unethical behaviour may be a betrayal of religion, but it does not imply irreligion. No doubt Sir Samuel was blind partly because he didn't want to see – he was too busy solving the problems of the Book of Genesis. But his blindness, and the blindness of archaeology, are more or less inevitable, for religions claim that the truth about reality is not to be found in physical appearances. The essence of religion is its inwardness. You can't conclude that religion isn't there just because there's nothing to see.

Religions are not merely a matter of explaining reality – how the world was created or how we came to exist – nor are they only a set of commandments or moral prescriptions. In these respects religions are no more than competitors with other explanatory systems like empirical science, or with

secular ethics. What is unique to religions is that they always
assert the possibility, of getting in touch, directly, with whatever is ultimately 'real'. The metaphors are endless, but I have
chosen one familiar in a number of religious traditions, 'inwardness'. Professor Evans-Pritchard writes of the Nuer:
'They can speak of their experience of Spirit but can tell us
nothing of Spirit itself,' and elsewhere: 'It is because Spirit
constantly manifests itself to men and intervenes in their en-
terprises and affairs that we have the subject of this book,
[Nuer] religion.'[42] Among the Aztecs, the 'laws of interior
preparation' were revealed by Quetzalcoatl. Mystic union
with the divinity could be achieved by successive steps as the
result of a life of contemplation.[43] (St Teresa of Avila, who developed the Spanish tradition to its greatest heights, in
Carmelite spirituality, was a little girl of four when Cortes
landed in Mexico.) It is also this same inwardness which we
can never reach directly in palaeolithic religion, though it is
implied in the religions of modern hunting peoples.

The word 'religion' has been around too long, and has
meant too many things to different people, ever to achieve a
satisfactory definition, as the debate among social scientists
shows.[44] They have tended to look at it in their own terms, defining it according to its indispensable (or dispensable) social
functions, or according to visible and concrete behaviour,
symbols, and publicly stated beliefs. A definition which describes in evaluative terms what religion 'really' is, is normally
considered 'inappropriate for the tasks of science'.[45] Nevertheless, this book will deal with the aspect of religion which
concerns personal experience of the presence or power of
whatever is conceived as ultimately real, whether named God,
the gods, Dharmakaya,[46] that which cannot be named, or anything else. I believe this is justified, because it is this inward
part of religion which is normally taken to be central by religious people themselves.[47] Whether they are right or wrong
in making it their primary concern, or in their notion of the
'ultimately real', is not the point at issue. I shall be asking
whether this kind of experience is still widespread in our own
industrial society; or is something which has probably been
with us since before the last Ice Age due to disappear entirely
from human consciousness?

2

Cultured Despisers

'Don't you hear the bell? Down on your knees!
The sacrament is being carried to a dying God!'

HEINRICH HEINE[1]

Engels

During the 1960s, a team of social scientists was working in
the Tambov district in Russia, giving practical aid to the local
authorities in spreading scientific atheistic propaganda. To try
to understand the problem they were facing, they decided on a
programme of interviews with people identified as believers.
Sometimes they were not quite sure how to deal with the
answers they got. For example, when they asked Baptists why
they had joined the sect, they were told over and over again
about 'visions, mysterious dreams and voices from heaven'.[2] A
typical comment was 'How did I adopt the faith? It was not I
who sought God, it was God who found me.'[3]

L. N. Mitrokhin, one of the research team, gave some
advice on handling replies like this. He pointed out that you
could not use the recorded views of a believer 'as the basis for
a profound conclusion'[4] because 'Religion is a form of dis-
torted consciousness, and the believer's opinions about it, as a
rule, do not coincide with its real essence . . . Such replies,
therefore, should be subjected to scientific analysis. The interviewer has to explain why the believer answers in this way.'[5]

Mitrokhin was only expressing in milder form what Lenin
had said more violently at the beginning of the century. For
him religion was 'stinking philistinism', 'ideological necrophily',
'filth', 'sanctified ignorance', 'degradation'. These expressions
of disgust escaped him in letters to his friend Maxim Gorky,

whom he suspected for a dreadful moment of being sucked into the religious morass. In his anxiety, he rises to the height of invective:

> Just because any religious idea, any idea of God at all, any flirtation even with a God, is the most inexpressible foulness, particularly tolerantly (and often even favourably) accepted by the democratic bourgeoisie – for that very reason it is the most dangerous foulness, the most shameful 'infection'.[6]

No wonder, then, about the efforts at spiritual fumigation in Tambov! But what had happened to make religion, that most universal and unquestioned of human phenomena, a thing to be despised and explained away? Of course, there is no simple, agreed answer. Nevertheless, in the early life of Friedrich Engels, co-founder of Marxism, we can see encapsulated the pilgrimage of many a modern atheist from faith to militant unbelief.

At the time of Engels's birth in 1820, the Wupper Valley, where he was brought up, was in the throes of a famous evangelical revival or 'awakening'. This rose to its climax in 1825 with the arrival in Barmen (which with Elberfeld forms the modern town of Wuppertal) of the pietist preacher F. W. Krummacher, who laboured in that particular vineyard throughout Engels's youth, before being invited by the Kaiser to Berlin and, eventually, the court at Potsdam.[7] Pietism was a reaction of the 'spirit' against the 'letter' and laid great emphasis on religious experience. However, at least in the form it took in the Wuppertal, it also held to an extreme stance on the literal truth of the bible.

Engels senior was both financially well off and deeply committed to the pietist cause. The style of his prose, in a letter to a friend about the birth of Friedrich, has a recognizable ring:

> The good Lord has heard our prayer . . . and presented us with a babe, a healthy well-shapen boy. We thank and praise Him from the fulness of our hearts for this child . . . May He be to the child as kind a Lord and Father as He has been to me, and grant that we shall yet rejoice before His Throne at his birth.[8]

Young Friedrich seems to have come up to his father's expectations, aided by strict discipline. Occasionally he kicked over the traces, being found at the age of fourteen with a 'greasy book' on the impious subject of thirteenth century knights. 'The careless way he leaves such books about in his desk is remarkable. May God watch over his disposition, I am often fearful for this otherwise excellent boy.'[9] But by and large he was thoroughly pious, being deeply moved by the experience of confirmation at the age of sixteen. In the same year he wrote a hymn which began with the lines:

Lord Jesus Christ, God's only son,
O step down from Thy Heavenly throne,
And save my soul for me.
Come down in all Thy blessedness
Light of Thy Father's holiness,
Grant that I may choose Thee.[10]

And on leaving school at the end of the year he received a reference from his teacher commending him for his religious feeling and purity of heart.

In July 1838, he was sent to an office in Bremen to continue his commercial training before joining his father's textile firm. It is from this point that we can chart the change in the young Engels's outlook. His office duties were light and he quickly involved himself in pleasures denied to him at home. He got caught up in the parochial in-fighting of the local newspapers by writing anonymous articles and poems of critical parody. And he launched into a vigorous and witty correspondence with two old school friends, Wilhelm and Friedrich Graeber, the sons of a pastor and themselves to become pastors.

In September 1838 he was voicing opinions that would make his father uneasy. The hymn book they used at his church in Bremen was dreadful, full of 'songs against cow-pox and all kinds of other nonsense. It is sheer barbarism unequalled anywhere.'[11] Soon, in a letter to Friedrich Graeber, he was writing sarcastically about the empty spiritualizing of pietism and the bigotry of F. W. Krummacher.

At the same time, under the pseudonym of 'Friedrich Oswald', he made his first important contributions to a newspaper, the 'Letters from Wuppertal',[12] in which he complained

of the way pietism had spread throughout the Wupper Valley[13]
and, in his opinion, smothered the life of the people. Engels
felt that mysticism was most prevalent among the craftsmen.
'It is a pitiful sight to see one of them in the street, a bent
figure in a very long frock coat, with his hair parted in the
pietist fashion.'[14] They sat in their workshops all day long
with a Bible open beside them, hardly working at all. But
what really incensed Engels was the close link he thought he
saw between the pietistic way of life and social distress. The
workers lived in conditions of terrible poverty and disease, yet
the pietists among the factory owners (which included his own
father) treated their workers worse than anyone else did.
'They use every possible means to reduce the workers' wages
on the pretext of depriving them of the opportunity to get
drunk.'[15] In later years, when he was living in Manchester,
Engels developed the theme of religion as an instrument of
social control, keeping the poor contented with their lot. It is
he who makes us detect a sinister note in this English religious
tract of 1854:

> I know I am poor; but what of that? I can still be
> honest. I can go to Sunday School, and there I can get
> many a tract and pretty book; and my teacher says, if I
> get the knowledge of Christ, I shall be richer than many
> a man who owns thousands of pounds.[16]

The bourgeoisie of Wuppertal were in no doubt of who was
being attacked. There was uproar. In a letter, the eighteen-
year-old Engels excitedly asked Friedrich Graeber to guess
who wrote the newspaper articles.[17] In the same letter, he let
slip a comment that foretold the end of his belief in the literal
truth of the Bible. He had been reading the work of David
Friedrich Strauss.

Strauss was a biblical scholar who in 1835 wrote *The Life of
Jesus*,[18] a book which changed the face of biblical study and
which remains a pivotal work to this day. Strauss treated the
Gospels as secular literature and exposed the contradictions
and inconsistencies within them. Although this had been
attempted partially before, the book was an extraordinarily
powerful and thorough-going piece of scholarship. Its effect on
Strauss's personal life was catastrophic. He was at once cut off

from any possibility of university preferment and he remained more or less ostracized by the orthodox for the rest of his life.[19] But, though constrained in body, Strauss and his friends felt their minds were freed. There is a moving story of him reminiscing with a friend, Vatke, in 1860:

> 'Do you remember, Vatke? There was a good wine in 1835!'
> 'Good thoughts too!' replied Vatke.[20]

Engels, however, was still in two minds: 'You do not know the weight of the burden one feels with the first doubt, the burden of the old belief, when one must decide for or against, whether to go on carrying it or to shake it off.'[21] Friedrich Graeber tried to keep up an intellectual debate on the contents of the Bible and on theology, but he was really unable to compete with his friend on these grounds. His religious experience was keeping Engels in the fold. 'I well know the happiness everyone has . . . who places himself in a close, heartfelt relationship with God.'[22] And it was this that brought tears to his eyes as he saw his faith slipping away.

By the beginning of 1840 he was thoroughly bored with theological debate, and his anger was directed more at the way the establishment used religion to further its own ends. Of Friedrich Wilhelm III he wrote: 'I hate him with a mortal hatred, and if I didn't so despise him, the shit, I would hate him still more.'[23] Ironically, later in the same year Friedrich Wilhelm IV mounted the throne and invited none other than the butt of Engels's satire, F. W. Krummacher, to Berlin to try to stem the attack on orthodoxy in the city. In 1841, Engels himself arrived in Berlin to complete his military service and it was here that he was able to make the final break with religion.

He had been reading the philosophy of G. F. W. Hegel, who dominated German thought at that time, but in the end it was the atheist theologian Ludwig Feuerbach[24] who gave him the knife which cut the knot. Hegel thought of man as an idea in the mind of God and Feuerbach made a 'daring inversion' – God is an idea in the mind of man! For Feuerbach, the Christian religion was a projection on to an imaginary God of all the best qualities of man, leaving him helpless and degraded: 'The more empty life is, the fuller, the more concrete is God.

The impoverishing of the real world and the enriching of God is one act. Only the poor man has a rich God.'[25] Why are people religious, then? Because religion offers comfort, what Marx called 'opium' and Lenin 'spiritual booze': 'It is pleasanter to be passive than to act, to be redeemed and made free by another than to free oneself.'[26] With his memories of the poor people of Wuppertal, pacified by a pietism encouraged by the factory owners, this attitude must have seemed familiar to Engels.

He had to take one more step before his thought became recognizably Marxist. Although, in Marx's opinion, Feuerbach was right about the origin of God as an idea, he (Feuerbach) was still not enough of a materialist to realize where the idea came from. It was one thing to decide that religion was just fairy stories, another to explain where the stories originated. Marx did this most concisely in his eleven 'Theses on Feuerbach'.[27] Feuerbach had started out with the notion of religion as 'self-alienation' – that what was asserted about God was really a statement about the human species. But the very fact that people project into the clouds what belongs in the real world, thought Marx, has to be explained by the material suffering and contradictions in existing class society. Opium is necessary because the world is painful, but as the class society is overcome and with it economic injustice, there will be no need for opium and religion will disappear. This was a view to which Engels at once assented, and which he continued to preach for the rest of his life.

What conclusion can be drawn, then, if religion continues to survive in the Soviet Union, more than sixty years after the revolution? Anxiety about this is perhaps what lies behind the militant atheism of Marxism–Leninism. Leninism, it has been said, is 'Marxism in a hurry',[28] and the fact that there may well be as high a proportion of formally religious people in the Soviet Union as, for example, Great Britain may explain why programmes of the type mentioned at the beginning of this chapter are promoted and why the Communist Party of the Soviet Union[29] encourages the spread of atheist clubs, films, museums, lecture programmes and posters. Soviet anger with religion sometimes makes the senses reel. 'One poster showed the pregnant Virgin Mary looking at a billboard advertising a film on abortion. In the caption she exclaims: "Oh, why didn't I know that before."'[30] On the other hand it is amusing to listen to the volunteer atheist lecturer who, with his syrupy piety, rather reminds one of some of his opposite numbers: 'What a joy to realize that your work helps people to break away from the path of religious ideology and renounce their faith in god!'[31]

Freud

As we have seen, the idea of religion as something corrupt, from which people must be saved, can be derived from Lenin, whose tone at times is not far short of hysterical. Hostile critics sometimes suppose that the vehemence of Lenin's denial is an indication of powerful but repressed religious feelings within himself.[32] Similarly, it has been suggested that Engels's attacks on the religious and civil authorities of his day gained force from displaced anger against his father, the first authority figure in his life. The reason that such explanations have any plausibility depends on the work of another great despiser of religion, Sigmund Freud. Now although Freud thought religious belief nonsensical, he never reached the point of advocating its destruction or believing very seriously that it would disappear. He even went so far as to advise his clergyman friend Oscar Pfister on the use of psychoanalysis in his pastoral work, a suggestion which Pfister (and successive generations of clergy) took up with enthusiasm.

Unlike Engels, Freud claimed no personal understanding of religious feeling or experience. His biographer Ernest Jones says that, though he came from a Jewish background, he grew up 'devoid of any belief in God'. 'The emotional needs that usually manifest themselves in adolescence found expression first in rather vague philosophical cogitations, and soon after, in an earnest adherence to the principles of science.'[33] One result of the religious 'blank' in his life was that he never stopped nagging at the problem and trying to make sense of it in secular terms.

In particular, he found religious ceremonial repellent. On one occasion, after watching a Jewish wedding in fascinated horror, he wrote a mocking sixteen-page letter to a friend, describing all the (to him) repulsive details. Indeed it was only with great difficulty that Freud would permit himself to undergo the ceremonies connected with his own wedding. Unfortunately for him, it was a requirement of Austrian law that for a marriage to be valid there had to be a religious service. He found the learning of Hebrew prayers the night before his wedding in 1886 an embarrassing and meaningless chore.

In 1907, Freud was able to give vent to his feelings. He published a paper, 'Obsessive Actions and Religious Practices', in which he compared the apparently meaningless rituals of obsessional neurotics with the religious ceremonies he himself found so empty. 'People who carry out obsessive actions or ceremonials belong to the same class as those who suffer from obsessive thinking, obsessive ideas, obsessive impulses and the like. Taken together, these form a particular clinical entity, to which the name of "obsessional neurosis" is customarily applied.'[34] These apparently pointless actions, he said, have an unconscious meaning which relates to repressed sexuality. He gives the following example:

> A woman who was living apart from her husband was subject to a compulsion, whenever she ate anything, to leave what was the best of it behind: for example, she would only take the outside of a piece of roast meat. This renunciation was explained by the date of its origin. It appeared on the day after she had refused marital relations with her husband – that is to say, after she had given up what was the best.[35]

So the compulsive action, as long as its latent meaning is not understood, helps the neurotic person to hide from the painful sexual truth. Freud found the analogies with religious ritual so striking that he began to think of religion as providing a sort of large-scale publicly available set of symptoms that people could use to cope with their repressed feelings. From then on he spoke of religion as a 'universal neurosis'.

But how had it become so universal? God, he said, is a projection of the father, and here of course he is elaborating Feuerbach's idea. When very young and helpless, we are full of anxiety about the cruelty and impersonality of nature and we feel utterly dependent on our fathers. They are like gods to us and we attribute superhuman powers to them. But when we grow up and realize that we no longer have their support, in our dependence we invent a 'Father-God' to help us to hide from our helplessness. Religious experience thus becomes an extreme case of the universal neurosis.

A young American doctor once had the temerity to write to Freud in an effort to turn him from his irreligious ways. Apparently, as a student, this doctor had once been tempted to doubt by the sight of the body of a sweet-faced old lady lying in a dissecting room. If there was a God, how could He allow her to be so dishonoured? He decided to finish with religion, except that an inner voice warned him to think well before denying God. He replied, 'If I knew of a certainty that Christianity was truth and the Bible was the Word of God, then I would accept it.' And in due course, the doctor wrote, God instructed his soul in the truths of religion and showed his reality by 'many infallible proofs'.[36]

Freud's response to this was characteristic. There seemed to be an obvious explanation. The corpse of the old woman reminded the young physician of his dearly loved mother. Freud believed that at a certain stage male children become aware of sexual desire for their mother and murderous resentment towards their father, whom they regard as a rival (the well-known Oedipus complex). But, as children grow up, because social survival would otherwise be impossible these feelings are repressed and continue to exist only in the unconscious. However, in the case of the young American, his unconscious desire for the destruction of his father came back into consciousness disguised as a doubt about the existence of God. His hidden longing for his mother could then come into the open as rage at the abuse of the body of the motherly old lady, especially since children believe that the father abuses the mother in sexual intercourse. However, in the case of Freud's correspondent, the destructive impulse appearing as religious doubt 'subsides under the tremendous pressure of inhibition. The psychic conflict ends in complete submission to the will of the Father-God.'[37]

Theodor Reik, an enthusiastic disciple of Freud, added a few points to this explanation which linked it more clearly with obsessional neurosis. The young doctor's statement 'If I knew of a certainty . . .' is little different, said Reik, from the typical neurotic's 'If the streetcar passes the lamppost before the automobile does, my father's operation will be successful.'[38] What distinguishes the doctor's case is the fact that, in Freud's opinion, he got a reply to his challenge via a 'hallucinatory psychosis'. Such an explanation, if true, would presumably apply to many so-called 'conversion experiences'.

Whether his American correspondent was devastated or unmoved by the proposed explanation is unrecorded, but Freud's attitude seems to suggest a gentle but firm attempt to force people to face up to some uncomfortable truths. Religious experience is merely the universal neurosis which has temporarily slipped into a hallucinatory psychosis.

On another occasion we find him in debate with his friend Romain Rolland on the validity of the experience of 'loss of self' undergone by Eastern mystics. This 'oceanic experience', he said, is probably 'nothing more'[39] than a regression back to the undifferentiated world of early infancy – a kind of acting-out in fantasy of the desire to get away from the threatening world, back to a place of complete safety. Later, another psychoanalyst was to imply that there was something abnormal about Buddhist meditation by calling it 'artificial catatonia'.[40]

So it would appear that a good place to find neurotics would be wherever two or three religious people are gathered together. But it is not as simple as that. Freud was well aware that in his native Vienna religious people were far less likely than others to suffer from neurotic complaints. Indeed, he even attributed the steep increase in neurotic illness in modern times to the declining influence of the church, which provided a 'crooked cure'[41] for all kinds of psychological upsets. As he repeated frequently down the years, it is *because* they suffer from the universal neurosis that religious people do not have to go to the trouble of constructing a private set of symptoms of their nervous infirmities.

Other students of the psychology of religious experience were not so subtle. Writing in 1929, the American psychologist James Leuba[42] had no doubt that the ecstatic experiences of St Teresa of Avila were due to the physical arousal of sexual feelings, though she may not have known it.

> The subject of the voluptuous excitement may not be aware of the participation of his sex-organs and may, therefore, regard his delight as spiritual . . . Very coarse manifestations of sex regarded as 'spiritual happiness' may be witnessed in persons mentally deficient.[43]

St Teresa's life story makes it hard to regard her as anything other than an extraordinarily competent woman, but the great mystics

> also had to live a life of continence and they were for years divided souls with regard to things which most matter to men. Because of the ideal they had formed and of the method of life they had chosen, their deepest instincts and desires could not be gratified in the ordinary way. And they aggravated repressions and conflicts, in themselves sufficient to produce a variety of psychoses, by excessive and persistent ascetic practices, and thus exhausted themselves to inanition.[44]

After that, in spite of his claim that the mystics are not really psychopaths, Leuba's protestations of admiration sound a bit hollow.

Although Engels and Freud between them represent two of the most powerful strands in the web of modern atheism, in public they seldom bothered to combat directly religion's claims to interpret the meaning of human existence. Mainly, this is because in their view the rationalists of the eighteenth century had thoroughly disposed of its intellectual content.

The European Enlightenment is usually taken to stretch from 1620, the year in which Francis Bacon's *Novum Organum* was published, but it reached its peak in the eighteenth century. At least from a secular perspective, the progress of the Enlightenment can be seen as a steady and coherent increase in the dominance of a rational and empirical model of reality. The heroes of this movement tend to be scientists like Copernicus, Galileo and Newton. And the philosophy which arose out of it is probably best represented as beginning when Descartes made doubt the first principle of philosophical investigation. There are one or two key notions which can be seen to pervade, unobtrusively, the world of the Enlightenment:

Firstly the autonomy of reason. Thus, the philosopher John Locke proposes that the lover of truth does not entertain any proposition with greater assurance than the proofs it depends upon will warrant. 'Whoever goes beyond this measure of assent, it is plain . . . loves not truth for truth's sake but for some other end.' Although Locke himself was a committed Anglican, for many it ultimately followed that autonomous reason has priority over biblical or ecclesiastical authority.

A second alteration is in the *function* of reason, which more and more becomes a tool of empirical investigation and less the constructor of a 'scholastic' body of truth.

Thirdly 'nature' as the matter for empirical investigation, becomes more central to human consciousness and the idea of its uniformity and orderly arrangement, derived from Newton, leads to an expectation that phenomena will be universally found. Therefore, cases where a phenomenon is restricted, as for example a specific religious system, leads people to doubt whether it can be considered fundamental.

Fourthly, a growing materialistic optimism caused people to see this as the 'best of all possible worlds', or if, like Voltaire, one were sceptical of that, to believe that things are, nevertheless, getting better. Concentration on another, better world, began to seem morbid. The idea of progress is closely linked with that, as is the opinion that the human emergence from darkness is due to the throwing off of the superstition and errors of Judas-Christian beliefs.

This mood pervades the writings of both Engels and Freud; in fact in 1922 Lenin was complaining that the Soviet Communist Party was failing in its duty to 'translate the militant atheist literature of the late eighteenth century for mass distribution among the people'.[45] Consequently, the populace was failing to get a decent grounding in atheist arguments.

The Communist Party leadership, however, could take all that for granted. Their problem was to explain the existence of such a huge mistake in human history. As we have seen, they took the only reasonable line, given their interpretation of reality. It must be some kind of illness, or, as Feuerbach put it, 'theology is nothing else than an unconscious, esoteric pathology'.[46] Furthermore, for Marx it was a pathology that was kept going by a conspiracy on the part of the ruling

establishment, as a means of pacifying the masses and holding
on to power. There certainly seemed to be plenty of evidence
for that, all over nineteenth century Europe.

Yet Engels paused, before making his final break, because
of the pull of his own 'experimental' religious knowledge. It
must have been this which attracted him briefly to the
writings of the theologian Schleiermacher. Friedrich
Schleiermacher published his celebrated speeches on religion
to its 'cultured despisers'[47] in 1800, and based his theological
system on man's religious experience. He attempted to
combat the attack on religion by the Enlightenment, by insist-
ing on the uniqueness and reality of this dimension of human
experience. Like Engels, he came from a pietist background,
but he had a liberal stance on doctrinal and biblical matters.
However, Engels had reached Schleiermacher too late, and
was too violently in conflict with his own pietist past.
Feuerbach convinced him that he could safely abandon
religion for good.

His decision meant that he had, in principle, to reinterpret
the thing he had labelled 'religious experience' as something
else. Whether he ever managed this consciously is not clear.
Perhaps, having got rid of religion at great cost, he did not feel
like investigating that particular corner again. Perhaps he
agreed with Feuerbach's analysis. Men have no 'sense' or
'organ' of religious awareness, says Feuerbach, any more than
they have an 'organ of superstition'. When people interpret
their secular experiences religiously, it is due to ignorance and
stupidity. 'The Caribs believe, for example, that an evil spirit
is at work in a gun . . . that a bad smell indicates the presence
of the evil spirit of the person.' 'When a comet appeared in the
sky after Caesar's death, the Romans . . . believed it to be
Caesar's soul.'[48] 'Psychological proofs' of the existence of God
were merely a matter of wish-fulfilment. And Freud pushed
this particular line of reasoning to its limit by suggesting that
man's longing for his non-existent God becomes fierce enough
to generate 'psychotic hallucinations' – for him, the true substance of religious experience.

Behind these attempts at explanation lies a prior assumption that religious ways of making sense are non-sensical. It is
because of this that religious experience, which as Engels knew

has *some* basis in reality, becomes a problem in need of an explanation. It is also for this reason that our Victorian forebears became fascinated by the question of the origin of religion.

3

Dreams and Origins[1]

'Myth narrates a sacred history; it relates an event that took place in primordial Time, the fabled time of the beginnings.'

MIRCEA ELIADE[2]

A new Genesis

If you didn't know any better, you might think that the following tale came from a tribal story-teller, crouched with his listeners round the fire, recalling memories of a time immeasurably remote, and chilling them with his imagery:

A huge old male, fierce-eyed, is placed in the central arena of the story. Violent and jealous, he prowls around protecting his property, the women of the tribe. In the outer darkness stand the sons, fearing him and hating him; desiring the women. Slowly a common decision crystallizes amongst the young men, and at an appointed moment they rush, screaming, upon the tyrant and kill him. Then they tear his body to pieces and devour it raw – blood, flesh and bones. In the act of eating him, they believe they gain his strength.

But almost at the height of their exultant blood-lust, the horror of what they have done begins to dawn on them. Perhaps the sight of the dead and helpless body dissipates their hatred and uncovers the love they felt for the man who gave them life. In the agony of remorse and guilt there seems to be no way to undo what has been done. From desperation they decide to act out a revised version of history to remove their guilt. So they choose a sacred animal, a totem, to represent their dead father, and make a covenant with it. In return for a promise from the totem that he will protect and care for them, they undertake from henceforth to consider him sacred

31

and to respect his life. At the same time, the men agree to forgo sexual intercourse with the women of their own tribe, so that they must find themselves wives from elsewhere.

So *that*, the storyteller concludes, is why incest is prohibited and that is how the tribe got its totem.

Indeed, for Freud, who first recounted this modern myth,[3] that is how mankind got its religion. It is not certain just how literally he expected his readers to take his account. The anthropological data on which it was based were soon found to be inaccurate, and the way totemism is understood nowadays is radically different from the way Freud understood it.[4] But if we take the story as a myth which is attempting to state, in symbolic terms, some underlying truth of human experience, we can see that Freud is expressing his opinion that man's religions have their roots in the experience of a particular kind of guilt. Oedipal guilt, according to Freud, is what I feel towards my father as a result of my unconscious desire to destroy him. In normal civilized society, part of the maturing process involves coping in a non-violent way with this wish, but perhaps in some hypothetical dawn of human kind the sons really did turn on their father and kill him. So, in Freud's words, 'In the beginning was the deed.'[5]

As we have seen in the previous chapter, the dismissal of religion necessarily involved explaining it, a task that Freud took up on several occasions. He comes towards the end of a long line of Victorians and Edwardians who attempted to get at the origins of religion, prompted by the crisis of faith. Most of the vigorous speculations came from men who felt they had emancipated themselves from religious belief. They, unlike others, were left with the puzzle of how the error could have been made in the first place.

Three important strands can be seen running through their explanations. First, they usually took it that religions had not been invented, as it were, out of nothing, as a kind of intellectual exercise. They must have arisen as the result of reflection on some kind of practical experience, because no set of ideas isolated from real human experience could be expected to survive as long as those of religion. Secondly, all explanations inevitably emerged beneath the vast shadow of evolutionary ideas. The notion that living species had evolved was widespread long before it was crystallized by Charles Darwin in *The Origin of Species*.[6] As we shall see, parallel views about the evolution of society were similarly gripping people's minds. Finally, it is possible to see an at times unconscious, autobiographical element in much of what was written. In their role as unbelievers, many of these authors could look back to an infancy in the bosom of religious orthodoxy, an orthodoxy from which they had steadily withdrawn as they grew older. Sometimes they seem to have imagined the child-hood of the race as like their own and to have thought of their remote ancestors as mentally like young children.

This is most explicit in the writings of Auguste Comte, philosopher of positivism and founder of an atheist religion.[7] Born into a devout Catholic home in Montpellier in 1798, he was rudely torn away from his family at the age of nine to go to boarding school and at the age of thirteen had totally cast off his religion. In adult life his most famous contribution to learning was his enunciation of the 'Law of Three Stages':

> According to this fundamental doctrine, all our specu-
> lations on every subject of human enquiry are bound to
> pass successively both in the individual and the race,
> through three different theoretical states, usually known
> as Theological, Metaphysical and Positive.[8]

What is interesting about this statement is the parallel Comte intentionally draws between the infancy of the individual and the infancy of the human species. And there is no doubt in his case that he is drawing on his own life story as the basis for in-terpreting the world. At the beginning of his huge multi-volume work on positive philosophy he writes:

> Then each of us, in contemplating his own history,
> does he not remember that he has been successively, with
> regard to his most important ideas, *theologian* in his in-
> fancy, *metaphysician* in his youth, and *natural philosopher*
> (physicist) in his manhood?[9]

So the infant Comte, like adults in the infancy of the species, attributed human qualities to every object he came across. The feeling that all objects have a life of their own, Comte called 'Fetishism', and he believed it to be the earliest form of religion, still to be seen as a survival in Africa.[10] As young Auguste grew a little older, however, he stopped attributing conscious life to objects themselves and transferred it to a set of fictitious and invisible beings, the gods, until eventually his theology took its final form in a belief in one God. It was at this stage that he (and mankind) began to notice that the phenomena of nature are actually subject to a set of invariable laws. The curtain was now ready to go up on the mature discovery that reality is only knowable through the senses and by the scientific study of the laws governing matter. According to Comte, there is between the 'theological' and 'positive' stages an unfortunate 'metaphysical' period, when people try to discover the essence of things by introspection and the 'spinning of doctrines out of the brain' instead of from practical experience, the only true measure.

Religion in this interpretation is a necessary but infantile stage that we all go through, and, according to Comte, relapse into in moments of misfortune. He gives as an example the case of 'the most eminent of thinkers' who fall into the naïvest fetishism if their ignorance happens for the time being to be combined with 'some vehement feeling', 'as when Jesus, in a moment of irritation, cursed the fig tree,'[11] or when Comte himself in middle age regularly visited the grave of the woman he loved, to communicate with her remains.[12]

Spiritual beings

The power of evolutionary ideas is also evident in the writings of Edward Tylor, whom we have already met in controversy with Samuel Baker. He quotes Comte with approval in his major work, *Primitive Culture*,[13] and in the second edition of 1873 apologizes in the preface for the sparse references to Darwin, even though the book insists 'so strenuously on a theory of development or evolution'.[14] Like Comte, Tylor came from a devout background, this time Quaker, and, somewhat less vehemently, half-withdrew from his childhood faith.

Perhaps because of the emphasis given to inwardness in Quakerism, Tylor looked to immediate personal experience as the source of religion. His famous definition of religion as 'a belief in spiritual beings' rested on the conviction that these experiences had given our prehistoric ancestors the clue from which all religion had evolved. Presumably his own contact with the Quaker 'inner light' did not include anything he could interpret as a direct awareness of God, because for him the primary experiences were of another kind. Firstly there is the moment when we see someone die. What is it that makes the difference between a living and a dead body? And, as subsidiary but related questions, what causes sleep, or trance, or disease? Secondly, who or what are the people that appear in our dreams or hallucinations? In Tylor's view the ancients first thought that every person had two modes of being, a 'life' and a 'phantom'. Their next step was to combine the two, to say that life and phantom are one, the 'spirit', a kind of disembodied 'soul'. It is these we see in our dreams.

Tylor's method is to pile up example after example drawn from primitive cultures. These illustrate the beliefs of people he presumes to be closest in outlook to our prehistoric ancestors. Then he backs up this material by showing that in their language and customs modern Europeans unwittingly reveal survivals of a similar past. For example, he takes the case of the concept of 'spirit'. He reminds his readers how in ancient Rome at the death of a man it was the custom of the closest kinsman to lean over and inhale the last breath of the departing. In this way he believed he was receiving the virtue of the dead man.[15] Turning to a much more geographically remote people he relates how 'the Karens of Burma will run about pretending to catch a sick man's wandering soul, or as they say with the Greeks and the Slavs, his "butterfly"'.[16] In many parts of the world, when anyone faints or dies, their spirit, it is believed, can sometimes be brought back by calling after it. So occasionally occurs 'the ludicrous scene in Fiji of a stout man, lying at full length, and bawling out lustily for the return of his soul'.[17] And in our own day, says Tylor, ideas like these remain in the form of everyday expressions such as 'being beside one's self', or 'out of one's self' or 'in an ecstacy', or in the phrase 'I met him in spirit'.

On the next rung up the evolutionary ladder, the doctrines of 'soul' and 'spirit' presumably spread to all other objects, leading to fetishistic beliefs like those described by Comte. We

have a survival of this, according to Tylor, when we talk of dis-
tillations of wine as the 'spirits of wine'. Gradually the idea of
free spirits which had never been attached to a material object
developed, so that we still talk of being 'taken over' by a spirit
such as the 'spirit of patriotism'; or a person can become
'enthused', that is, be possessed by a god (from the Greek *'en
theos'*) and so exhibit 'enthusiasm'.

The next step was for gods or spirits to be related to particular types of object: forests would be presided over by the god of
trees, and perhaps a large-waisted and belching god would be
in charge of beer. Again Tylor sees a remnant in the way we
speak of inanimate objects in 'animate' ways: 'We say of a
dozen similar swords, or garments or chairs that they have the
same *pattern* (patronus, as it were, father), whereby they were
shaped from their *matter* (materia, or mother substance).'[18] At
this point in the evolution of thought we have reached the
stage of 'polytheism' and it is then, thought Tylor, a compara-
tively short step to the final summit of religious evolution, the
belief in one god, 'monotheism'.

Social effervescence

Such explanations of the origin of religion depend basically on
reflection on individual experiences, whether of guilt, dreams,
someone's death or the attribution of consciousness to objects.
In that sense they are psychological. But according to one
theorist, the most important element may be social.

Let me illustrate this. Several years ago I was driving
through Northamptonshire on a Sunday morning, when I
came across a sign to the village of Bugbrooke. At that time a
nonconformist chapel in the village had achieved some fame
as a centre of religious revival. Curious, I turned off the main
road, searched for the chapel and found a grey, barn-like
building packed to the doors with people taking part in a Bible
service. Many of them were in their teens or early twenties and
they eagerly found me a space to squeeze into.

The mental stance I proposed for myself, that of detached
observer of religious phenomena, turned out to be unrealistic. By
virtue of being born into a community which retains some connection with Christianity, I already had some preconceptions

with which to clothe the experiences I had in the chapel. These included a knowledge of some of the things that are 'supposed to happen' at a revival meeting. Recalling it now, the images which I retain are of an almost feverish excitement as the preacher declaimed his message. During his sermon there were continued cries of 'Yes, Lord', 'Amen', 'Hallelujah', etc., and beneath that an undertow of humming or muttering which I eventually realized was coming from people who were 'speaking in tongues'. With the heat and the emotionally charged atmosphere I began to feel semi-hypnotized and a bit 'high'. It was a curiously pleasurable emotional state, being carried along on a tide of effervescent feeling. I imagine the mood in Bugbrooke chapel would have been not unfamiliar to Engels from his boyhood experiences in the Wuppertal.

Although I was intrigued by the atmosphere and did not find myself particularly hostile to the sentiments expressed by the preacher, nevertheless there was a part of me which stayed 'on guard', perhaps because of what I knew of the writings of the French sociologist Émile Durkheim. Born in 1858, Durkheim was the son of a rabbi, but had fully broken with the faith of his childhood when he wrote his book *The Elementary Forms of the Religious Life*,[19] which sets out to explore the social origins of knowledge, especially religious knowledge, via the religions of the Australian aborigines. But as one of its early reviewers said, it 'is also meant as a general theoretical enquiry into the principles of religious experience'.[20] I can imagine that Durkheim, had he been seated in Bugbrooke chapel with his 'serious and somewhat cold appearance',[21] would have 'observed the facts, analysed them and explained them fully by laws' drawn from his book. For him,

> The sentiment of the divine is evoked in collective ceremonial, during which, as a result of the intense emotionality and involvement which is generated, the individual feels himself swamped by action of an entity superior to himself. Although this force emanates from the collective assembly, it only realizes itself through the consciousness of the individual, who feels it to be both transcendent over him and yet immanent in him.[22]

He claimed that

In fact anyone who has really practised a religion well knows that it is the cult which gives rise to those impressions of joy, internal peace, serenity and enthusiasm which are for the believer a kind of experimental proof of his faith.[23]

And the preacher himself can get caught up:

Sometimes he actually has the feeling that he is dominated by a moral force greater than himself, for which he is merely the spokesman . . . Now this extraordinary growth in power is very real; it derives from the very group which he addresses.[24]

In a sense, Durkheim took the experiential basis of religion more seriously than many who had gone before him. He even said there were no religions which were false. They were true 'in their own fashion'. However, though he did not think that accounts of religious experience were 'purely illusory', he certainly did not accept them as they stood. Thus, he would have been unable to take seriously the explanations and justifications of their beliefs and practices by the congregation at Bugbrooke. If invited to address them, he would probably have explained that the feelings of 'effervescence' that had swept through the church that Sunday morning were really 'society becoming conscious of itself'. The assembled worshippers, though they believed they were worshipping God, were in fact paying homage to another awesome entity, 'society'. Society, like God, is the milieu in which we live and move and have our being; society existed before us and will do so after we die; it is from society that we learn our code of ethics, and society has the power of life and death over us. In summary, 'Forces which are generated by human association are represented in the individual mind as the product of supernatural essences or beings.'[25] 'Man,' Durkheim would say to the people of Bugbrooke, 'can never be anything but religious, because he will always be the creation of society.' But now that he (Durkheim) has revealed the source of our religious feelings, it will be necessary to revise and get rid of its mythological aspects.

If, rather crestfallen, individuals decided to go home and pray privately, Durkheim would have some other words of wisdom. The secrecy of one's room, behind a closed door, is a favoured spot for religious exercises like prayer.[26] Nevertheless, such activity is not much more than a faded remnant of the public cult:

> . . . fasts and vigils or retreat and silence . . . are nothing more than prohibitions put into practice . . . [but this negative cult] does not contain its reason for existence in itself; it introduces men to religious activity, but it supposes this more than it constitutes it . . . In fact it is in group life that they [sacred beings] are formed . . . but when the assembly has broken up and each man has returned to his own particular life, they progressively lose their original energy.[27]

The fading of the myths

It is ironic that it was Auguste Comte, one of the first modern delvers into the origins of religion, who labelled curiosity about impossible problems as indicative of a primitive mentality: 'At their first rise, all human speculations necessarily take a theological shape. They are marked by a predilection for the most insoluble questions relating to subjects that no investigation can ever decide.'[28] The problem of getting at the origins of religion seems as good a candidate as any for the label 'insoluble'. There simply is no way to reassemble those remote human societies where religious consciousness presumably made its first appearance.

For a time the early anthropologists thought they could reconstruct these beginnings by analogy. As we have seen, they believed that by examining the religions of contemporary human groups living at a very simple cultural level, they could see what religion was like in primeval times. The trouble with that approach is that it assumes that simplicity of material culture necessarily implies primitiveness of religion. And while Edward Tylor was turning up examples of primitive animism in savage tribes, his pupil, Andrew Lang, was finding examples of monotheism amongst similarly primitive peoples.[29] During the first part of the twentieth century, Lang's discoveries were taken up vigorously by the anthropologist Wilhelm Schmidt.[30] This Austrian priest, a contemporary of Freud's (and for whom Freud seems to have had a hearty dislike[31]), claimed to show that monotheism was present in a considerable number of culturally very backward human groups. He opposed the prevailing evolutionary theory and claimed instead that animism, polytheism etc. were regressions from a once universal primitive monotheism. Naturally, it did not escape public attention that in his role as Catholic priest Schmidt would be quite pleased to be able to prove this was so.

People found it easy to be suspicious of Schmidt's findings because of his obvious bias, but it was not as clear at first that the work of many other anthropologists could also be accused of bias, though in the opposite direction. Schmidt himself pointed this out, choosing for severest criticism those who, like Comte and Durkheim, had given up an earlier faith:

> If religion is essentially of the inner life, it follows that it can be truly grasped only from within. But beyond a doubt, this can be better done by one in whose own inward consciousness an experience of religion plays a part . . . Renan[32] perceived this; he however believed that a still better investigator was one who had formerly been religious and had since abandoned his creed. This cannot be allowed. Renan commits himself thereby to the most emphatic expression of judgement concerning truth, and so forfeits all claim to objectivity.[33]

And indeed a majority of scholars were implying an emphatic judgement. For them, the kinds of experience which they thought had generated religious ideas might well have been convincing to primitives, the uneducated, or the stupid, but a grasp of modern science enabled one to explain these things in a much more satisfactory way. There was a general tendency to equate 'primitiveness' with stupidity,[34] and it may have been a kind of filial piety on the part of university dons like Tylor and J. G. Frazer[35] to suggest that the ethical monotheism of their parents was the most highly evolved way to be mistaken.

Scholarly 'explainers away' generally practised detachment towards both hypothetical 'primitive savages' and modern believers. There were, however, one or two early students of religious origins (apart from Schmidt) who did not set a gulf between themselves and the objects of their studies. Two Victorians who retained their openness to religion while being fully involved in the intellectual movement of the times were Friedrich Max-Müller and Andrew Lang.

Max-Müller[36] was a fellow of All Souls at Oxford, an expert in Sanskrit and a supporter of the 'nature-myth' theory of the origin of the gods. This held that the gods of the past were really personifications of natural phenomena like the sun or the moon. But Max-Müller felt that the experience of such phenomena awakens an awareness of the divine, rather than that the gods 'are' those things. Here again, biography is involved. Referring to his childhood in Dessau in Germany, he recalls a vivid experience of nature reminiscent of Wordsworth:

> On this Easter day . . . the old church with its grey slate roof, and the high windows, and the tower with the golden cross, shone with marvellous brightness. Suddenly the light which streamed through the high windows began to wave and seem alive. But it was far too bright to look at; and as I shut my eyes, the light still came into my soul, and everything seemed to shine and be fragrant, and to sing and sound. I felt as if a new life began in me, as if I had become another being . . .[37]

In his life-long devotion to the ancient Vedic literature of India, it is possible to see a continuing fascination with this kind of experience. Writing to a friend in later life, he says:

> The *Veda* alone of all works I know treats of a genesis of God-consciousness . . . we see it grow slowly and gradually, with all its contradictions, its sudden terrors, its amazements, and its triumphs . . . As God reveals his Being in nature, in her order, her wisdom, her indestructibility, in the eternal victory of light over darkness, of spring over winter . . . so man has gradually spelt out of nature the Being of God.[38]

In a similar fashion, Andrew Lang, though early a critic of his Presbyterian childhood,[39] found analogies in his own experience with the religious world of the 'savage'. On at least four occasions in his life he believed himself to have come in

contact with the supernatural. For example, while a don at
Merton College in Oxford, he was convinced that he saw the
ghost of a professor standing opposite the entrance to Oriel
College. At that very moment, it later transpired, the professor
(Conington) was dying at a place far removed from the site of
Lang's vision.[40]

I have already mentioned that Lang believed he had identified examples of primitive tribal monotheism. In his opinion
the two chief sources of religion were:

> (1) the belief, how attained we know not, in a power-
> ful, moral, eternal, omniscient Father and Judge of men.
> (2) the belief (probably developed out of experiences
> normal and supernormal) in somewhat of man which
> may survive the grave.[41]

Therefore, Lang suggested, there is a way of investigating the
origins of 'savage beliefs about visions, hallucinations, clair-
voyance, and the acquisition of knowledge apparently not
attainable through normal channels of sense. They should be
compared with attested records of similar experiences among
living and educated civilized men.'[42]

The theories of Lang and Müller thus differ from most of
those we have looked at. Both men appealed to aspects of
human experience which were religiously convincing to themselves as well as some of their contemporaries. But in fact their
status as accounts of the remote origins of religion were no
more verifiable than any of the others.

The futility of the search for origins became more and more
obvious as the twentieth century wore on. What was left behind was a large set of ingenious and curious modern myths,
which reveal more about the inner life of their authors than
anything else. For this very reason they do retain a certain
amount of interest in that they might help to explain why
people in our own era of history either take up or discard
religion.

On the face of it, the second alternative would seem to be
the popular one, at least in Europe. To our ears, furious intellectual battles over religion have a dated, nineteenth century
ring. Perhaps the lessons taught by the scholars we have been
examining have sunk in. Though it is still quite easy to find

remaining symbols of its former influence, institutional religion often has a beleaguered quality, apparently isolated from the mainstream of modern life. The religious images of the past have lost their relationship to most people's inner experience and become merely works of art. 'THIS IS NOT A MUSEUM' says a notice in Cologne Cathedral, presumably because to many visitors that is precisely what it is.

In the next chapter I shall be illustrating the decay of publicly available symbols of religion, while pondering the effect of this on people's inner experience.

4

Disappearing Symbols

' "There's a church in Salford, at the top, St Simon's, you ought to go and see it, it's your cup of tea. Up your street." So I didn't do it. Naturally. Never do today what you can put off till tomorrow . . . "You'll really have to go and see that St Simon's Church. It's your cup of tea and it's going to come down very soon." So I went up and made a drawing, and went again in another month's time to check on it, and it had gone absolutely flat.'

L. S. LOWRY[1]

An appearance of power

'The city is the image of the soul', said St Catherine of Siena, who lived and died there during the second half of the fourteenth century. When she walked its streets she could not fail to come across symbolic representations of religion in practically every corner.[2] Set on an eminence in the centre was the black and white marble of the gothic cathedral, a building which was continually being extended for practically the whole of her lifetime. Around the edges of the city lay the great monastery churches of the religious orders, San Francesco, San Domenico, Sant'Agostino and Santa Maria dei Servi. Within these buildings another layer of symbols reminded the faithful that they lived in a God-filled universe. The cathedral pulpit, carved by Nicolò Pisano, depicted, in stone, scenes from the life of Christ, God's manifestation on earth. Lower down on the same structure stood single figures representing the spiritual virtues it was necessary to cultivate so that the individual could meet his God. Adorning the walls and altars of the churches were paintings of religious subjects by some of Italy's most eminent painters, including Duccio, whose picture

44

'The Glorification of the Madonna' decorated the high altar in the cathedral.

Yet another layer of symbolism existed, in the consciousness of the Siennese of their own religious history. St Catherine herself was part of that tradition in that she was recognized as a saint and received in her body the stigmata, or wounds of the crucifixion. She had the power to influence Popes, for it was she who persuaded Gregory XI to leave Avignon and return to Rome in 1377. The stories about her and her successor, St Bernardine, along with the many tangible memorials to their presence added yet further embellishments.

But perhaps the most powerful expression of religion in Siena was the sheer numbers of people professionally involved in the life of the church. Statistics are available for Rome which show that the percentage of priests, monks and nuns in the population of the city was consistently extremely high from the fourteenth to the seventeenth century.[3] It seems quite likely that the same was true for Siena. At any rate, according to a modern Italian historian,[4] as late as the eighteenth century, with the French Revolution just round the corner, more than one in every eight people living in the town were occupied in some form of religious activity. Siena of course was the seat of a bishop and could therefore expect to attract an unusually large number of clerical officials. Even so, their impact as they filled the town, many of them with the distinctive garb of their orders, would have been at least as strong as that of the dons and undergraduates on the university town of Cambridge at the present day.

It is certainly true that Siena was exceptional, though other Italian cities could boast of figures not all that much lower.[5] And competition to enter the religious orders was fierce. In 1492, Marcello Crescenzi, Bishop of Assisi, had the task of selecting two out of fourteen applicants for a sought-after position, in this case as a nun in the convent of Santa Chiara.[6] In eighteenth century Italy as a whole, including the countryside, where clergy were very much more thinly spread, it has been calculated that out of a total population of 13½ million, probably a quarter of a million were in religious life.[7] Even with so many people in the ranks of the clergy, anti-clerical feeling, though undoubtedly widespread, did not make itself felt in the statistics of public practice. Rome, of course, as the official centre of Christendom, is a special case. For the same reason it also has figures for the numbers of people attending communion stretching back to before the eighteenth century. In 1702, out of a total population of 106,740 eligible to receive communion, only 148 failed to do so.[8]

So here we have a series of images displayed publicly which speak of a society shot through with an awareness of a transcendent dimension to life. Siena, for instance, is often represented with its familiar churches, towers and streets brooded over by an immense benign figure of the blessed virgin, her cloak spread out to encompass and protect its walls.

Internal decay

But the accumulation of sacred symbols is not necessarily the best indicator of the religiousness of a society. Beneath the 'sacred canopy', the inward awareness out of which religion grows can become disconnected from its outward artefacts. The motives for entering the religious life during much of the period under discussion were very mixed, ranging from a sincere desire to get to heaven to a cruder straining after financial and political power, or perhaps merely an easy life. Probably a high proportion of monks and nuns at that time were children of the aristocracy who had little prospect of inheritance (or, in the case of girls, of marriage) and who were provided for by being professed. This, naturally enough, would lead to anti-clericalism amongst the poor, or, in the event of church endowments being removed, to a dramatic decline in vocations. Giovanni Fabroni, writing in the eighteenth century about the fecklessness of many of the people of Turin, had no hesitation in including its 2,000 monks and priests amongst the idlers who live off the labours of others.[9]

Strong religious imagery can co-exist with violent anti-clericalism and also fairly radical unbelief, and there is evidence of this stretching back in Christian Europe to well before St Catherine of Siena's time. Vivid first-hand accounts exist from the early fourteenth century of attitudes and opinions which have a very modern, sceptical tone. The future Avignon Pope, Benedict XII, was Bishop of Pamiers in what is now Southern France from 1318 to 1325. In this role, he set himself the task of stamping out the Cathar heresy, which at that time survived most strongly in the village of Montaillou in his diocese. His inquisitorial records include verbatim accounts of peasant opinion, such as the following:[10] 'The priests talk nonsense when they tell us to give alms for the salvation of souls. All that is rubbish! When a man dies, the soul dies too. It is just the same as with animals. The soul is only blood . . .' (Shades of Sir Samuel Baker's conversation with Commoro here!) Another peasant says, 'The weather, following its course, causes cold and the flowers and the grain, and God can do absolutely nothing about it.' Raymond de L'Aire of Tignac doubted the virgin birth: 'Christ was created through fucking and shitting, rocking back and forth and fucking, in other words through the coitus of a man and a woman, just like the rest of us.' Admittedly, that upset people. His neighbour, Raymond Segui, said, 'If you don't stop it, I'll break your head open with my pick-axe.'

It is because of the obsessive interest of a bishop that we have these records, but they reflect a kind of earthbound commonsense which was no doubt to be found quite widely in medieval Europe, though usually hidden from us by the dominant orthodoxy.

At any rate, towards the end of the eighteenth century the decay of the institution in Italy must have been very far advanced. Revolutionary ideas were widespread, and, apparently catalysed by the revolution in neighbouring France, there was a sudden, permanent and catastrophic decline in the numbers of religious vocations in Italy. For example, throughout the seventeenth and eighteenth centuries the number of ecclesiastics per hundred inhabitants in the city of Bologna never dropped below five. In 1791 the average was 5·3 per hundred. Meanwhile, the French Revolution was under way and the beginning of a new world was symbolized by renaming 1792 the year 'One'. The news got through to the clergy of Bologna, for by 1799 (old reckoning) there was less than one clergyman left per hundred people in the city.[11]

Protestant England in the sixteenth century began to exhibit a different set of religious symbols from Catholic

Europe of the same period. Nevertheless, for a long time the differences remained more superficial than real. Like Catholicism in the Mediterranean states, in England after the Reformation 'the Anglican Church was nothing less than society itself in one of its most important manifestations'[12] and contained inside itself all the divisions of society. The historian Keith Thomas points out how religious symbols both penetrated, and therefore united, every aspect of social life and at the same time emphasized its subdivisions. In the sixteenth century it was a crime punishable by law to stay away from church on Sunday, and once there your place was assigned: women on one side, men on the other; the wealthy in the front, or, as in Breedon church in Leicestershire, in a huge ornate pew sailing like a galleon at one side of the church; the poor in the pews at the back, or standing. God was sometimes called 'the great landlord' and in some places social divisions extended to differences in quality of communion wine for the differing classes. No doubt with an eye to eliminating the possibility of social embarrassment in heaven, one Anglican divine even explained that there were three sub-sections in paradise assigned respectively to the 'very poor', 'men of mean estate' and finally 'great men'.[13]

These symbolic subdivisions do not appear to be supported by the New Testament, nor do they seem to have been thoroughly popular with the people. In spite of the law, the evidence suggests that churchgoing never reached anything like universality. Cases are reported from the sixteenth and seventeenth centuries where less than half the communicants turned up on Sundays. Even when they got as far as church, their behaviour sometimes left much to be desired, as the records of the ecclesiastical courts of the time reveal. Keith Thomas lists, amongst other kinds of unseemly behaviour, 'jostling for pews, nudging neighbours, hawking and spitting, knitting, making coarse remarks, telling jokes, falling asleep and, on one occasion, letting off a gun'.[14] There are reports of occasions when, as the vicar began his sermon, most of the parishioners would disappear to the ale house to refresh themselves. Or, if some of the lower elements stayed in, the preacher might be subjected to heckling and catcalls, 'loathsome farting, striking and scoffing speeches'. These

entertainments were often to the delight rather than to the dis-
comfiture of the rest of the congregation. As Thomas remarks,
there is something very reminiscent here of the behaviour of
difficult classes of schoolchildren in an inner-city school, and
we may guess that the motives are somewhat similar. Com-
pelled by law to attend what they do not understand or find
irrelevant to their ordinary lives, they either play truant or
take refuge in the only available defence, which is ridicule.
When a preacher in Essex in 1630 spoke of 'Adam and Eve
making themselves coats of figleaves, one loud mouthed
parishioner demanded to know where they got the thread to
sew them with'.[15] Many modern schoolteachers would find
familiar the combative spirit of a bored schoolboy trying to
catch the teacher out.

On the whole we may be inclined to imagine the treatment
of the church and the vicar with a kind of belligerent contempt
as little more than irritation with a divinely sanctioned social
order which got in the way of people's down-to-earth interests.
But there is no doubt that it shaded into outright disbelief and
atheism at times, even though it is impossible to say how frequent this was. Thomas[16] mentions that in 1600 the Bishop of
Exeter was claiming that the existence of God was commonly
debated in his diocese. There are also a number of accounts of
isolated individuals who were executed for denying fundamental religious doctrines such as the divinity of Christ. Nevertheless, the complaint which consistently appears amongst
churchmen is of ignorance of religious doctrine and carelessness about church attendance. These defects were attributed
particularly to the poor peasants and workmen, and Thomas
writes:

> It is small wonder that in the seventeenth century the
> godly came to see themselves as a tiny minority in an un-
> regenerate world and regarded the lower ranks of the
> people as the greatest enemies of true religion. 'If any
> would raise an army to extirpate knowledge and re-
> ligion,' declared Richard Baxter in 1691, 'the tinkers and
> sow-gelders and crate-carriers and beggars and barge-
> men and all the rabble that cannot read . . . will be for-
> wardest to come into such a militia.' 'The far greater

part of the people,' he thought, 'hated practical
godliness.'[17]

The Victorians

'Soapy Sam' Wilberforce was a pillar of the nineteenth
century religious establishment who, while Bishop of Oxford,
had the misfortune to be trounced in a famous debate with
T. H. Huxley on the theory of evolution. In 1829, as a young
man, he had almost taken a parish in the middle of industrial
Lancashire. To his father's relief he decided against it, feeling
that the atmosphere would not be conducive to devotion and
the cultivation of the spiritual life.[18] So the service of the poor
was left to others.

However ignoble Wilberforce's attitude to social ethics,
there was certainly some substance to his decision, at least as
far as the nineteenth century working-class view of religion
was concerned. Here, it seems, the religious disaffection of the
seventeenth-century poor was more fully displayed. In the
East End of London in Victorian times: 'Any form of religion
(except perhaps Roman Catholicism which could be seen
merely as a harmless form of Irish eccentricity) was seen as . . .
a sign of weakness and qualified its professor both for bullying
and general suspicion.'[19]

Hugh McLeod[20] describes the 'machismo' culture of male
working-class London in those days. It included as part of its
package an image of religion as soft and effeminate, acceptable at
best amongst wives and daughters. Since the London Irish, who
had a most unfortunate reputation for roughness, did not share
this view of religion, though their practice was careless, it is clear
that cultural differences are operating here. At any rate, missionaries attempting to spread their message could expect harsh
treatment from the men in the docks or workshops by the river,
and at most a contemptuous tolerance in the pub. The greatest
difficulties, the missionaries felt, were with groups of men who
were out of touch with a 'home-environment'. Defiance and
blasphemy were the prerogative of 'sailors, railway navvies,
brickmakers, residents of common lodging houses'.[21]

It is noticeable in this connection that religious groups, like
the nonconformists, which achieved some success in hard,

poverty-stricken environments did so by preaching a fiercely evangelical religion which engendered a mirror image of toughness by emphasizing the blood sacrifice of Jesus, endurance in the face of temptation and stern abstinence from strong drink, swearing and tobacco. In a broader perspective, however, the rejection of religion as effeminate seems to be a rejection of a passive contentment with fate and the fatalistic view that poverty and starvation were the will of God. Survival required a more aggressive resilience than was commonly preached by the clergyman. Engels believed that the English working classes were aware that the established church operated as a mouthpiece of the ruling classes. It was for this reason that men with clerical collars were liable to be given short shrift by the poor. Bishop Wilberforce was right: in these stern communities, interpretations of reality which made much of notions of inwardness and contemplation could only seem bizarre and laughable, suitable perhaps as a pastime for the idle rich, or women.

Head-counting

In 1851 any mythology which may have existed about the religious loyalty of the British was finally shattered. At the time of the national census for that year, an inquiry was launched to discover what proportion of the populace attended places of religious worship on a Sunday. According to K. S. Inglis, in many of the largest towns in England it was found that less than one in ten of the people attended church on Sunday. In particular, the official report noted of the working classes, 'These are never or but seldom seen in our religious congregations.'[22]

Since those days, accurate statistics have been kept concerning the membership of most religious bodies in the British Isles.[23] Over that period, the figures show an overall steep decline. The legal and social pressures to become an active member of a church have decreased continuously over the last 300 years. In itself this may be taken as a sign of the weakening of the power of the religious institutions. However, the most catastrophic decay in membership of the major protestant denominations set in during the mid-1920s. At that point, with a rising national population, they not only failed to increase their membership, but actually began to decline in absolute numbers.

Thus there were estimated to be just under 6,000,000 protestants in Britain in 1927; the figure had slipped to less than 4½ million by 1970.[24] In the Church of England, baptisms reached a total of over 600,000 in 1920, while in 1978 the estimated number was 214,000. Confirmations, around the 200,000 mark in 1920, were less than 100,000 in 1978. Marriages numbered over 220,000 in 1919 and had dropped to somewhat over 155,000 in 1972 (the figures for civil marriages in those years were just over 85,000 and over 190,000 respectively).

Concealed behind these statistics is the fact that there were large decreases in the membership of the Church of England during the two world wars, followed by recovery. However, after the Second World War the recovery was only very partial. The speed of decline over the past twenty years has been very rapid. Between 1960 and 1978 baptisms approximately halved, and the confirmations per thousand of the population aged ten to twenty years dropped by more than half. Similar declines can be documented for all other major denominations with the exception of the Roman Catholics. A recent survey shows that about 40 per cent of the Roman Catholic population in England and Wales attend weekly mass.[25] Membership numbers and baptisms have approximately doubled since the 1920s, though this is usually attributed to immigration and perhaps to the large size of Catholic families. In the case of several small sects such as the Seventh Day Adventists and Jehovah's Witnesses there has been a steady and continuous growth up to the present time.[26]

Looking at the figures more closely in an inner-city working-class area illustrates just how far the established church has declined. In a recent book,[27] Leslie Paul documents the situation in the Anglican Deanery of Battersea in London. A survey in 1965 showed that 'less than 1 per cent of the population of the deanery was in an Anglican Church on an average Sunday'.[28] In 1970 he reported only one in 144 persons present. Over a five-year period the number of baptisms in the deanery dropped by over 50 per cent and in seven years weddings declined by nearly 40 per cent.

The image that comes to mind is of a tiny community within Battersea, highly eccentric and on the point of disappearing.

Health?

The changing fortunes of formal religion in countries with a Christian tradition present an extraordinarily complicated pattern. What is to be made of the resilience of Polish Catholicism, for example, or the disappearing church in Sweden?[29] It is usually assumed that in all cases the churches are having to struggle against the process of 'secularization',[30] a process which continues more or less successfully in different regions. The United States is often taken as an example of an industrial nation which remains highly religious. In the 1950s for example, not far short of 50 per cent of all Americans would be found in church on an average Sunday and amongst Roman Catholics the figure was 75 per cent.[31] Writing in 1953, the Cistercian monk Thomas Merton reflected on the paradoxical situation created in his monastery of Our Lady of Gethsemani in Kentucky when the national religious enthusiasm hit it. Traditionally, a Cistercian Abbey

> is a quiet, out-of-the-way place – usually somewhere in France – occupied by a community of seventy or eighty men who lead a silent energetic life consecrated entirely to God. It is a life of prayer and of penance, of liturgy, study and manual labour . . . The life is usually quiet. There is no conversation. The monks talk to their superiors or spiritual directors when necessary. In the average monastery, Trappist silence is an all-pervading thing that seeps into the very stones of the place and saturates the men who live there.[32]

But within four or five years in the early fifties, 'two hundred and seventy lovers of silence and solitude' were jammed into a building meant for seventy, and at times the monks were camping in tents in the grounds to make room.

Phenomena like this were repeated throughout the mainline American denominations, and President Eisenhower probably spoke for the majority of the nation when he said: 'Our government makes no sense unless it is founded in a deeply felt religious faith – and I don't care what it is.'[33] In spite of this, many modern commentators are inclined to think that the boom of the fifties was deceptive. There were factors affecting the situation which had little to do with 'proper religious motives'. For instance it was a time of high social mobility, with many people moving into the middle classes for the first time, and still having in their heads the connection between churchgoing and respectability. We have seen that this can be traced back at least to post-Reformation England. There was a lot of geographical mobility as well, and the churches provided a focus for newcomers to be integrated into the community and perhaps to find others from the same ethnic background. With the post-war baby boom, parents sent their children in droves to Sunday School in the hope that they would obtain some moral instruction. In summary, says the sociologist Peter Berger,[34] what the churches were doing was providing comfort in a time of rapid social change. Once in church, people found they could relax and decide that the world, and especially the American way of life, was 'O.K.'.

So American religious institutions were doing very well in the fifties, and continue to do so today even when there has been considerable erosion of numbers (in 1976, only 42 per cent of the population attended a weekly service, and amongst Catholics it had dropped to 55 per cent).[35] But according to Berger, this success was at the expense of 'real' religion. By becoming highly bureaucratic socializing agencies, the American churches had been secularized from within. They had sold out on their reason for existence, their links with a transcendent God.

Desolation

There is something rather odd about an argument which insists on talking about 'secularization' whatever the circumstances, so that even high levels of church attendance can be shown to support rather than weaken the case.[36] Nevertheless it would be hard to dispute the evidence for many parts of Europe. The Italian sociologist S. S. Acquaviva makes the point concisely when he remarks that in many parts of modern

Italy, 'the percentage of those who attend church . . . is much lower than the percentage who wore the habit, not only in the Renaissance but even as late as the eighteenth century'.[37]

In the stark vistas of L. S. Lowry's paintings of urban Salford[38] we seem to come to the end of a long line leading from the densely layered religious imagery of a city like Siena. The symbols, or what remains of them, take on a different kind of meaning. There is a deep ambiguity of feelings aroused by the dark rows of houses and factories, the hurrying people with poverty expressed in the posture of their bodies. In Lowry's depictions of black isolated churches there is the same uncertainty – whether to love them or hate them. Perhaps it would lead to an easing of the mind if they were knocked down so that they could be forgotten. I came across one of these decayed buildings recently. In the middle of a slum clearance area beside rows of new council houses, it stood with weeds growing out of the brickwork, windows boarded up, corrugated iron nailed over the doorways. The corrugated iron had been wrenched away from one entrance and there was a dank, rotting smell from the interior. Bags of decayed rubbish lay around. A small sign indicated that it had been a mosque for a time, but in a stone carving on the wall its origins were revealed: Methodist New Connexion, 1876. After a series of reunions between its various subdivisions,[39] including the Methodist New Connexion, the Methodist church had a membership of nearly 770,000 in 1933. By 1960 it had declined by almost 100,000 and in the next ten years to 1970 by another 100,000. Buildings like this express those figures. (It has since been demolished.)

Richly expressive, too, is the 'death of God' theology which became popular in the 1960s. It is as if theologians, finding themselves out of a job because their employer is missing, presumed dead, reverse the old fairy tale of the 'emperor's new clothes' and continue to make fine new clothes to put on a non-existent emperor. Peter Berger comments on the surrealistic quality of these theologies:

> The phrase 'secular theology' itself strikes with intriguing dissonance, while phrases such as 'atheist theology' or 'religionless Christianity' seem to come from

a script for the theatre of the absurd. The strangeness of the spectacle does not disappear on closer scrutiny. Professional theologians begin with the pre-supposition that there is no God . . . To an outside observer, say a Muslim scholar of Western religion, all this might well appear as a bizarre manifestation of intellectual derangement or institutional suicide.[40]

Lastly, there is the image of clergyman as idiot. Perhaps in the light of the foregoing it is not surprising that one of the most popular caricatures of an English vicar portrays him as a goofy-toothed fool.[41] Not merely is he unable to comprehend the modern world, he is so out of touch that he doesn't even realize it exists. Only by such blindness, the implication runs, is he able to maintain his role. On the other hand, the frequent appearance of a man in a clerical collar in commercial advertisements which trade on nostalgia at least leaves the clergy with some of their ancient image of innocence.

We have been looking at the decline or disappearance in large parts of the traditionally Christian world of symbols and institutions which remind people of the sacred. In one sense, it is those symbols which constitute a religion. The anthropologist Clifford Geertz defines a religion as

A system of symbols which acts to establish powerful, pervasive and longlasting moods and motivations in men by formulating conceptions of a general order of existence and clothing these conceptions with such an aura of factuality that the moods and motivations seem uniquely realistic.[42]

At least, from the picture handed down to us, we can gather that the system of symbols in fourteenth-century Siena was particularly rich. A man born and brought up in Siena at that time could hardly fail to have his moods and motivations powerfully pervaded by the religious imagery that surrounded him. Especially if he were an ordinary citizen, rather than a scholar with links outside his native city, the world picture into which he was born could seem nothing less than reality itself. Give or take a liberal addition of pre-Christian and magical beliefs, the general order of existence as prescribed by the church must have been, for most people, self-evident.

Much of the modern argument about secularization has been about sets of symbols, in particular those connected with Christianity. Have they been disappearing? How fast have they been disappearing? If they are still there, has their meaning been changed or lost? In this chapter I have tried to illustrate the undeniable fact that in large parts of the Christian world they have disappeared or lost their meaning.

But there is another question, perhaps deeper than this. Preoccupation with institutions and symbols may blind us to the claim of religious people that there is a sacred dimension to human experience which is prior to all symbols. Without this, it could be argued, all other dimensions of religion are emptied of their meaning. To this question we shall now turn.

Part Two

What is the
Experiential Dimension?

5

Religion: Public and Invisible

'. . . a great deal of our modern study of religion attempts to give an account of a response without any reference to the stimulus.'

Religious institutions

Durkheim was right. There is something overawing about great institutional gatherings. Looking at a photograph of the opening ceremonies at the Second Vatican Council in 1962, it is hard not to be impressed by the serried ranks of bishops, disappearing afterwards in the immense perspectives of St Peter's in Rome.

On closer examination, however, the photograph begins to reveal the rather more mundane aspects of the assembly. High up in the building are untidy rows of floodlights. The ancient stonework is cluttered with cables, evidence that the building must have been swarming with electricians in overalls, putting in the lights. At ground level, microphones and loudspeakers give further clues to their activity, and an army of joiners has obviously been working overtime, building the banks of seats which run like football stands along either side of the nave. Somewhere in the background, radio and TV men from around the world must be desperately trying to get decent coverage for their home audiences.

Bureaucrats must have been busy for months, arguing over contracts for renovations, working out costs, fighting for cash, hiring staff, organizing sleeping accommodation for bishops, arranging eating facilities, lavatories and washrooms, fixing ways for the princes of the church to get their laundry done. Thousands of letters and information sheets have filled the

61

post-boxes of Rome, en route for destinations round the world.
Back in their home dioceses the bishops have been working
out who is going to do their work while they are away and how
they are going to get to Rome. Prelates from wealthy
American dioceses will probably go by luxury jet, others will
have to try to hitch a ride in a ship headed in the right
direction.

While they are waiting, some will be engaged in speculation. Those with a political cast of mind will be trying to fore-
cast the outcome of the council. Which is the best way to
jump? Who is worth supporting? There will be humbler preoccupations. Will it be possible to understand what is going on
at such a vast meeting?[2] What will the translation facilities be
like? Will Roman food cause indigestion? Will there be a
chance for a bit of sightseeing?

No doubt to almost all the bishops the council was something special, but the bureaucratic side of life would not be
anything new to them. From their beginnings as newly
appointed parish priests they would have been involved in an
endless round of committees, fund raising, building plans;
hiring and firing teachers, cleaners, architects, gravediggers,
musicians, gardeners; buying furniture and hymn books; in-
specting schools, influencing local politicians, cajoling people
into doing jobs, writing references, witnessing legal
documents.

It may be asked in what material way all this activity differs
from that of a member of any other bureaucracy? The answer
is, not at all. The German sociologist Max Weber includes the
Roman Catholic Church, especially in its developments since
the end of the thirteenth century, as one of his examples of 'distinctively developed and quantitatively large bureaucracies'.[3]
It shares this distinction with five other types of organization,
including 'public corporations' and 'large-scale capitalist en-
terprises'. For Weber, one of the salient characteristics of
bureaucracy is the 'levelling' or equalization of the 'governed'
by the centralization of power in the hands of a group of permanent bureaucratic officials. In the Catholic church,

first the feudal and then all independent local inter-
mediary powers were eliminated. This was begun by

Gregory VII and continued through the Council of Trent the [first, 1870] Vatican Council, and it was completed by the edicts of Pius X.[4]

In fact, the most famous single issue debated at the 1870 Council was the doctrine of papal infallibility, but associated with it, and at times becoming confused with it, were arguments about the nature of the Pope's claim to have primacy of jurisdiction over the universal church. As Weber remarked, issues of bureaucratization were involved, and the canon which gained the consent of the council read (rather breathlessly):

> If anyone says that the Roman Pontiff has only the office of inspection or direction, but not the full and supreme power of jurisdiction over the universal church, not only in things pertaining to faith and morals, but in those that pertain to the discipline and government of the church spread through the whole world; or that he has only the principal part, but not the full plenitude of this supreme power, or that this power of his is not ordinary and immediate, whether over the churches all together or individually, or over pastors and faithful all together or individually; let him be anathema.[5]

The debate leading up to the proposal and passage of this canon was humanly many things: dreary, exciting, off the point, laughter-provoking, clever, ironic.[6] Bishop Verot of Savannah, sometimes labelled the *enfant terrible* of the council, was annoyed by the centralizing of power in the hands of the Pope, and there is more than a hint of sarcasm in the proposal he made that there should be a new canon, 'If anyone says that the authority of the Pope in the church is so full that he may dispose of everything by his mere whim, let him be anathema.' His speech was accompanied by laughter and it brought the president of the assembly, Cardinal Capalti, to his feet to complain that 'We are not in a theatre to hear buffooneries, but in the church of God to transact the serious business of the church.'[7]

Whether in the Catholic church or elsewhere, once it is established, felt Weber, a bureaucracy is very difficult to get

rid of. 'The individual bureaucrat cannot squirm out of the
apparatus in which he is harnessed' unless there is a move
from the top of the hierarchy. At the time of the Second
Vatican Council, even the man at the top, John XXIII, felt
trapped by the maze of 'rationally established norms . . .
enactments, decrees and regulations'[8] which Weber saw as the
triumphant end-point of bureaucracy. '*Sono nel sacco qui*' ('I'm
in a bag here') the Pope is reported as saying to an American
cardinal.[9]

Of course, the centralization of power turned out not to be
the whole story. When the Second Vatican Council met, it saw
itself as completing the work of the 1870 Council, which had
been cut short by political events in Italy. One of the un-
finished tasks was the assertion of the importance of middle
management – the bishops – in the document it produced on
the church, 'Lumen Gentium'.[10]

In a large institution, reform of the machinery of government may be a pressing task, if it is not to grind to a halt. It
may also be true that the consciousness of an ecclesiastical
bureaucrat is mostly filled with his responsibility to maintain
the complex network of regulations, which, after all, was origi-
nally constructed to make things run smoothly. Indeed, it is
because of their preoccupations that officials have collected,
over the centuries, statistics of church attendance, communion
taking, numbers of clergy and so on. As we have seen, these
figures can be very useful in helping us to gauge the state of
the institution at different times during history, and it is
annoying to find that numerical estimates are absent because
the bureaucrats of the time were careless or thought the task
not worthy of their time. Nevertheless, reform of government,
facts, figures and keeping the great wheels turning are certainly not the central issue in religion.

From a religious person's point of view there are other,
more serious purposes for the existence of the institution.
Sociologists themselves have begun to feel more dissatisfied
with an approach which uses management structure and
head-counting as the major criteria for making judgements
about the state of religion. In recent years this has led to the
proposal that there are a number of different dimensions along
which people can be religious.[11] The flat images of the past are

being replaced with pictures which reflect more accurately the many ways in which people express their religious experience. Although he is not a sociologist, Ninian Smart has made a helpful subdivision into six categories[12] which I shall use in this chapter.

Dimensions of religion

1. The social
This covers the bureaucratic, plant-maintaining aspect that we have just been discussing. Clearly, this is a preoccupation for every large institution, however secular. There are other, more specific reasons for the existence of religious bodies.

2. The doctrinal
In their persons, and in the person of Pope John XXIII, the Catholic bishops at the Second Vatican Council represented a gathering together in one spot of the teaching authority of an organization which makes claims to universal assent. One might feel that in such a circumstance an appropriate manifestation of the voice of God would be an earthquake which left a gaping crack in the fabric of St Peter's, for future pilgrims to marvel at. In fact, the public face of what went on was much more mundane. As they had been at the 1870 Council, the intrigues and manoeuvres surrounding the production of the documents were a source of great interest to the general public, and have been entertainingly described more than once.[13] The texts finally passed by the bishops are full of administrative advice and practical instruction.[14]

There is an obvious sense in which the debates and publications of the council were political, but to concentrate on the politics is to ignore entirely what the bishops believed themselves to be engaged in – their religious intentions. Their arguments rested on varying interpretations of the New Testament. During the 1870 Council, there had been a strong emphasis on the 'Petrine texts',[15] which were deemed to show that Jesus had given all authority in the church to St Peter, and hence to his successors, the Bishops of Rome. On the other hand, the doctrine of collegiality[16] proposed in 'Lumen Gentium' was based on the view that Jesus had given collective responsibility for the direction of the church to all the apostles as a single unit. The evidence for this was drawn partly from the Acts of the Apostles, where they are shown receiving divine power as a body on the day of Pentecost[17] and thereafter making joint decisions, though with Peter as the accepted leader. As modern descendants of the apostles, therefore, the bishops were jointly responsible for running the affairs of the church. This belief in a particular interpretation of the New Testament was being acted out by their very presence at the council.

There is an important intellectual aspect to this. The debates amongst the bishops were not simply a matter of spontaneous argument on sacred subjects. The discussions were on draft documents which had been laboured over by committees of theologians and sent to the bishops before the debates took place. An appropriate image of many of the preparatory committees might be that of a group of academics trying to make rational sense of what the fundamental beliefs are about. Because religions frequently contain a large number of apparently irreconcilable beliefs, the attempt to achieve doctrinal clarity can be the cause of great tensions. Thus, the question of papal primacy was, and continues to be, a source of numerous violent disputes and splits within Christianity. In recent years the related question of papal infallibility has led to heated arguments within Roman Catholicism itself.[18]

Doctrinal arguments are of course a feature of all large-scale religions, a fact which is illustrated by their many subdivisions. Even within a notably peaceable faith like Buddhism, there was an early split between the southern Hinayana and northern Mahayana, almost a hundred years before the birth of Christ. In the thirteenth century the Japanese Buddhist sectarian Nichiren labelled all other religious groups as 'Hell . . . devils . . . ruin . . . traitors',[19] and the largest modern Japanese sect, the Soka Gakkai, which follows some of the teachings of Nichiren, set itself up as a separate body only in 1931.

But the need for doctrinal clarity is not a peculiarity of religious groups. Practically any body of people with the wish to promote an idea finds itself involved in doctrinal disputes, whether they concern what Lenin really meant, vegetarianism, environmental conservation or nuclear disarmament. Arguments amongst politicians lead to party expulsions or splits because of squabbles over doctrine. Sometimes the divisions, particularly those on the radical left, appear, to an observer unacquainted with the underlying implications, nit-picking in the extreme. The wish for clarity over the things that matter seems to be a universal human characteristic, and is not found only in religious organizations.

3. The mythological
But in religion, doctrinal arguments are concerned with the meaning of sacred stories or mythologies. Every religion has as its centrepiece a collection of stories which treat the most mysterious and disturbing of human problems. Why is there something rather than nothing? Where do we come from? Why is there suffering? What happens when we die?

From all over the world come cosmic creation stories, some bizarre, some strangely familiar to Western ears, many with a haunting beauty.[20] The Omaha Indians of North America conceived of the universe beginning in God's thought, with the creations of his mind searching in space until they find a place in which they can take on material existence. For the Maidu Indians of California the initiator of the earth came down from the sky on a rope of feathers to find that everywhere there was water. He was assisted in the creation of dry land by a turtle which dived to the bottom of the ocean and brought up earth in its claws. In one African tribe, the Boshongo, the first ancestor created the universe by vomiting it up, beginning with the sun and ending with man.

There are also stories of religious heroes, and in the account of their lives, their exploits, their teachings and their deaths, believers feel that they find material to grapple with the profound problems of existence. The stories are revered because they give meaning and coherence to life and awaken the motivation to strive after goals. It is because they know the story of the Buddha's enlightenment under the tree at Bodh-gaya that Buddhists feel encouraged to seek after personal enlightenment. When Jews or Christians read the account of Moses bringing the tablets of the law down from Mount Sinai, or when Christians read the Sermon on the Mount, they feel they have a vivid basis on which to build a system of ethics. The dramatic moment in the synagogue, when Jesus stood up and announced the beginning of his mission by saying that he was bringing good news to the poor, has inspired many individuals and groups down the centuries to identify themselves with the cause of the oppressed, one example in our own era being the theologians of liberation in South America.[21]

But how different are these religious stories from all kinds of secular myths? The word 'myth' is another of those problem words over which scholars argue at great length.[22] I am choosing to use it to refer to 'truths people live by', that is to say, beliefs that are held with conviction by particular individuals. In itself the word 'myth' is a neutral term which makes no reference in an absolute sense to the truth or falsity of a belief. Myths are true for those who believe in them. They are profound metaphors for life without which no one, religious or irreligious, could lead anything but an aimless existence. In this sense 'scientific truths' have mythological significance. Curiosity about origins is provided for by physical theories of the cosmos, and notions about an original 'big bang' or of 'continuous creation' have their own awesome strangeness.

Likewise, in the extraordinary life stories of modern secular heroes there is often a strongly mythological quality. For the radical, there is the story of Lenin, passing through Germany in a closed train, and as in a dream, stepping down from it at the Finland station at St Petersburg, almost, as it were, inaugurating a new era. Or think of the famous image of Lenin addressing the masses from a high platform, leaning forward, chin jutting, cloth cap clutched in hand, bringing good news to the poor. Such depictions help to urge on the flagging spirits of the tired revolutionary. The essence of mythology, that it should be seen to be saying something true about deep issues, seems to be met here. This is the case even where the provisional nature of truth is what is proclaimed, as in the scientific myth.

4. The ethical
Questioned about the true importance of religion, many people will refer to its function as a means of inculcating a

sense of right and wrong. Parents who no longer practise their faith may send their children to Sunday School, and it is assumed that they are hoping their offspring will be given a usable moral code. Religious officials themselves frequently give the ethical dimension greatest emphasis. The most prominent inscription in many an English parish church is the ten commandments, perhaps displayed on a huge pair of boards above the chancel arch or on either side of the altar. By following these, the implication runs, Christians can be sure they are obedient to their creator.

In a somewhat parallel way, immediately after his enlightenment at Bodh-Gaya, the Buddha laid down the Four Noble Truths, which, if systematically meditated upon, would bring enlightenment and release from suffering. The fourth truth describes the eightfold path towards release: right views, right intentions, right speech, right conduct, right livelihood, right effort, right mindfulness, right concentration. Although in the first case the wilful breaking of a commandment is defined as a sin against God, and in the second case avoidance of the eightfold path is to choose to remain in ignorance, in both, what is proposed is an individual and social ethic. The central practical tasks of the Judaeo-Christian and Buddhist religions are enshrined in these two codes.

We noted earlier that General Eisenhower believed religion to be the ethical cement of society. Indeed it may be, if a single religion is commonly held by a majority of the population. But the continuing violent history of religious wars suggests that it does not always succeed in this role. In any case, it is not true that religion, *per se*, necessarily inculcates what is usually regarded as virtuous by Westerners. To the hopeful eye of those concerned to find a common ethic underlying all religions, it is evident that there are basic similarities between Buddhism and Christianity. But though religions have developed attitudes to every dimension of practical life, they can be utterly contradictory, even on issues of the profoundest moral significance. As we have seen, the killing and eating of their fellow human beings in huge numbers was a religious duty for the Aztecs of Mexico. On the other hand, according to Jain mythology, one of its greatest heroes, Mahavira, died of self-starvation as a result

of his desire not to harm any form of life around him. Ninian
Smart writes of the Jain monk:

> The monk must strain his water before drinking; he
> wears a gauze mask over his mouth to prevent the un-
> intentional inhalation of innocent insects; the monk is
> required to sweep the ground before him as he goes, so
> living beings are not crushed by his footsteps; and always
> he treads softly for the very atoms underfoot harbour life-
> monads.[23]

In Western culture, religious people who dedicate themselves to God quite often take a vow of celibacy. Similarly,
followers of the Jain religion who become monks renounce
sexual intercourse, as part of their programme to reach enlightenment. Yet devotees of Tantric Buddhism practise a
type of yoga involving sexual intercourse to achieve spiritual
awakening.

Strict Calvinists sometimes believe that it is morally wrong
to attend the theatre. In Aberdeen, where in one part of the
city a library, a church and a theatre lie alongside each other,
local people refer to them jokingly as 'Education, Salvation,
Damnation'. Yet the theatre has religious origins and was
prominent in the miracle plays of medieval British religion.

Quite apart from this, many people would claim that
religion is neither the only nor the rational source of morality.
Numerous attempts have been made to develop a system of
ethics on another basis. For example, utilitarians believe that
the basis of moral behaviour should be those principles or
actions which provide the greatest happiness for the greatest
number. Karl Marx held the view that the dominant morality
in any society had more to do with maintaining the interests of
the ruling class than with abstract religious notions of virtue.
Hence only by abolishing class differences would an uncorrupt
ethical system be possible. So there are many contenders for
the right to establish what moral behaviour is, and not all of
them are religious.

5. The ritual

When we turn to ritual we seem to be approaching the heart-
land of religion. This was certainly the view of Durkheim and

Freud. The Second Vatican Council had, as its opening event, the most significant of all Christian rituals, a mass or communion service. Anyone who doubts the power of this particular ritual in European history need only consider the huge collection of architectural and artistic creations connected with it which are scattered all over that continent,[24] and anywhere that a European influence has been felt.

Robert Bocock[25] defines ritual action as 'the symbolic use of bodily movement and gesture in a social situation to express and articulate meaning'. Sociologists often see the mass as expressing primarily a sense of social solidarity, whether the congregation consists of two or three people or a vast assembly of hundreds of thousands. This solidarity is not merely a matter of numbers present, it is a statement of community with all co-religionists, a prescribed and repeated action known to be taking place elsewhere. And the links are also historical, because the drama centres on the most intense moment in the upper room when Jesus shared out bread and wine with his disciples and stated that he was giving them his body and blood. Amongst Roman Catholics even the boundaries of time are abolished, because the modern mass is said to be 'the same sacrifice'.

So the mass is a symbolic presentation of a Christian event, but it is also a vehicle for doctrine and ethics which are expressed by practically every detail of dress, every movement, every change in tone of voice, every material object used.[26] Somewhere a priest in the clothes of a workman may be presiding at a mass round a kitchen table, using bread and wine from the local supermarket and kitchen crockery. Though the ritual may look simpler than high mass in a cathedral, it may also be expressing a multitude of meanings. For example, it could be an ethical statement that the virtues of humble brotherhood and sisterhood are more true to the heart of the Christian story than hierarchic splendour. Onlookers in cathedral or kitchen may be impressed or scandalized depending on the meanings they personally attach to the symbols.

Another kind of religious ritual, apparently found in every culture, is that connected with important transitions in a person's life.[27] So Christians have their infants baptized, get married in church and arrange for their dead to have a funeral service. But need these 'rites of passage' necessarily be religious? It certainly seems to be true that, whether they are formally religious or not, people like to mark important phases in their life with ritual. In the Soviet Union the communist party has made strenuous and to some extent successful efforts to construct secular ceremonies which will appropriately express the seriousness of these occasions.

Furthermore, if rituals are symbolic expressions of meaning, there are many examples of totally secular performances of this kind. Dances, theatrical performances, pop-festivals, sporting displays, military spectacles may all be expressive of secular, political or ethical points of view. Roland Barthes[28] gives an ironic account of French all-in wrestling as having the nature of 'Greek drama', presenting in exaggerated gestures a view of justice and the battle between good and evil. In the area of politics, the function of ritual in showing group solidarity is very obvious. Marches and demonstrations accompanied by bands and banners are expressing precisely that. It cannot therefore be said that ritual is the preserve only of religion.

6. *The experiential*

There are, then, plenty of examples of secular institutions with their own special doctrines, myths, ethical systems and rituals. Frequently the examples I have used have been drawn from Marxism. Indeed, because the parallels are easy to draw, Marxism is sometimes taken to be a kind of religion. But I suspect that the association of these phenomena with a political movement is nothing to do with religion. It is to do with the fact that the movement expresses a consensus on matters of major importance amongst a very large number of human beings.

The most obvious way that religion differs from the secular is in its intention. Religions always intend to be the social expression of an inner experience of the sacred or the holy.[29] This experiential aspect of religion is the last and most crucial of Ninian Smart's dimensions. Without it, the other dimensions may retain a meaning of sorts, but it will not be religious.

Thus, to take the ritual dimension, our discussion of the mass lacked any consideration of what the participants thought they were doing. Rightly or wrongly, Durkheim believed the intention behind ritual was the worship of society. Rightly or wrongly, in the mass, Roman Catholics believe they are communicating with God. At the moment of communion, for the believer, there is a reliving of the mysterious occasion when Christ gave himself to the disciples. When the ritual loses this inner meaning for a person, at best it remains a source of aesthetic pleasure, at worst it becomes a cause of embarrassment or hostility.

For religious people, the sacred is not primarily a theoretical category which can be deduced or refuted by debate. Religious myths are, in their view, the public side of an inner religious experience. In many cases, as for example in the life stories of the Buddha or Jesus, they refer to the religious experience of the founder. Religious heroes are not merely great men, they are people who either are believed to have had direct experience of, or are themselves the manifestation of, the sacred. From time to time, followers claim that they personally obtain a kind of experimental confirmation of the truth expressed by the myth. Believers also hold the view that those who make doctrinal statements, if they are to be valid, must be assisted by divine power. Sometimes Christians claim that a theologian can make a genuine contribution to doctrine only if he is himself a man of prayer. I have heard Indians make a similar statement about an admired guru: 'What he speaks, he knows.'

In the same way, ethical insights are seen by believers as gaining their imperative power, in the end, from religious experience.

> You know me through and through,
> From having watched my bones take shape
> When I was being formed in secret
> Knitted together in the limbo of the womb,[30]

says the psalm. People from a Judaeo-Christian background who believe themselves to have had direct experience of an intimate relationship with the sacred feel the force of these lines, when they are grappling with the ethical dilemmas surrounding the question of abortion on demand.

Finally, the experiential aspect of religion can sometimes be powerful enough to lead to the other dimensions being ignored. Throughout history, religious people have attacked religious institutions, rituals, doctrines, myths and codes of ethics in the name of their inner experience. Within Christianity, such people have come in time to seem like both saints and demons, as in the case of Luther, or the millenarian peasant leader Thomas Müntzer, or George Fox, the founder of the Quakers. A similar disregard for public forms characterized Bodhidharma, founder of Zen Buddhism, even though the modern Zendo is not without its rituals. So it seems that people have a deep regard for religious institutions because they express publicly, and correspond to, something profoundly personal. But they can also despise them because they find no answering echo in personal experience. The paradox, of course, is that without the language provided for us by the religious or mystical traditions, it is well nigh impossible to express religious experience.

Of course the very term 'religious experience' arose out of specific cultural origins in Europe. To try to understand what it meant, and has since come to mean, we shall have to return into Protestant history and, in particular, its effect on the New England consciousness.

6

The New England Connection

'There is some new sensation or perception of the mind, which is entirely of a new sort, and which could be produced by no exalting, varying or compounding of that kind of perceptions or sensations which the mind had before . . .'

JONATHAN EDWARDS[1]

Calvinist and Pietist Origins

William James is generally credited with initiating the widespread modern currency of the term, 'religious experience', when he published *The Varieties of Religious Experience* in 1902. But in spite of his cosmopolitan upbringing, James' understanding of the term was very strongly coloured by the peculiarities of the history of Christianity in New England. In this chapter we need to have a look at some of these antecedents if we are to understand both the richness and the limitations of what James had to say on the subject.

Like many New Englanders, William James came from a Calvinist background, though both his father and himself had moved away from their religious origins. Nevertheless, some understanding of Calvinism is necessary to see how James may have been affected by it.

In his *Institutes of the Christian Religion*, John Calvin discusses the way men relate to God. His first premise is that we cannot know God in his Essence, and yet it is vital to know God in more than an abstract way, such as might be deduced from philosophy. This more direct knowledge, says Calvin, comes from scripture, but again, it is not enough to read the scriptures like a secular book; they have to be read with faith. Of itself, says Calvin, the Bible is simply an historical document with no more authority than any other document. If it is to speak personally to the reader as a 'living word', there must be some intervention of the Holy Spirit. The Spirit uses the scripture dynamically in the here-and-now of the reader's experience to convince him or her that it truly is the Word of God:

> For as God alone is a fit witness of His word, so also the Word will not find acceptance in men's hearts before it is sealed by the inward testimony of the Spirit. The same spirit, therefore, who has spoken through the mouths of the prophets must penetrate into our hearts to persuade us that they faithfully proclaimed what had been divinely commanded.[2]

Calvin is implying here a kind of 'spiritual knowing' which frees the believer from dependence on an external authority, particularly, from a Reformation perspective, the Roman Catholic Church. In addition, according to Calvin the Holy Spirit acts in an homologous way when He gives people predestined to salvation inner certainty of their adoption by God. The elect are thus given a certainty through faith, of their election. On the other hand, those predestined by God to eternal damnation, are not aware of their condition, though Calvin allows that we can perhaps guess on the basis of their unresponsiveness to the Gospel or to preaching.

It would be a violent distortion of Calvin's thought to describe the action of Divine Grace as a matter of feeling, or even religious experience; for him it approximated much more to an intellectual conviction. The twentieth century sociologist Max Weber has described with incomparable power his perception of the impact of this doctrine on the believer:

> In its extreme inhumanity this doctrine must, above all, have had one consequence for the life of a generation which surrendered to its magnificent consistency. That was a feeling of unprecedented inner loneliness of the single individual. In what was, for the man of the age of the Reformation, the most important thing in his life, his eternal salvation, he was forced to follow his path alone to meet a destiny which had been decreed for him from eternity. No-one could help him. No priest, for the

chosen one can understand the Word of God only in his own heart. No sacraments, for though the sacraments had been ordained by God for the increase of His glory, and must hence be scrupulously observed, they are not a means to the attainment of Grace, but only the subjective *externa subsidia* of faith. No Church, for though it was held that *extra ecclesiam nulla salus* in the sense that whoever kept away from the true Church could never belong to God's chosen band, nevertheless the membership of the external Church included the doomed . . . Finally, even no God. For even Christ had died only for the elect . . .[3]

Sooner or later, for the committed believer, the crucial question, 'Am I one of the saved?' must have forced other questions into the background. The anxious search for cast-iron certainty, according to Weber, became of dominating importance and, even against the central thrust of Calvin's doctrine, there began a search for some kind of infallible criteria by which membership of the elect could be confirmed. In addition there was a pressure on people engaged in pastoral work to find a means of dealing with the suffering caused by the doctrine.

Weber interpreted the rise of capitalism in Western Europe as one major response, resulting from the recommendation to embark on intense worldly activity as a means of assurance that one is a tool of the Divine will.

Another response, more directly concerned with our subject, and perhaps influenced by the Enlightenment emphasis on the priority of direct experience in achieving truth, is the appearance within English Puritanism in the seventeenth century of a new emphasis on 'feeling' as a testimony to election.[4] The history of English Dissenting religion is extremely complex and obscure,[5] and the key figure in this shift was not himself a dissenter, but an Anglican, William Perkins.

In Perkins' writing we see appearing the idea of conversion as something which is the end point of a psychological process. The first requisite was the experience of self-condemnation:

None can be a lively member of Christ till his conscience condemn him, and make him quite out of heart in respect of himself. And the want of this is the cause why so few perceive any sweetness or comfort in the Gospel.[6]

The normal route by which this experience came about was by hearing the preaching of Divine law. At the same time, preaching offered a way of escape from the despair induced by repentance, and the discovery of the love of Christ towards a man:

> Herein stands the power and pith of true religion, when a man by observation and experience in himself, knows the love of God in Christ towards him.[7]

At much the same time that Perkins' influence was being felt within English dissenting religion there was a parallel emphasis on the importance of religious feeling appearing in Lutheran Germany. It seems to have been a response to the dry and intolerant Spirit that appeared in Protestant Orthodoxy on the Continent after the death of Luther in 1546. One of the notable figures in this movement was Philip Jacob Spener, who, like Perkins, gave attention particularly towards the necessity for a direct, inner, psychological illumination in conversion.

With the appointment of Auguste Hermann Francke, on the advice of Spener, to the new University of Halle in 1692, Pietism developed in a direction which will be familiar to modern ears. The basis of Francke's faith was his experience of conversion in 1687, described movingly in his autobiography and underlining the sudden nature of the change:

> I cried to God whom I still did not know nor trust, for salvation from such a miserable state (asking him to save me), if indeed he was a true God. The Lord, the Living God, heard me from His Throne while I yet knelt . . . my doubt vanished as quickly as one turns one's hand; I was assured in my heart of the Grace of God in Christ Jesus and I knew God not only as God but as my Father . . . when I knelt down I did not believe that there was a God but when I stood up I believed it to the point of giving up my blood without fear or doubt.[8]

Because of Francke's role at Halle, the University quickly became a centre of Pietist mission, one continuing evidence of which is the familiarity of his phraseology in our own day. It was with the background of his own experience that Francke made central Jesus' requirement that we be 'born again'. Like many a modern evangelical preacher, Francke also advised that there are special moments which come in individuals' lives where they have the opportunity to 'decide for Christ'.

Pietist influence affected North America through missionary effort and immigration, but more specifically in New England it had a powerful influence on the understanding of religious experience through its 'step-child', Methodism. John Wesley, as is well-known, received his religious awakening through contact with Moravian Pietists during a visit to Georgia in the winter of 1735–36, and was finally converted in London on the 24th of May 1738 when he,

> . . . went very unwillingly to a religious society in Aldersgate Street, where one was reading Luther's Preface to the Epistle to the Romans. About a quarter before nine, while he was describing the change which God works in the heart through faith in Christ, I felt my heart strangly warmed. I felt I did trust in Christ, Christ alone, for salvation; and an assurance was given me, that He had taken away *my* sins, even *mine*, and saved me from the law of sin and death.[9]

Two years later, in 1740, Wesley's evangelist colleague, George Whitefield, was preaching in Northampton, Massachusetts to the congregation of the Reverend Jonathan Edwards.

Jonathan Edwards

We shall see later that Edwards had a very direct influence on William James' understanding of religious experience. Edwards had no doubt about its reality. It is because of a failure to recognize spiritual reality directly, a mistaken appropriation of the words and symbols used to refer to the reality as if they *were* that reality, Edwards believed, that there was so much religious apathy in his community. For Edwards, spiritual understanding is never merely intellectual or theoretical; religious knowledge derives from a direct, first hand encounter with sacred reality.

The totally novel quality of 'religious experience' led Edwards to reject the normal five senses, and the mind's reflection on them, as the basis for an explanation of such experience. Nevertheless, as someone keenly interested in the philosophy of John Locke, yet remote from the sceptical currents of thought in Europe, he proposed a further supraphysical 'sense of the heart'. It is the 'infinite excellency of God' which is perceived by this sense, and Edwards goes on to claim that this is not simply a perception of a fact, it is also a perception of meaning and value. Whilst it is true that there are often 'external ideas' in attendance at spiritual experience (the beauties of nature, etc.), for Edwards these are not part of the experience any more than 'the motion of the blood, and beating of the pulse, that attend experiences, are a part of spiritual experience'.[10]

It is important to note that Edwards is not attempting a wild speculation here; he is trying to account for the sense of intense meaningfulness associated with the religious experience he himself had as well as those to whom he preached. Spiritual knowledge for him is a kind of insight. Faith is perception, not an admission of ignorance, and Edwards goes on to propose that it is the 'whole man' and not merely a particular faculty which does the perceiving. It was in an attempt to produce the conditions necessary for the moment of insight that Edwards developed his hell-fire preaching. These methods have lately been interpreted in Freudian terms[11] but Edwards himself had no doubt that conversion brought about an 'inward firm persuasion of the reality of Divine things, such as they don't use to have before their conversion'. They had, claimed Edwards, 'seen and tasted', 'intuitively beheld' and 'immediately felt' the 'Divine excellency and glory of the things of Christianity'.

From Edwards to James: Calvinism Transformed

The historian H. C. Goddard remarked that, 'the history of American thought is, in its largest outline, identical with that of Europe, though generally, save in politics, America lagged several decades, sometimes near a whole century, behind.'[12] Whilst in Western Massachusetts Calvinist orthodoxy

continued to flourish well into the nineteenth century and influenced some of William James' scientific contemporaries, a
drily rationalistic religion had arrived in the sophisticated
world of Boston and Cambridge, rather late, in the form of
Unitarianism. It was in response to this that the New England
Transcendentalists appeared. Ralph Waldo Emerson, the
greatest of the Transcendentalists, was born in 1803, the son
of a Congregationalist minister, and he himself entered the
Unitarian ministry, but resigned on the pretext that he felt unable conscientiously to administer Holy Communion. During
a subsequent trip to Europe, he underwent a profound
personal change which, phenomenologically, amounted to a
conversion, or an experience of rebirth, in Calvinist terms.

The rationalism of nineteenth century Unitarianism
became an anathema to Emerson. He spoke of it as 'an ice
house' and attacked the 'corpse cold Unitarianism of Harvard
College and Brattle Street'.

In one dimension his reaction was very remote from the
Calvinism of his ancestors. He moved into the world of
modern comparative religion by espousing a monism which
comes from the Hindu Advaita philosophy. His best known
description of what purports to be his own transcendental experience, appears in his essay on *Nature*:

> Standing on the bare ground – my head bathed by the
> blithe air, and uplifted to infinite space – all mean
> egotism vanishes. I become a transparent eyeball. I am
> nothing; I see all; the currents of the Universal Being
> circulate through me; I am part or parcel of God.[13]

The Pantheism of this final sentence became more pro-
nounced in later years and laid him open to quite a bit of
satire, as did remarks like,

> I am God in nature, I am a weed by the wall.

The point that matters in what he says, with regard to the
development of our modern understanding of the term
'religious experience', is his belief that religious truth is intuitively available to all people. Discovery did not depend on
academic learning or the assimilation of religious doctrine.
His ideal was to build a new faith, which abandons dependence
on historical models of religion. As he writes in *Nature*,

> Our age is retrospective. It builds the sepulchres of the
> fathers. It writes biographies, histories and criticism.
> The foregoing generations beheld God and nature face to
> face; we, through their eyes. Why should not we also
> enjoy an original relation to the Universe? Why should
> not we have a poetry and philosophy of insight and not of
> tradition, and a religion by revelation to us, and not the
> history of theirs?[14]

No doubt Jonathan Edwards would have abhorred his creed
and, doctrinally, the chasm between their views is unbridge-
able. Yet it appears that at the level of personal style and motivation, there are clear continuities between Edwards'
Calvinism and Emerson's effort to confront face to face the
Divine Presence in the physical universe 'without the inter-
mediacy of ritual, of ceremony, of the Mass and the con-
fessional'.

Emerson could be seen, in effect, as an Edwards whose faith
in historical Christianity has been destroyed by rationalism.
'Religious experience', with its assurance of salvation to the
Puritan, is what Emerson claims is available to all. Transcendentalism's voice of God in the intuition of the heart has come
to mean for Emerson, Edwards' 'Divine and supernatural
light immediately imparted to the soul by the Spirit of God',
now extended from the elect of John Calvin to include the
whole human race.

Participation in the Divine 'Over-Soul' implied both indi-
vidualism and self reliance; 'speak your latent conviction and
it shall be the universal sense'. It also encouraged the demo-
cratic view of human talent and the idea that there were other
valid sources of knowledge than the scientific method.
Emerson's anti-intellectualism and his democracy of the spirit
have been seen by some as *the* philosophy of ordinary
Americans. Though his views were revolutionary, they advised a revolution within the individual, and man's alienation
as an alienation of the well-springs of religious experience.
The popularity of Emerson's views perhaps helps to explain
the openness of the next generation of New England
academics to the scientific study of religious experience.

William James

The personal and intellectual life of the James family was closely associated with Transcendentalism and with Emerson, who was a personal friend of the elder Henry James, William's father. But William's intellectual universe was still further secularized than that of Emerson, in that Darwinian ideas had reduced the plausibility of rationalist arguments for the existence of God, based on design.

His empiricism, at first sight, would not have been congenial to Emerson and was also the cause of fierce arguments with his own father. 'Empirical science', Emerson had said in his essay on *Nature*, 'is apt to cloud the sight, and by the very knowledge of functions and processes to bereave the student of the manly contemplation of the whole . . . A dream may let us deeper into the secret of nature than a hundred concerted experiments'.[15] Yet Emerson's mysticism implies the sort of enlarged empiricism for which James argued. It was a pragmatic mysticism in that it insisted on testing all truths by experience. James adhered to the 'religious hypothesis' on the grounds that 'God is real because he has real effects'.

There is in James a final reversal of priorities that had been begun by Emerson in his revision of Calvinist logic. Whilst Edwards used scripture to interpret the meaning of natural phenomena, Emerson argued from his experience of nature to scripture: 'what is a farm but a mute gospel?' Only in methodology did James differ from Emerson, in that his intent was to collect specific observations to demonstrate the validity of the general truths enunciated by the latter.

With all his commitment to empiricism, James conducted no studies of his own on accounts of contemporary religious experience. However, when he was invited in 1896 to prepare a series of Gifford Lectures to be presented in Edinburgh University, he began a sporadic collection of materials from an extremely wide variety of sources. To a great degree his examples were culled from the historical writings of the world religions, but he also quoted extensively from the research findings of his student E. D. Starbuck[16] as well as several others of his scientific contemporaries. Their work, which laid the basis for the modern empirical study of reports of religious experience, will be referred to later in this book.

The work of preparing the lectures was carried out in trying circumstances. By 1899, James' health was so bad and his spirit so depressed that he talked of 'getting safely out of the Gifford scrape'.[17] He tried to resign his appointment but on being pressed, made do with a postponement and eventually delivered the first series in 1901. The struggle seems to express something of the ambivalence in him towards both his father and to religious belief. At the time of his father's death in 1883, he had written to his brother Henry,

> As life closes, all a man has done seems like one cry or sentence. Father's cry was a single one that religion is real. The thing is so to 'voice' it that others shall hear – no easy task, but a worthy one, which in some shape I shall attempt.[18]

The difficulty was to transcend the history of argument and disagreement between father and son. The elder Henry found science repellant and claimed never to have known a moment of scepticism in his life. But William had been trained as an empirical scientist and taught philosophy in the modern critical sense, that is to say, *beginning* with scepticism. Nevertheless, employing the pragmatism which he endorsed for others, he worked his way towards his father's position. In 1891 he wrote, 'Father would find in me today a much more receptive listener – all *that* philosophy has got to be brought in'.[19]

James' purposes in presenting the Gifford lectures were outlined in a letter to a friend.

> . . . first, to defend (against all the prejudices of my 'class') experience against philosophy as being the real backbone of the world's religious life – I mean prayer, guidance and all that sort of thing immediately and privately felt, as against high and noble and general views of our destiny and the world's meaning; and *second*, make the reader or hearer believe what I myself invincibly do believe, that, although all the special manifestations of religions may have been absurd (I mean its

creeds and theories) yet the life of it as a whole is mankind's most important function. A task well nigh impossible, I fear, and in which I shall fail; but to attempt it is *my* religious act.[20]

Too much weight has been put on the fact that this act was one of filial piety towards his father. No doubt the judgement is partly true, but the evidence in the *Varieties* points to a more direct religious need than that. Though a delightful companion, James was frequently sick in body and soul, and, still rooted in his Puritan origins, he was involved in a passionate search for individual salvation. His religious affinities can be traced back to Edwards, and in spite of his sophistication he was no religious liberal, referring to himself on one occasion as a 'crass supernaturalist'.

His refuge seems to have been in 'numinous uneasiness',[21] a sense of having strayed on to the boundaries of mystical experience, without having properly entered therein. In 1898, with the Edinburgh lectures very much on his mind, he had what would nowadays, following Abraham Maslow, be called a 'peak experience', whilst camping in the Adirondack Mountains,

> . . . the streaming moonlight lit up things in a magical chequered play and it seemed as if the gods of all the nature mythologies were holding an indescribable meeting in my breast with the moral gods of the inner life . . . The intense significance of some sort, of the whole scene, if one could only *tell* the significance; the intense inhuman remoteness of its inner life, and yet the intense *appeal* of it; . . . in point of fact I can't find a single word for all that significance, and don't know what it was significant of, so there it remains, a mere boulder of *impression*. Doubtless in more ways than one, though, things in the Edinburgh lectures will be traceable to it.[22]

This account which is Wordsworthian in its romanticism, seems remote from the Puritan conversion experience, though it is not alien in tone from some of Jonathan Edwards' more lyrical descriptions of his personal experience.

It has been observed,[23] that James' concern with salvation leads him in his lectures to conflate improperly an extraordinarily wide range of accounts of experience from 'saints, philosophers, artists and ordinary people, from Protestants and Catholics, Jews, Buddhists, Christian Scientists, Transcendentalists, Quakers, Mormons, Mohammedans, Melanesian cannibals, drug takers, atheists and neurotics, including himself in the guise of an anonymous Frenchman'. Nevertheless, it is inappropriate to discount James' scientific ambition to postulate a psychological hypothesis, rooted in the biological nature of the species which would account in general terms for this realm of human experience.

In the light of what has gone before, I suggest that James stands at the end point of an implicit humanism in New England Puritanism, first postulated in Jonathan Edwards' 'sense of the heart'. Edwards' lack of embarrassment at what appeared to be the proposal of a psychological 'sense' linking creature and transcendent God continued through a number of mutations up to the time of James. It opened the possibility for James' religious empiricism as a distinctively New England phenomenon.

In this respect James was able, with a number of his pupils and academic contemporaries to prevent a complete split between religion and religious experience on the one hand, and the tradition of empirical enquiry on the other. His assiduity in the collection of accounts of religious experience and his refusal to be reductive in his interpretations, make him in some ways a forerunner of the twentieth century phenomenologists of religion, but his roots are in the Calvinist tradition emanating from Jonathan Edwards.

By the time he was writing it was no longer possible for a well-educated American to remain isolated from the sceptical winds heralded by the European Enlightenment. James' personal competence, childhood environment, and life history, therefore, meant that he bore in his body a bewilderment and anxiety about religion which still speaks to many who share his cultural antecedents. He was too honest and too sensitive a man to accept secular dismissals of his religion, and on the other hand, he found no easy resting place for it in the intellectual tradition as it stood.

Part of the difficulty is that the realm of religious experience is not only difficult to define, but the experience itself is very strange and difficult to describe, as we shall see in the next chapter.

7

Strange and Difficult to Describe

'This is the way It [Brahman] is to be illustrated:
When lightnings have been loosed:
  aaah!
When that has made the eyes to be closed:
  aaah!'

From the KENA-UPANISHAD[1]

A particular kind of experience

We think of religions as starting with a bang. I suppose this is
because the opening scene of so many religious mythologies is
a panorama of the creation of the universe. But where we are
in historical touch with a founder, rather than the vast remoteness of cosmic beginnings, the reference is to an overwhelming
experience.

Muhammad, it is said, came to love solitude at a certain
stage in his life, and would withdraw for several nights to a
cave in a mountain near Mecca. One night, as he was praying
in the cave, the truth came unexpectedly to him:

> He (i.e. Gabriel) came to him saying: O Muhammad,
> thou art Allah's Apostle. Said the Apostle of Allah –
> upon whom be Allah's blessing and peace: 'Thereat I fell
> to my knees where I had been standing, and then with
> trembling limbs dragged myself along till I came in to
> Khadija [his wife] saying: Wrap ye me up! Wrap ye me
> up! till the terror passed from me. Then (on another
> occasion) he came to me again and said: O Muhammad,
> thou art Allah's Apostle, (which so disturbed me) that I
> was about to cast myself down from some high mountain
> cliff. But he appeared before me as I was about to do this

and said: O Muhammad, I am Gabriel and thou art Allah's Apostle.'[2]

In the New Testament the scene when Jesus was baptized in the river Jordan is described as follows:

> No sooner had he come up out of the water than he saw the heavens torn apart and the Spirit, like a dove, descending on him. And a voice came from heaven, 'You are my Son the Beloved; my favour rests on You.' Immediately afterwards the Spirit drove him out into the wilderness and he remained there for forty days . . .[3]

The modern New Testament scholar James D. G. Dunn[4] sees in this event the moment when Jesus gained an existential conviction that he was God's son. His 'baptism by John was probably the occasion for an experience of God which had epochal significance for Jesus'.[5] Following this experience, he began his mission.

According to the Buddhist scriptures, the inauguration of the Buddha's career as a teacher was the shattering personal experience he had as the result of deep meditation under a tree. In the *Dhammapada* his hymn of victory tells how he experienced the loss of ego, the limiting 'tent-designer':

> Tent-designer, I know thee now;
> Never again to build art thou;
> Quite out are all thy joyful fires,
> Rafter broken and roof-tree gone;
> Into the vast my heart goes on,
> Gains Eternity – dead desires.[6]

Reflecting on these descriptions, the question comes to mind: are the experiences of these great founders so extraordinary as either to be unbelievable or to have no echo in the lives of other people? By analogy, theories of origins in geology and biology used to speak of a primeval cataclysmic event which threw up the mountains and continents and peopled them with living things. But then the suggestion was made that the slow processes of earth movement and natural selection which are still going on could equally well explain the nature of the earth. Perhaps, in a comparable way, it would be possible to make a search to find out whether in contemporary human experience there are phenomena out of which religion grows. If they exist, are they at all common, or in any way like those described in ancient stories?

Types of experience

But first I would like to try to specify in more detail what sort of experience modern scholars might consider as falling into the category of 'religious'. It would be foolhardy to try to set sharp boundaries to the kinds of physical events which people have defined for themselves as religious, because there are no areas of experience which at some time have not been so called. This is a question we shall be returning to in a later chapter. But what if there is a particular kind of occurrence in the life of members of our species which leads them to feel that they are directly aware of or being influenced by a transcendent presence or power? Perhaps this is the raw material, as it were, of religious consciousness.

Ninian Smart suggests that there are two major strands of human experience which do fall into this category.[7] They are sometimes called 'numinous' and 'mystical' experience, and both of them have a profound strangeness which makes them very difficult to describe.

The man who coined the term 'numinous' was Rudolph Otto, a German theologian–philosopher who died in 1937. He is described as an erect military-looking figure whose formality was not over-reassuring to diffident visitors.[8] Nevertheless, his writing shows him to have been a man of intense and subtle feeling. In his book *The Idea of the Holy*[9] he attempts to get away from the word 'holy' because it is tangled up in people's minds with virtue or piety, as when we speak of a holy man. There may even be an aura of hypocrisy about it; a person who gives the impression of slimy sanctimoniousness is sometimes called a 'Holy Willie'.[10] So Otto invents a new word to refer to a particular kind of experience which is *sui generis* and not reducible to something else. In a parallel way, 'seeing' cannot be reduced to anything else, for example by saying that it is nothing but a string of electrical impulses.

The problem about this special kind of experience is that it is very difficult to see how to explain it to someone who doesn't already share a knowledge of it. Otto opens the third chapter of his book with the disappointing statement:

> The reader is invited to direct his mind to a moment of deeply felt religious experience as little as possible qualified by other forms of consciousness. Whoever cannot do this, whoever knows no such moments in his experience, is requested to read no further . . . We do not blame such an one, when he tries for himself to advance as far as he can with the help of such principles of explanation as he knows, interpreting . . . 'religion' as a function of the gregarious instinct and social standards, or as something more primitive still.[11]

These discouraging remarks are, of course, an encouragement to read on. The author appears to be leaping over the sort of theoretical explanation we have already discussed, to appeal directly to the reader's experience. In a way, he is a little like a science teacher who is getting beginners to look at their experience of the world and analyse it more carefully. If readers can find in their life histories a moment when they have been overwhelmed by strangeness or total 'otherness', this '*mysterium tremendum*' is what Otto is driving at. A second quality is a feeling of the 'awfulness' of the experience, in the sense of a dread or even of a terror which can make the flesh creep. Thirdly there is an element of being overpowered, of being 'dust and ashes' before the divine. Fourthly there is the feeling of being caught up in the power of unbridled energy – 'The love of God is a consuming fire'. Finally, in spite of the fearfulness, there is a powerful element of fascination or alluring charm.

Still struggling to communicate with his reader, Otto suggests reading the Book of Isaiah. 'If a man does not *feel* what the numinous is when he reads the sixth chapter of Isaiah, then no "preaching, singing, telling", in Luther's phrase, can avail him.'[12] This is the way the chapter opens:

> In the year that King Uzziah died, I saw also the Lord sitting upon a throne, high and lifted up, and his train

filled the temple. Above it stood the seraphims: each one had six wings; with twain he covered his face and with twain he covered his feet and with twain he did fly. And one cried unto another and said, Holy, Holy, Holy is the Lord of Hosts: the whole earth is full of His glory. And the posts of the door moved at the voice of him that cried, and the house was filled with smoke. Then said I, Woe is me for I am undone; because I am a man of unclean lips, and I dwell in the midst of a people with unclean lips: for mine eyes have seen the King, the Lord of Hosts.[13]

The aftermath for Isaiah was a feeling of being cleansed or purged:

Then flew one of the seraphims unto me, having a live coal in his hand, which he had taken with the tongs from off the altar: And he laid it upon my mouth, and said, Lo, this hath touched thy lips; and thine iniquity is taken away and thy sin purged.'[14]

Otto, drawing from a totally different tradition, says that, indeed, if the question is asked 'Who is the Lord of Hosts?' the answer is the same as for 'Brahman', 'that in whose presence we must exclaim "aaah"!'.[15]

These numinous experiences by definition involve the feeling of being in the presence of someone or something sacred or holy. But they shade into another large group of experiences which are called 'mystical' by modern scholars.[16] The difference is that in a mystical episode the experiencer feels that, in an extraordinary way, all things are One. At its profoundest it is totally indescribable, since the language and thought which would be used in a description have already divided the world into 'you', 'me', 'that over there' and so on. Sometimes mystics try to point to the experience:

It cannot be called void or not void,
Or both or neither;
But in order to point it out,
It is called 'the Void'.[27]

To a Western ear, the search for the void has a coldness about it which is not borne out in the life of its practitioners, for whom enlightenment brings 'bliss unspeakable':

Hawklike, the roshi scrutinized me as I entered his room, walked towards him, prostrated myself, and sat before him with my mind alert and exhilarated . . . 'The Universe is One' he began, each word tearing into my mind like a bullet. 'The moon of truth –' All at once the roshi, the room, every single thing disappeared in a dazzling stream of illumination and I felt myself bathed in a delicious, unspeakable delight.[18]

I said that there was a shading from numinous into mystical experience because, within religious traditions which emphasize the separateness of God, there are often 'mystics' for whom the distinction between God and his creation becomes a very fine one. Jalal al-Din Rumi, a Sufi mystic of the thirteenth century, says in a poem:

What is to be done O Moslems? For I do not recognize myself.
I am neither Christian, nor Jew, nor Gabr nor Moslem.
I am not of the East, nor of the West, nor of the land, nor of the sea . . .
I am not of this world, nor of the next, nor of Paradise, nor of Hell.
My place is the placeless, my trace is the Traceless.
'Tis neither body nor soul, for I belong to the soul of the Beloved.
I have put duality away, I have seen that the two worlds are One.
One I seek, One I know, One I see, One I call.[19]

Meister Eckhart, the fourteenth century German Dominican mystic, got himself into trouble for such 'monism'. Speaking of nature, he said: 'All that a man has here externally in multiplicity is intrinsically One. Here all blades of grass, wood and stone, all things are *one*. This is the deepest depth.'[20] When it came to the crunch, however, he saved his orthodoxy, as in this description of inner experience: 'Though she [the soul] sink all in the one-ness of divinity she never touches bottom. God has left her one little point to get back to herself and know herself as a creature.'[21]

Sometimes the shading goes the other way. Although the Buddha made no claim to be a god, and in Western terms

Buddhism is a non-theistic religion, in practice things are not as clear-cut. In Sri Lanka, at the Temple of the Tooth, one of the verses addressed to the Buddha image is: 'Forgive me my transgression committed through carelessness by body, word or thought, O Tathāgata of great wisdom.'[22]

Implied here is an awareness of a numinous presence, personalized, which is able to forgive sins. In northern, Mahayana Buddhism, this tendency towards theism is even more obvious. Members of the Pure Land Sect achieve liberation through faith in the power of the Buddha of Boundless Light, Amitabha.

Context and experience

The difficulty with this realm of supposed human experience is that it is forever wriggling away from the possibility of neat definitions. For example, there is a Hindu poem to the God Vishnu which seems to be expressing mystical and numinous experience at the same time:

> You are everything, earth, water, fire, air, and space,
> The subtle world, the Nature-of-All,
> *And* the person who stands for ever aloof.[23]

Now this is taken from a literary work, so it is possible that the writer is talking about his experience of Vishnu on two separate occasions or simply making an abstract theological statement.

But what may appear still more paradoxical is the idea that all these experiences from different cultures are, at a deep level, of the same kind. This is a view which has been implicit in what I have written so far, and is sometimes called the 'common core' theory. The best-known popular exponent of this view was Aldous Huxley. In his book *The Perennial Philosophy*[24] he drew together a fascinating selection of mystical writings from the major world religions in an attempt to show that they were basically in agreement, even in the language they used in their descriptions. Modern writers on mysticism tend to be critical of this opinion, explaining it as being rooted in a sort of missionary or 'ecumenical' desire to find common ground between the world religions. A well-known Roman

Catholic scholar, Raymond Pannikar, who wrote a book called *The Unknown Christ of Hinduism*[25] attempting to show that Christian experience was implicit in Hinduism, would allegedly fall under this criticism.

A more sophisticated version of the common core view is that of Ninian Smart, whose concept of 'types' of religious experience found naturally in all cultures we have already discussed. The language may be different, but the experiences are the same. The American philosopher Steven T. Katz, however, reminds us that there is no such thing as an uninterpreted experience – and everybody interprets their experience in their own way. So how can we know that all these experiences are the same? Much informed opinion would nowadays hold that our experience takes place in a context which affects even the way we perceive the world in the first place.

Thus, foremost in the consciousness of a Jewish mystic is

> his conception of God as the sort of being who is in some sense personal and even more, is ethically and evaluatively personal, i.e. a God who is affected by good deeds and acts of obedience . . . The Jewish conditioning pattern so strongly impresses that tradition's mystics (as all Jews) with the fact that one does not have mystical experiences of God in which one loses one's identity in ecstatic moments of unity, that the Jewish mystic rarely, if ever, has such experiences.[26]

On the other hand, the young Buddhist is taught that his goal,

> *Nirvāna*, is not a relational state in which the finite self encounters a saving or loving transcendental being – God . . . That there is no encounter of any sort results from the fact that he is taught there is no real self and no transcendental other self . . . There is no intelligible way that anyone can legitimately argue that a 'no-self' experience of 'empty' calm is the same experience as the experience of intense, loving, intimate relationship between two substantial selves, one of whom is conceived of as the personal God of Western religion and all that this entails.[27]

Katz is differentiating between two kinds of experience, 'numinous' and 'mystical', which Smart himself distinguishes.

But Katz implies that there are not just two or a few types of religious experience; there are at least as many as there are religious traditions.

However, there is another side to this coin. Almost all the illustrations given above have been taken, intentionally, from classical religious sources, most of them well over a thousand years old. Each of them is tied to a massive cultural tradition with a unique social and psychological history. Yet, at least to some of our contemporaries, there is a curious sense of mutual recognition. Even looking across that widest of cultural divides, between Western Christianity and Eastern Buddhism, those whose professional concern is to lay themselves open to religious experience find there are meeting points.

Here are some examples. A Benedictine monk in Yorkshire practises Zen meditation as part of his programme of Christian contemplation.[28] A Belfast-born Jesuit teaches Zen meditation in a Japanese university.[29] A Theravadin teacher gives his pupils the fourteenth century English mystical work *The Cloud of Unknowing* as an introduction to *vipassana* (Buddhist 'awareness' meditation).[30] Another Jesuit, this time Japanese, finds that his background in Buddhist meditation gives him insights into what the Bible is getting at.[31] Perhaps these people are a little like the sixteenth century Spaniards and Aztecs, who recognized that they shared the common category of religion. This time the recognition, even under all the weight of cultural differences, is of an experience which has fundamental elements in common.

There appear to be other similarities in the 'preparations' for religious experience. The study of the electrical activity of the brain has shown that it is constantly emitting faint impulses which can be recorded by an electroencephalograph (EEG), a machine which can amplify the brain rhythms several million times so that they can be picked up from electrodes pasted to the skull and transmitted on to sheets of paper as wavy lines. Four main kinds of waves are produced by the brain, conventionally labelled alpha, beta, delta and theta. The alpha waves are the ones which interest us, because they appear particularly strongly in people who are meditating. At the Langley Porter Institute in San Francisco, work has been done on this, using adepts from various Asian religions, including Zen. William Johnston, the Irish Jesuit mentioned above, when visiting the Institute,

> asked in a flash of Irish chauvinism why they didn't test some Christian monks. They replied that they did. They tested some Catholic clergymen. But whereas the yogis and masters sat silently in majestic splendour registering exquisite and impeccable alpha, the clergymen read the Bible, sang hymns, wandered round the room and fouled up the machines. On hearing this, I blushed for the Holy Roman Church.[32]

Johnston suggested that they had tested the wrong people. Maybe if they did the experiment with Cistercian or Carthusian monks, who have a tradition of silent meditation, they would get different results. And indeed, Johnston himself was able to make the test with a group of Christian contemplatives, all of whom exhibited high-amplitude alpha during contemplation. So it looks as if at least when committed religious people from these utterly different backgrounds perform their most characteristic religious exercises, they enter into surprisingly similar physiological states.

In talking about the electrical state of the brain, we are no longer merely in the realm of sociology or psychology; biology comes into it too. Biologists would argue that what we experience depends first of all on physiology and only secondarily on cultural and psychological factors: 'From the great cake of reality, every living organism cuts a slice, which it can perceive and to which it can react, owing to its psychophysical organization, i.e. the structure of receptor and effector organs.'[33]

Of course the way we perceive the world changes according to our physical state. For example, when we suffer from a fever the rate at which time passes subjectively slows down. This is connected with the fact that the chemical processes in our bodies speed up when our temperature rises. For the same reason, as we get older and our metabolic rate slows down, time passes more quickly. We can also change our body chemistry artificially and so alter our perceptions. People who take drugs like LSD, for example, experience the world in radically different ways from those of everyday existence.

Sometimes these experiences with 'acid' are very similar to what we have been describing as religious experience. Professor Huston Smith once illustrated this by playing the following game with a group of Princeton students:

> Below are accounts of two religious experiences. One occurred under the influence of drugs, one without their influence. Check the one you think *was* drug-induced.

I

Suddenly I burst into a vast, new, indescribably wonderful universe. Although I am writing this over a year later, the thrill of the surprise and amazement, the awesomeness of the revelation, the engulfment in an overwhelming feeling wave of gratitude and blessed wonderment, are as fresh, and the memory of the experience is as vivid, as if it had happened five minutes ago. And yet to concoct anything by way of description that would even hint at the magnitude, the sense of ultimate reality . . . this seems such an impossible task. The knowledge which has infused and affected every aspect of my life came instantaneously and with such complete force of certainty that it was impossible, then or since, to doubt its validity.

II

All at once, without warning of any kind, I found myself wrapped in a flame coloured cloud. For an instant I thought of fire . . . the next, I knew that the fire was within myself. Directly afterward there came upon me a sense of exultation, of immense joyousness accompanied or immediately followed by an intellectual illumination impossible to describe. Among other things, I did not merely come to believe, but I saw that the universe is not composed of dead matter, but is, on the contrary, a living Presence; I became conscious in myself of eternal life . . . I saw that all men are immortal: that the cosmic order is such that without any praedventure all things work together for the good of each and all; that the foundation principle of the world . . . is what we call love, and that the happiness of each and all is in the long run absolutely certain.[34]*

* The answer is given in the notes.

In one of these experiences, the mere ingestion of a chemical was the apparent trigger for an experience which, though extraordinary, is expressed in comprehensible language and uses concepts familiar to religious people. There seems to be an interaction between biology and culture. Joachim Wach, who was a student of comparative religion at the University of Chicago, expressed it this way:

> We have to understand the situational character of religious experience, that is, we must conceive of it in its particular context. When seen historically, culturally, sociologically and religiously, our experience and its forms are always conditioned. An absolutely spontaneous religious experience is as inconceivable as its counterpart, an absolutely determined one.[35]

Common ground

In spite of our cultural conditioning, thought Wach, all kinds of religious experience, whether classified as numinous, mystical or anything else, would fit a set of general criteria.

Firstly, it always feels to the experiencer that he is responding to a 'given'; that it is not just something to do with his everyday self. William James described it thus:

> It is as if there were in the human consciousness a *sense of reality*, a *feeling of objective presence*, a *perception* of what we may call 'something there' more deep and more general than any of the special and particular 'senses' by which the current psychology supposes existent realities to be originally revealed.[36]

In a way, James is contradicting Feuerbach's remark that there is no 'organ of religious experience'; not by physically identifying one, but by claiming that religious experience is a matter of total bodily awareness. Wach's second point expresses this. Religious experience is a matter of total involvement. It is not just a case of intellectual or aesthetic 'bits' of a person becoming aware; the whole person is involved in something 'other than' themselves.

Thirdly, the experience is intensely real, more so than everyday experience. It is as if the mental clutter of ordinary life was cleared away to leave behind merely what is 'here and now'.

Finally, because of the vividness and totality of these experiences, they have consequences for practical life. This could be simply at the level of seeing life differently after the experience, or it could have effects which are revolutionary for the personality. The Old Testament prophet Jeremiah sometimes regretted bitterly the outcome of his encounter with Jaweh:

> The word of Jaweh has meant for me insult, derision, all
>   day long.
> I used to say, 'I will not think about him,
> I will not speak of his name any more'.
> Then there seemed to be a fire burning in my heart,
> Imprisoned in my bones.
> The effort to restrain it wearied me,
> I could not bear it.[37]

The kinds of experience I have been describing and which Wach tries to pull together as one category may strike you in a number of ways. Perhaps they seem bizarre, or even moving and beautiful, but mistaken; or from another place and another time and nothing to do with the mainstream of modern life. But there is no reason, biologically speaking, to suppose that any particular way of perceiving the world is right or wrong. The average twentieth century north-west European may feel that the representation of the world which they have is normal. But, as Bertalanffy points out, that is really just another kind of imperialism: 'To consider all other sorts of experience that are equally vivid as merely abnormal, fantastic, or at best a primitive precursor to our "objective" world picture [has a nineteenth century ring to it].'[38] This is not to deny that there is, as it were, an 'objective' world, but what we perceive of it is a small selection of the possibilities.[39]

There is no reason to suppose, either, that the pictures of the world we build up in our different cultures fit all that closely to what is there. But in the long run the fit has to be reasonable, otherwise we would not survive:

> The categories of experience have arisen in biological
> evolution, and have continually to justify themselves in

the struggle for existence. If they would not in some way
correspond with reality, appropriate reaction would be
impossible and such organisms would quickly be eliminated by selection.[40]

The example that Bertalanffy gives is of a group of schizophrenics who share their illusions. They might easily get on
well with each other. Nevertheless, because their picture of the
world is askew, they are not able to adapt themselves to 'real
outside situations'. That, of course, is why they are put into
mental hospitals. Bertalanffy's choice of illustration is an interesting one, because some modern psychiatrists are not sure
that schizophrenia should be dismissed as simply maladapta-
tion to reality. Schizophrenics' perceptions, it is argued, could
in fact be an accurate rendering of the splintered and contradictory social world in which they find themselves.[41] Is,
then, the religious experience that we read about in the
classics of mystical literature based on an aberrant perception
which doesn't correspond to the real world? Or were these
people, when, to their evident amazement, they came across
such experience personally, actually colliding with a part of
reality which they had heard about, but never met before?

There may not be a satisfactory answer to such questions. It
would be interesting, however, to find out whether these experiences or anything remotely like them occur at all commonly today. Modern religious professionals, like contemplative monks, presumably do feel they come across this realm of
experience, but they are a very tiny fraction of humankind.
What about ordinary people? Do such things happen, as it
were, spontaneously in their lives? How many, and what sort
of people are they? What does their experience consist of? How
do they explain it? Does it affect their lives? In Part Three of
this book I shall be looking at the way scientists during the
twentieth century have tried to explore the religious experience of ordinary people.

Part Three

Modern Explorations

Part Three

Modern Explorations

8

Entering the World of
Personal Experience

*'One cannot help feeling that the study of Yoga and of mysticism generally,
through EEG, ECG and similar methods, is like studying art through
films of the eye movements of art viewers.'*

FRITS STAAL[1]

The rise of modern interest

At the turn of the century, if you were a scientist interested in
religious experience, the place to be was New England.
During the 1890s Edwin Diller Starbuck, a student of William
James at Harvard, started asking people about their experience of religious conversion.[2] Science, he reasoned, has con-
quered one field after another, so why should he not enter the
most complex and sacred of domains, religion? 'The wind
bloweth where it listeth and thou hearest the sound thereof,
but canst not tell whence it cometh or whither it goeth,' he was
warned by wiser and older men, including initially James himself. However, in his brash way, Starbuck reflected that
meteorologists were nowadays studying the comings and
goings of the wind quite successfully, and decided to struggle
on.

He felt the best way to go about his task was to collect sets of
religious autobiographies from members of the general public,
by asking them to write answers to a standard set of questions.
Some of them were fairly intimate, by the standards of the
Victorian era. His first question was:

> What religious customs did you observe in childhood
> and with what likes and dislikes? In what ways were you
> brought to a condition to need an awakening: – faulty
> teachings, bad associations, appetites, passions etc?

103

What were the chief temptations of your youth? How were they felt, and how did you strive to resist? What errors and struggles have you had with (a) Lying and other dishonesty, (b) Wrong appetites for foods and drinks, (c) *Vita sexualis*; what relation have you noticed between this and moral and religious experiences? (d) Laziness, selfishness, jealousy, etc?

And question four asked:

How did relief come? Was it attended by unnatural sights, sounds, or feelings? In what did the change consist? – breaking pride, public confession, seeking the approval of others, feeling God's forgiveness, sudden awakening to some great truth, etc? . . . What part was supernatural or miraculous?[3]

Starbuck hoped that he would get 'a true picture of conversion in modern Christian communities'. The people he asked to reply to his questions were almost all Protestants, the largest single group being Methodists, with such groups as Baptists, Presbyterians, Congregationalists and Quakers well represented.

It is interesting to note that the point where Starbuck shyly lapses into Latin in his first question is on the links between sexuality and conversion. I think this hints at the strength of his intuition that religious conversion might have something to do with the appearance of sexual feelings in adolescence. In this he may have been guided by another of his teachers, G. Stanley Hall, president of Clark University at Worcester in Massachusetts, and also professor of psychology there. Hall was himself deeply interested in the psychology of conversion, which he saw to be a pivotal issue in the New England community to which he belonged. Brought up in a small farming village in Massachusetts, his environment was still heavily influenced by the theology of someone we have already met, the eighteenth century preacher and philosopher Jonathan Edwards[4]. It will be recalled that on the basis of his personal experience, Edwards came to the conclusion that the centrepiece of Christian piety was a moment of conversion when one became aware of the presence of God.

The method that Edwards used on many occasions was to awaken a fear of hell in his listeners: he may have been the master of the hell-fire sermon. In his writings on conversion, Hall recalls part of Edwards's most famous oration, 'Sinners in the hands of an angry God', where he is discoursing on the agonies of the damned:

> There will be no end to the exquisite, horrible misery. The inhabitants of heaven and all the universe will look on and praise God's justice. No prayer will mitigate God's hate and contempt, for he can no longer pity. You would have gone to hell last night, had he not held you like a loathsome spider over the flames by a thread. Every moment of delay accumulates wrath.[5]

Edwards's legacy was still very strong in the Massachusetts of Hall's youth, and he himself went through an experience of conversion while he was a student. Although he became very liberal in theological matters, he never repudiated his conversion, but he was curious about the links between it and feelings of guilt such as those that Edwards played upon. Hall recalled those feelings from his own adolescence very candidly. In his autobiography he writes about the agonies he went through over the bullying of his younger brother and sister, but more particularly over masturbation. The implication that his biographer[6] draws is that he found at least a temporary resolution of his sexual difficulties in his religious conversion. It is certainly true to say that the main body of statistics he collected in relation to conversion illustrated the fact that the age range at which it happened coincided, to within a very few years, with the age of sexual maturation.

As one of his tasks, Starbuck checked on the typical age of conversion and his results agreed with others collected by Hall. William James was not happy about the supposed links between conversion and sexuality and launched a broadside against it in his Gifford Lectures.[7] But he was pleasantly surprised by the wealth of descriptive material that Starbuck had managed to collect.

Among other things Starbuck noticed that women are much more likely to report external social pressure as a factor in their conversion, whereas men tend to refer it to an inner conviction of sin. Six times as many women as men reported that they were converted at a church service or prayer meeting, whilst twice as many men as women were converted at home, and generally when they were on their own.

Phenomenologically, the moment of conversion appeared typically to have an emotionally pivotal quality, though high emotion was not always in evidence. Starbuck quotes one man as saying, 'There was no emotion, it was a calm acceptance of the power of Christ to save'.[8] Significantly, Starbuck noted that although the moment of conversion was traditionally depicted in allegorical terms as a battle between the powers of darkness and the powers of light, with the individual as a kind of onlooker, the experience was never described that way by his respondents. Nearly all descriptions interpreted it as an internal psychological event, though still couched in conventional theological language.

His interpretations were not only psychological but also physiological. And he attempted an explanation of the phenomena of conversion in terms of alterations in neural pathways in the brain. Thus, he found that it was almost universally reported that there was an increase in feelings of altruism following conversion. What had previously been 'reflex' responses to religious and moral precepts, became 'real' and personally appropriated. It was as if what had existed as 'reflexes in the lower nerve centres' had been taken up as factors in 'higher cerebral activity'. This change, Starbuck observed, took place at the point where the young person is about to enter adult society and where 'physiological awakening has announced the possibility of parenthood and citizenship'.

The appearance of altruism in connection with religious conversion was thus viewed by Starbuck as, however inexplicable in physiological detail at the time he was writing, a perfectly normal and natural process which had evolutionary survival value,

> It is natural (from an evolutionary survival perspective)
> that in adolescence there should be a rapid development,
> which either furnishes some of the elements that directly
> enter into religion, or brings the individual suddenly into

such ripeness of mental capacity that religious impulses may have an adequate organ for their reception and expression.[9]

Difficulty and decline

Starbuck's was probably the most extensive attempt by someone benevolently disposed towards religion, to bring the study of religious experience under the umbrella of natural science. He was much less interested than even William James in the sociological side of the picture and the great interest of New Englanders in conversion, though understandable, imposed limitations on the scientific study of religious experience in general.

Even so, it is extraordinary how aware Jonathan Edwards himself had been of the deep influence of expectation on how people defined their experience. James quotes him on the 'rules' governing conversion in revivalist circles:

A rule received by common consent has a very great, though to many persons an insensible influence in forming their notions of the process of their own experience . . . Very often their experience at first appears like a confused chaos, but then those parts are selected which bear the nearest resemblance to such particular steps as are insisted on; and these are dwelt upon in their thoughts, and spoken of from time to time, till they grow more conspicuous in their view, and other parts which are neglected grow more and more obscure. Thus what they have experienced is insensibly strained, so as to bring it to an exact conformity to the scheme already established in their minds.[10]

The question was: 'How strained?' Out of all recognition?

When Starbuck brought out his work on the psychology of religion, his aim had been 'to bring conciliation to the feud between science and religion'. At that time, in an atmosphere of relative benevolence towards religion, this seemed a possibility, and James' interpretations seemed to point that way.

James' central contention concerning the origin of religious experience was that it was to be located in what would nowadays be referred to as the 'unconscious'. The basis for this was F. W. H. Myers' conception of the 'subliminal self' which indeed has similarities to Freud's more familiar metaphor. It gave structure to James' understanding of the unique quality of the content of religious awareness, in that it seems to invade the consciousness of the individual from some other region:

> Let me then propose, as an hypothesis, that whatever it may be on its *farther* side, the 'more' with which in religious experience we feel ourselves connected is on its *hither* side the subconscious continuation of our conscious life.[11]

And as to truth,

> . . . we have *in the fact that the conscious person is continuous with a wider self through which saving experiences come*, a positive content of religious experience which, it seems to me, is *literally and objectively true as far as it goes*.[12]

Mystical experiences 'carry authority for him who has them', but for no-one else. Nevertheless, 'they break down the exclusive authority of rationalistic states'. Outsiders should judge the religious experience by its,

> 'pragmatic-therapeutic' value. That is, the meaning or truth of religious experience consists in its power to heal the divided soul and to enable the individual to confront the world in a coherent and 'lively' manner.[13]

But soon events were to conspire to prevent the continuance of this movement of reconciliation between science and religion. In 1909 Stanley Hall succeeded in inviting Freud and several of his most eminent colleagues to visit the United States and lecture at Clark University. This was the first occasion on which psychoanalysis was given international recognition, and it had a strong effect on the minds of many of Hall's contemporaries. Soon, psychoanalytic articles would appear in journals, attempting to show the illusory nature of religion and its origins in repressed sexuality. Starbuck's hopes for conciliation began to look dimmer.

A second influence was the rise in popularity of the behaviourist psychology of J. B. Watson.[14] On the first page of his book *Behaviorism*, he selects William James as one of his prime examples of wrong-headed psychology, because of his interest in the 'inner' experience of people. There is no tangible evidence for inner experience, says Watson, any more than there is evidence for the existence of a soul. Only behaviour is visible. 'The raw fact is that you, as a psychologist, if you are to remain scientific, must describe the behaviour of man in no other terms than those you would use in describing the behavior of the ox you slaughter . . .'[15] Anyone convinced by Watson would have to abandon thoughts of collecting accounts of religious experience.

As time passed, those who nevertheless continued to make a scientific study of religious experience became more and more polemical, a move which, in the end, destroyed the hopes of the early students. The main outlet for research work and articles was the *Psychological Bulletin*, a journal which continues to be published today. However, it published its last major review on the psychology of religion in 1933. Abraham Cronbach, the author of the review, writes with a scarcely disguised sarcasm about many of the papers:

> From the analysis of a psychotic Buddhist, Pfister comes to pronounce Buddhism a flight from life's conflicts . . . In various ancient vows and sacrifices, Reik is struck by their resemblance to modern insurance schemes . . . For Selbie the defense of religion consists in discrediting every psychological pronouncement that seems at variance . . . with current or traditional theological views. The widespread admixture of the non-scientific in works supposed to be scientific or in works that otherwise are scientific has made the construction of this list no easy matter.[16]

The problem of bias

The anthropologist Clifford Geertz has remarked that one of the main methodological problems in writing about religion scientifically is to 'put aside the tone of the village atheist and

the village preacher'.[17] At first the difficulty seemed to be with
the preachers. The psychological intensity surrounding the
conversion experience which interested so many of the New
England psychologists suggested that anyone who had been
through it would have great difficulty in being cool and
rational about it. Furthermore, the links with sexuality which
both Hall and Freud thought they had uncovered led others to
the suspicion that religious people were, almost by definition,
repressing the sexual truth about themselves. If that were so,
any attempt they made to study religious phenomena scientifically must, at the very best, be suspect, since it might be no
more than an elaborate defence mechanism to maintain a
fragile ego. Then again, there was the matter of allegiance to a
religious institution. How, it might be asked, could someone
belonging to a church take an unbiased stance on these issues?

An illustration of this difficulty is in the strained relations
between James Leuba, a pupil of Hall's and the Belgian Jesuit
writer on the psychology of mysticism, Joseph Maréchal.[18] In
Europe, at the same time as the developments in New England,
there had been an increasing interest in the psychology of Christian mysticism amongst Roman Catholic scholars, led by
another Jesuit, Auguste Poulain.[19] Leuba, a Swiss by origin, was
rather more interested in mysticism than many of his American
colleagues, and, as we have seen in a previous chapter, believed it
was often possible to trace a sexual element in the ecstasies of the
famous European mystics. Maréchal combated this view in a
chapter entitled 'Professor Leuba as a Psychologist of Mysticism', in which he castigates him amongst other things for his
rudeness about Catholic saints: 'Many of his readers will be
indignant about these odious pages.'[20] Leuba, reviewing the
book in which this chapter appeared, affected not to notice it,
simply mentioning that the author is a Roman Catholic and that
the book bears the *imprimatur* of his church. The book, he says, is
interesting as an example of the usual efforts of Roman Catholics
to discredit the results of the scientific study of mysticism: 'Ironic
points of exclamation occasionally take the place of refutation.'[21]
Personal polemic is of course not unknown in the cool halls of
scientific discourse, but the elaborate gamesmanship shown by
Leuba and Maréchal is very remote from the canons of rational
debate.

A closer examination of the backgrounds of those engaged in the explaining away of religion illustrates that they too can hardly be called unbiased. J. B. Watson, who wanted to define consciousness out of existence as far as psychology was concerned, came from a revivalist background not unlike that of Stanley Hall. His second name, Broadus, was that of a famous preacher, and his mother apparently extracted from him at a very early age a promise that he himself would become a minister. During adolescence he had the same struggles as Hall over sexuality, but rebelled and spent much of his time in hooliganistic behaviour. Paul Creelan sees Watson's 'radical rejection of traditional psychological phenomena such as those of "consciousness" as residing in the context of a vehement antipathy towards traditional religion and the closely related doctrine of "soul"'.[22] This becomes understandable when we know of the suffocating repression of sexuality which seems to have occurred in Watson's rigorously evangelical childhood. Perhaps the only way to break free was to assert the primacy of the flesh over the spirit.

We have already seen that Freud's feelings towards religious ritual amounted to a physical nausea, and it may be because of this that his descriptions of religious experience hardly ever go beyond what is necessary to prove his point. He therefore dismisses, without comment, aspects which would be considered highly relevant to a believer. In Freud's opinion, 'Where questions of religion are concerned people are guilty of every possible kind of insincerity and intellectual misdemeanour.'[23] I guess he had in mind 'believers' rather than those who sided with his own views, but it seems, on closer inspection, to be rather easy to let feeling run away with reason on either side of this argument.

Looking at the phenomenon again

It is important to know whether what I have called 'religious experience' does give people valid information about the world. Therefore it is natural that people will argue vigorously over its presumed links with sexuality; or, if indeed related to sex (or for that matter alienation, or other natural phenomena), whether that makes any difference. But the emotional heat generated over these questions more or less killed off the budding psychology of religious experience in the 1930s.

By the 1960s the mood was beginning to change. At the most basic level, it became legitimate again to look at the phenomena of consciousness. In spite of Watson's contempt for it, people found it very hard to ignore the fact that they seemed to *be* conscious, and that consciousness loomed very large in everyday life. At the very moment when the psychology of religion was dying down, L. L. Thurstone[24] was inventing what was to become one of the most widely used attitude scales in psychology. Ironically, the first version was designed to measure attitudes to the church. Since then a huge industry has built up within psychology and sociology concerned with finding out the contents of people's consciousness. Opinion pollsters are often laughed at when they get their political predictions wrong. Nevertheless, most of the time they are surprisingly accurate, and very complex and subtle methods of interviewing people are now used as a matter of routine by social scientists.

Apart from the legitimacy of asking people to talk about their experience and opinions, the problem of bias, though still large, began not to seem so overwhelming. Once it is accepted that *everybody* has a life history and therefore a set of biases, it becomes possible to try to cooperate to reduce them to a minimum. One way is to try to 'bracket out' preconceptions about the meaning of what people are saying. Instead of listening to someone describing their religious experience, eagerly trying to pick out the vital section that will support your religious or anti-religious point of view, the perspective is changed. The task is to get as detailed and accurate a description of the individual's experience as possible, and to find out how that person himself makes sense of his experience. It is important of course that the person being interviewed tells you the truth about his experience as he sees it. At this point, whether he 'really' was, for example, in the presence of God is not important. This method is referred to as 'phenomenological psychology and proceeds along strictly descriptive lines. No feature pertaining to an act of consciousness can be disregarded; conversely, nothing must be imputed to or foisted on an act that the latter does not actually exhibit.'[25] It is a fantasy to suppose that all bias is cut out by this method, but at least there is a better chance of collecting adequate descriptions of experience before the inevitable testing of pet theories is started.

A third difficulty which might deter people from asking about religious experience is that it may be taboo, rather like talk about private sexual habits. However, this particular barrier was broken during the 1940s by Alfred C. Kinsey and his associates when they began interviewing Americans about their sexual behaviour.[26] The initial difficulties put in their way by people in positions of authority were considerable, including attempts to have Kinsey thrown out of his job at Indiana University. Some of those who assisted him were given the sack, and one medical group organized a campaign against him. In spite of that, his group successfully collected over 12,000 histories of male sexual behaviour and went on to do the same sort of study for women. Although his methods have been criticized as inadequate, it was the first large-scale attempt, and he found that ordinary people were prepared to help him to a surprising degree. Kinsey seems to have been able to build very good trusting relationships with those he interviewed. The sentimentality of his comment about this nevertheless reveals his delight at how cooperative most people were:

> . . . the little grey haired woman at the cabin door, out on the Western plain, epitomized what we have heard now from hundreds of people: 'Of all things –! In all my years I have never had such a question put to me! But – if my experience will help, I'll give it to you.'[27]

As will become clear, a similar willingness to help has been found by those studying religious experience, even though nowadays talk about religion is, if anything, more taboo than talk about sex.

In 1969 Sir Alister Hardy, formely professor of zoology at Oxford University, set up the Religious Experience Research Unit in a house forming part of the property of Manchester College in Oxford. Though a zoologist by profession he was not especially attracted towards the research already being done with EEG machines on meditators. For one thing, it was not possible to get anywhere near someone's personal experience by merely recording electrical impulses in their brains. Such impulses show that something physiologically distinctive is going on when people meditate, which suggests that they are right to talk about the special nature of their experience, but there is no evidence about the subjective content. For another thing, Sir Alister was really interested in the apparently spontaneous religious experiences which happen in the lives of ordinary people from time to time. As is recorded in his books on the subject,[28] his first attempts to gather examples were not very successful. He decided to advertise in religious periodicals, asking people to write to him at Manchester College if they felt they had ever 'been aware of or influenced by a presence or power, whether they called it God or not, which was different from their everyday selves'. The initial response was disappointingly small, but when he decided to publicize his programme in the secular press the response was enthusiastic. There are now over 5,000 accounts of experience in the files, and many of these have been analysed and grouped into categories.[29] Hardy saw his role as that of the natural historian, collecting and classifying specimens, somewhat like a Victorian naturalist laying down the factual basis for the theories of twentieth century biology. Hardy's book *The Spiritual Nature of Man* should be consulted for a wide range of examples of the sorts of experiences that people sent in to the Unit. The following brief selection merely gives some sense of the mood of the descriptions:

> I have a growing sense of reality and personal identity, which comes from being united to something more powerful than myself, something that is helping me to be what I want to be.

> As far back as I can remember, I have never had a sense of separation from the spiritual force I now choose to call God ... From the age of about six to twelve in places of quiet and desolation this feeling of 'oneness' often passed to a state of 'listening'. I mean by listening that I was suddenly alerted to something that was going to happen. What followed was a feeling of tremendous exaltation in which time stood still.

A friend persuaded me to go to Ely Cathedral to hear a performance of Bach's B Minor Mass. I had heard the work, indeed I knew Bach's Choral works pretty well. I was sitting towards the back of the nave. The Cathedral seemed to be very cold. The music thrilled me . . . until we got to the great *Sanctus*. I find this experience difficult to define. It was primarily a warning. I was frightened. I was trembling from head to foot, and wanted to cry. Actually I think I did. I heard no 'voice' except the music; I saw nothing; but the warning was very definite. I was not able to interpret this experience satisfactorily until I read some months later – Rudolph Otto's *Das Heilige*. Here I found it – the 'numinous'. I was before the Judgement Seat. I was being 'weighed in the balance and found wanting'. This is an experience I have never forgotten.

I am aware of a sort of 'consciousness' outside of my own. I sense it . . . when I am in a state of happiness and well-being, and I feel there is a 'presence' whose hand I should like to grasp in affection and gratitude.

I find it difficult to define my experience, only to say that it seems to be outside of me and enormous and yet at the same time I am part of it, everything is. It is purely personal and helps me to live and to love others. It is difficult to describe, but in some way because of this feeling I feel united to all people, to all living things. Of recent years the feeling has become so strong that I am now training to become a social worker because I find that I must help people; in some way I feel their unhappiness as my own.

At one time I reached utter despair and wept and prayed God for mercy instinctively and without faith in a reply. That night I stood with other patients in the grounds waiting to be let into our ward. It was a very cold night with many stars. Suddenly, someone stood beside me in a dusty brown robe and a voice said, 'Mad or sane, you are one of my sheep'. I never spoke to anyone of this but ever since (twenty years) it has been the pivot of my life.

I realize that the form of the vision and the words I heard
were the result of my education and cultural background
but the voice, though closer than my own heartbeat, was
entirely separate from me.

The beginnings of survey work

Fascinating as these accounts were, there was, however, one
serious problem about the method adopted. Those who cared
to reply to Hardy's appeals in the mass media almost certainly
did not adequately represent the general public. In fact the
group was heavily overloaded with elderly and female respondents. It could be of course that these are the groups in British
society that, more than others, believe they have had religious
experiences, but there was no way of being sure. Another
question unanswered was the total numbers of people in
Britain who would say 'yes' if asked whether they had ever
had one of these experiences. There was a fair amount of cir-
cumstantial evidence pointing to the possibility that the
number would be very small indeed compared to the total
population of Britain. It is estimated that in 1965 only about
10–15 per cent of the population of England was likely to be in
a church of some sort on a Sunday, so that, if experience had
strong links with church attendance, the total would probably
be less than that. In addition, even within the fold of religion,
the predictions were pretty negative. Writing in 1965 about
the problems facing teachers of religion, Ronald Goldman
could say: 'The mystics, who claim to have direct sensations of
the divine, are exceptions, but as they are extremely rare
cases, rarer in adolescence and practically unknown in childhood, we shall not explore their significance here.'[30] Perhaps
the Religious Experience Research Unit already had all contemporary examples of direct sensations of the divine stacked
away in their files. Certainly the 'atheist' theologians would
have been prepared to accept that as perfectly possible.

In the winter of 1975 the Unit mounted its first national
survey of reports of religious experience in Great Britain,
which I directed from Nottingham University. It was then
that my research assistant Ann Morisy and myself first went out
on to the streets of Nottingham, armed with clipboards, to

test our potential survey questions on the general public. Our difficulties when we began will illustrate some of the problems of conducting research in this area.

We considered asking the question Sir Alister had used in his appeals through the mass media, but at first we were rather unhappy with it. It seemed rather complex and perhaps incomprehensible to people in the street, so we tried a number of others. But they didn't work as well. If, for example, you ask people directly whether they have ever had a religious experience you are liable to get two kinds of extreme reply. Deeply devout people will say 'All experience is religious'. Now that could mean that in all their doings they are permanently aware of a sacred presence. As we shall see, a small number of people do claim that, but more usually it means something like: 'By definition, God created and sustains the world, therefore, by deduction, all experience is religious.' Cases of the latter, though interesting, were not what we were primarily concerned with. At the other end of the spectrum, atheists might say in response, 'Certainly not! Religion is bunk!' Yet there is quite a lot of evidence that people who claim to be atheists sometimes do feel they have enjoyed mystical experiences. One very good example is Marghanita Laski, who in 1960 published an excellent study of 'secular and religious experiences'.[31] She felt such experiences were supremely valuable, without thinking that they necessarily required a religious explanation.

Questions about 'numinous' or 'mystical' experience tended to be met with a blank stare, because these terms are technical and not well known outside the circle of those professionally interested in such things. In the end we decided that Hardy's question did the best job. Almost everybody said they understood it, though they quite often doubted if anybody else would, which suggested perhaps that we were touching on a rather private world of experience. The other good thing about the question was that most of the people who replied to it affirmatively, when asked to give descriptions, spoke about experiences which did more or less fall into the 'numinous' or 'mystical' categories, though not necessarily exhibiting all the features that the theorists required. So in the end the main question we asked was:

> Have you ever been aware of or influenced by a
> presence or power, whether you call it God or not, which
> is different from your everyday self?

The 'whether you call it God or not' clause had the function of
allowing people whose interpretations of experience were not
religiously orthodox to say 'yes' if they felt they had been
aware of a presence or power.

Primarily we were interested in finding out what sorts of experience a cross-section of the British public would talk about
and how they would interpret them. But the first job was to
find an answer to the 'how many' question. So we approached
National Opinion Polls Ltd and arranged to put some questions in one of their 'omnibus surveys', which now take place
once a week in Britain. N.O.P. interviewers contact a random
sample of approximately 2,000 adults all over the country, to
ask their opinions on a variety of questions. Anyone can buy
space in a survey, for example to check on the popularity of a
commercial product or perhaps a TV programme. In August
1976, our group of questions on 'religious experience' was included in a mixed bag of other inquiries.

Apart from Hardy's question, we also asked about 'psychological well-being', using a scale invented by Norman M.
Bradburn of the National Opinion Research Center in
Chicago.[32] By a stroke of luck, Andrew Greeley and Bill
McCready of N.O.R.C. had recently been asked about
'ecstatic' experiences amongst a national sample of
Americans.[33] We took the chance to do some comparisons
with the United States, and arranged to include in the same
survey the question they had used:

> Have you ever felt as though you were very close to a
> powerful spiritual force that seemed to lift you out of
> yourself?

Of course we were curious to know about links with religious belief and church attendance, so we included questions
on that. Perhaps these experiences had something to do with
how important people felt the spiritual side of life was, and we
asked about that too. Questions about age, sex, education and
wealth were automatically included by N.O.P., along with

geographical area, so that we could see if there were variations in different parts of the country. In the next chapter I shall describe what we found.

9

The Common Experience[1]

'A light that might be mystic or a fraud
Played on far hills beyond all common sight.'

PATRICK CAVANAGH[2]

Some figures

In 1965 secular theology was in full swing. That was the year
two sociologists at Berkeley, Charles Glock and Rodney Stark,
published the results of their study of church members in
Northern California.[3] One of the questions they asked their
sample of nearly 3,000 people was whether they had ever had
'a feeling that you were somehow in the presence of God'; 45
per cent of the Protestants and 43 per cent of the Roman
Catholics said they were 'sure' they had, and a further 28 per
cent of Protestants and 23 per cent of Catholics 'thought' they
had. Overall, that makes more than two-thirds of this group of
church members who at least thought they had been in the
presence of God.

Though they were both professional students of religion,
based at the University of California, Glock and Stark were
more than a little surprised:

> There are few cues in the culture which would lead an
> observer to predict so high a rate of supernaturalism in
> what seems to be an increasingly modern, scientific and
> secularized society. For example, characters in contem-
> porary literature rarely undergo such encounters with
> the divine; and when they do, it is usually clear that they
> are odd people, old fashioned, simple, demented and the
> like.[4]

They had not bothered to include any questions on ecstatic or revelational experiences (broadly corresponding to Otto's 'numinous' category) because they hadn't foreseen 'how frequently modern Christians would report religious experiences'. They went on to speculate that the feeling of having been in the presence of God would almost certainly be closely linked with church membership. It seemed very unlikely that people outside the religious institutions would share such experiences. Further, a positive answer to Glock and Stark's question may not have meant a great deal – it could easily have been given by somebody merely assenting when the clergyman opens a service with words such as 'We come before you Lord, this Sunday morning . . .'

However, there are other pieces of evidence that suggest that at least some of those answers meant more than that. Also during the 1960s, two other sociologists, Kurt Back and Linda Bourque at Duke University in North Carolina, became interested in some technical problems of social surveying. They wondered whether ordinary commercial opinion polls could be used to inquire about deeply personal matters which might involve strong feelings.[5] Kinsey had been successful in asking about sexual behaviour during the forties. But he and his associates had trudged round the United States, literally for years, arranging long personal interviews in which they had the time to build up trust and rapport. What would happen if questions about something equally private, and concerning experience rather than behaviour, were slipped into a Gallup poll? Back and Bourque examined answers to a question about religious experience put into three ordinary Gallup surveys in 1962, 1966 and 1967. It asked:

> Would you say that you ever had a 'religious or mystical experience', that is, a moment of sudden religious insight or awakening?[6]

In 1962, 20½ per cent said 'yes', in 1966 nearly 32 per cent, and in 1967 just over 41 per cent. At first Back and Bourque couldn't make sense of it. People's explanations of their experiences showed that they had understood the question, so why was there a steady increase in positive response?

They came to two conclusions. Firstly, alongside the enthusiasm for secular religion among the theologians, there was a rising interest in mysticism. It was the decade of the hip search for the mystic revolution and the pilgrimage was on, via drugs and the journey into Eastern religion. 1967 was the year in which a motley crowd of 'witches, warlocks, holymen, seers, prophets, mystics, saints, sorcerers, shamans, troubadours, minstrels, bards, roadmen and madmen' tried to levitate the Pentagon as the centrepiece of a huge anti-war demonstration.[7] Perhaps the new atmosphere allowed people to admit to something they would have been too shy to speak of in previous years.

The other reason involved developments in the interviewing technique. In the first survey there had been only one question about religious experience, in the second there were three and in the third a total of eleven. So in each successive poll there was more time for the people being interviewed to get used to these rather unusual questions. Back and Bourque also noticed that their best interviewers – those who could handle difficult and unusual questions – were the most likely to obtain reports of 'transcendental' experiences. What seemed to be happening in successive polls was that a better level of trust was developed between interviewer and interviewed. Because of this, what is a highly taboo subject became a little more accessible to the surveyors.

It is interesting to note that the Princeton Religion Research Center, a subsidiary of Gallup Polls, asked a very similar question in a national survey in 1978.[8] Its positive response, of 35 per cent, was somewhat down on 1967. However, that still means that something like fifty million adult Americans believe they have had a religious experience.

While these American figures were rather surprising to us, we realized that, proportionately, between three and four times as many Americans as Britons were regular church attenders, and we had no reason to suppose that reports of religious experience in the two countries would be any more likely to correspond. With these thoughts running through our heads, we waited with mounting curiosity for the results of our British national opinion poll.

British and American Figures

Total numbers

As it turned out, rather more than 36 per cent of the sample of people approached by N.O.P. in Britain said that they had at some time been aware of or influenced by a presence or a power.[9] In a repeat survey carried out for the Alister Hardy Research Centre by Gallup Poll, London, in 1985, a total of thirty-three per cent of the population answered 'yes' to the same question.[10] On that basis we can predict that about fifteen million adults in this country would say the same; that is to say, over a third of the population aged sixteen or over. As we shall see in the next chapter, the results of the poll probably underestimate the actual totals of those who believe they have had this kind of experience.

TABLE 1: *'Have you ever been aware of or influenced by a presence or a power . . .?'*

Once or twice	18%
Several times	10%
Often	6%
All the time	2%
TOTAL	36%

This is a very common human experience. Yet in any one person's life history it is usually not at all common. As the figures in Table 1 show, half of the people who claim to have had a religious experience say it has happened only once or twice during their lifetime. Less than a quarter say it is something they have experienced often, or are aware of all the time.

From the comparative point of view, the most exciting results came from the question supplied to us by the National Opinion Research Center in Chicago. Greeley and McCready had collected national data in 1973 to show that 35 per cent of Americans would claim to have had what they called an 'ecstatic' experience.[11] As Table 2 shows, in Britain the positive response was 31 per cent, and the detailed pattern of frequency is very similar on both sides of the Atlantic. In the

TABLE 2: '*Have you ever felt as though you were very close to a powerful spiritual force that seemed to lift you out of yourself?*'

	Great Britain	United States
Once or twice	17%	18%
Several times	9%	12%
Often	5%	5%
TOTAL	31%	35%

comparative survey done for us in 1985 by Gallup Poll, there was a 43 per cent positive response by American adults as compared with 33 per cent positive response by British adults to Hardy's question. Though the American response was greater, there was still no comparison with the difference in Church attendance in the two countries.[12] We began to wonder about the supposed connections with churchgoing.

Differences betweeen men and women
Things are rather more what we might expect when we look at sex differences. The common idea that women are 'more religious' than men seems to be borne out: 41 per cent of the women interviewed reported experiences of a presence or power, compared with 31 per cent of the men. This is almost exactly the ratio we found between women and men who attended church services regularly.

There are other pieces of information which fit in with our findings. Women are more likely than men to hold traditional religious beliefs and to say regular daily prayers.[13] But this is something that varies from group to group. For example, if the proportions of men and women attending church services in the different Christian denominations are compared, there are huge contrasts. One study in the United States showed that while Eastern Orthodox and Roman Catholic congregations contained approximately equal numbers of men and women, amongst Christian Scientists there were more than three times as many women as men present.[14] Depending on which religious group people belong to, it seems to be more or less acceptable to be male and an active member.

Perhaps something similar could happen with religious experiences. As we said in an earlier chapter, these experiences always have the quality of a 'given'. To be open to and able to accept a given experience involves being passive and receptive, characteristics which in Western society are associated with femininity. A traditional way of putting this, amongst religious people, is to say that 'the soul is always feminine to God'. In our culture, it may be more difficult for a man than a woman to take up a vocation to the contemplative life. With the rise of the women's liberation movement and the parallel increase in the acceptability of feminine qualities amongst men, it could be that there will be an alteration in the proportions of men and women prepared to claim religious experience. To date, all the Gallup surveys in the United States agree in finding a majority of women reporting such an experience. Curiously enough, Greeley and McCready found a small majority of men in their survey.[15] Whether this is a sign of changing social mores it is impossible to say.

Links with age
Another result which did not surprise us was that older people were more likely to report religious experiences than the young: 29 per cent of people aged between sixteen and twenty-four years said 'yes' compared with 47 per cent of those aged sixty-five and over (Table 3).

TABLE 3: *'Have you ever been aware of or influenced by a presence or a power . . .?': age links*

Aged 16–24 years	29%
25–34	35%
35–44	33%
45–54	36%
55–64	43%
65+	47%

One obvious explanation of the increase with age is that the longer somebody lives, the more likely they are to have had one of these experiences; but there are other possibilities.

Many studies have shown that as people get older they tend to become more interested in religion. They are much more likely to practise private prayer than the young; they are very much more likely to believe in an after-life.[16] Apart from growing concern about the meaning and the fleetingness of life as death comes nearer, there is another factor which differentiates old people from the young, at least in Britain. During the lifetime of the elderly there has been a very speedy decline in the power and influence of the religious institutions. Old people are much more likely to have come across religious ideas and values as children than are their modern counterparts. Therefore they are more likely to expect to come across religious experience. Three American studies have compared reports of this kind of experience with age, and their findings support our general argument. Greeley and McCready found only a slight increase in numbers of reports with increasing age,[17] while Gallup Polls, in two surveys conducted in 1976 and 1977,[18] and also in their 1985 survey, found no link whatsoever with age. This is exactly what we would predict, because there has been no decline in church-going in the United States during the twentieth century comparable to the steep drop in Britain.

Links with education and social class
We found that the more education people have, the more likely they are to claim to have had religious experience (Table 4): 56 per cent of those who had gone through some form of higher education reported it, while only 29 per cent of those who left school at fifteen said 'yes'. The 35 per cent positive response from people who left school at thirteen or fourteen at first looks as if it contradicts the general trend. But this group is almost certainly a special case. The school leaving age was raised from fourteen to fifteen years in 1947, twenty-nine years before our survey was done. This means that everybody in the group was either forty-three years of age or over when they were interviewed, and, as we have just seen, report of religious experience is more frequent amongst older people. Quite possibly the effects of age have completely masked the contrary effects of reduced years of education.

TABLE 4: *'Have you ever been aware of or influenced by a presence or a power . . .?': education links*

Education ended at 13–14 years	37%
15	29%
16	37%
17–19	44%
20+	56%

When we looked at social class (Table 5) the trend was to increased report of experience moving from working-class to middle-class people. Nearly half of those in the middle-class and upper-class replied positively, compared with not quite a third of the skilled working-class, unskilled labourers and people living at subsistence level.

TABLE 5: *'Have you ever been aware of or influenced by a presence or a power . . .?': social class*

Unskilled labourers and subsistence	32%
Skilled working class	31%
Lower-middle class	41%
Middle class	49%
Upper-middle class	47%

This link with either higher education or social class, or both, is also found in several of the American studies, including those of Greeley and McCready and Gallup Poll's 1978 report.[19] Robert Wuthnow, working in the same department as Glock and Stark at the University of California, surveyed religious experiences in a large sample of adults in the San Francisco Bay area[20] during the mid-seventies. He too found they were reported more commonly by the well-educated. In my own department at Nottingham University I found that, of a random sample of 100 postgraduate students, 65 per cent claimed to have been aware of, or influenced by, a presence or power.[21] At the time I was rather staggered, but in the light of the findings just quoted this high percentage does not seem very surprising.

The reason for my initial surprise was that when social scientists think of 'experiential' religion they tend to have in mind a variety of pentecostal and messianic sects, of a type which are usually found among people who have been socially deprived.[22] As well as that, working-class people seem to be more superstitious than others. They are more likely to have a lucky mascot, have a lucky number, to have visited a fortune-teller, to read their horoscope regularly, and to believe in ghosts.[23] Sometimes people are inclined to lump religious experience and superstition together, but on this evidence it looks as if they should be treated separately.

One or two pieces of the American evidence contradict the pattern I have just been describing. For example, Back and Bourke found that their most poorly educated group were also more likely to report religious experience, though there was also an upturn at the upper end of the educational scale. In their 1978 survey, Gallup Poll found their highest positive response rate with the lowest income group, but again, paradoxically, when people were classified according to occupation, there was a steady increase of report moving up from manual workers to members of the professional and business classes.[24]

These paradoxes are puzzling, but they do not necessarily count against my previous conclusion. What may be happening here is that there is a 'confounding' of two or more contradictory factors. In the United States, black people are more likely to report religious experience than white people. The same is true for members of evangelical branches of Christianity such as the Southern Baptist Church. Because blacks and evangelicals are found more frequently in the less well off social classes in the United States, the high figures for report of religious experience must be, at least partly, attributed to these facts.

Of course it still remains necessary to explain why blacks and evangelicals report more religious experience than others and it could be interpreted in Marxist fashion, as a response to deprivation. The story must be rather more complex than that, however, as the pattern is not consistently repeated in survey work in the United States (appearing to depend to some degree on the form of the question asked[25]), and does not appear at all in Britain.

Once again, the pattern of report of religious experience coincides with that for church attendance. As we saw in an earlier chapter, middle-class people in Britain are much more likely to have direct links with religious institutions than members of the working-class. And of course, because the middle-classes tend to be better educated, we would expect, and do find, that better educated people are more likely to be church attenders than others.[26]

Geographical distribution

The part of Britain with the highest proportion of people who claim to have had religious experiences is Wales. Of those interviewed there, 46 per cent responded positively (Table 6). Next in frequency are South-West England and Scotland, with 41 and 40 per cent respectively. At the other end of the scale, Yorkshire and Humberside, followed by the West Midlands, are the least likely to yield positive responses, with 23 and 27 per cent each.

TABLE 6: *'Have you ever been aware of or influenced by a presence or a power . . .?': geographical distribution*

England	
North-West	35%
North	29%
Yorks and Humberside	23%
West Midlands	27%
East Midlands	30%
East Anglia	28%
South-East	34%
South-West	41%
Wales	46%
Scotland	40%

In American studies that have looked at geographical distribution,[27] the highest positive responses come from the Southern States. Large American cities with over a million inhabitants are lowest in report of religious experience; small towns of 2,500 people or less are where it is reported most commonly.[28] Broadly speaking, in both Britain and the United States the most frequent reports of religious experience come from those areas where people are also most likely to be church attenders.

Religious orthodoxy and religious experience
We have seen that reports of religious experience are probably commonest amongst women, older people (in Britain), the well-educated, the middle-classes and amongst people from rural or small town areas. These are of course exactly the parts of society where traditional religious institutions retain their strongest hold. Perhaps Glock and Stark are right: experience is connected with church membership. I think our results show that they are partly right, but they do not tell the whole story. For one thing, as we have already noted, although these experiences are reported almost as commonly in Britain as in the United States, there is a very big difference in the level of formal churchgoing in the two countries.

But there are other curious findings. For example, one of the things we asked people was whether they accepted a religious denominational label or not. In Table 7 the links between self-description and report of experience show there are wide differences between groups. Amongst people willing to be given a religious label, Anglicans had the lowest positive response rate at 33 per cent. This is not really surprising, since, as the established church, Anglicanism provides the title most likely to be

TABLE 7: *'Have you ever been aware of or influenced by a presence or a power . . .?': religious denominations*

Anglicans	33%
Nonconformists	44%
Roman Catholics	41%
Other Christians	68%
Jewish	39%
Other non-Christians	60%
Agnostics	23%
Atheists	24%
Don't Know	23%

espoused by those whose religion is merely conventional. At the opposite end of the scale, the 'Other Christian' group, which was relatively small in size, presumably consists of members of the pentecostal and millennial sects which were mentioned above. The 'Other non-Christian' group, also very small is probably made up mainly of adherents to Asian religions.

In the United States the distinction between 'Protestant' and 'Catholic' is rather clearer than in Britain. Protestants are more likely to report religious experience than are Catholics. Thus in the 1978 Gallup survey, 46 per cent of American Baptists reported religious experience, whereas only 19 per cent of Catholics and 15 per cent of Episcopalians reported such experience.[29] My interpretation of this is not necessarily that members of ritually inclined churches are less likely to have experiences falling into this general category. Perhaps in their case, as has been suggested to me by a priest/sociologist friend,[30] the experience tends to be mediated *through* public ritual. It may be that the questions that have been used by surveyors so far are rather 'Protestant' in orientation, deriving (as they tend to) from the traditions of New England, and fail to tap the dimension as it is manifested commonly within Catholicism.

Another point of interest is the replies of those who don't want to be given a religious label. Of the groups who ask to be called 'agnostic', 'atheist' or say they 'don't know', not far short of a quarter claim to have had an 'awareness of a presence or a power'. The atheists obviously don't call their experiences religious and the agnostics are at least doubtful, but they raise interesting questions of interpretation which we shall go into later.

We have seen that positive responses vary from denomination to denomination, but simply labelling yourself as a member is a pretty poor measure of commitment to a religious institution, at least in Britain. So we also asked about church attendance. Some people never go to church, except perhaps for a wedding, or their own funeral. This group, on the basis of our survey, makes up about 65 per cent of the adult population of Britain. The remaining 35 per cent go at least occasionally, implying some attachment to formal religion, and we compared these two groups (Table 8).

TABLE 8: *'Have you even been aware of or influenced by a presence or a power . . .?': church attendance*

Attend church occasionally	56% (367 people)
Never attend, apart from weddings, funerals etc.	26% (311 people)
TOTAL	(678 people)

The first point worth noticing is that only 56 per cent of churchgoers say they have had this kind of experience. Our figures show that all the remaining 44 per cent definitely say they have not. We looked at the figures for the small group of people who attend church weekly (12 per cent of the national sample), and of those there were still 41 per cent who said that they had never had an experience like this. Churchgoing does not necessarily imply report of religious experience.

We turn now to those who never go to church if they can help it. Just over a quarter (26 per cent) claim to have had experiences of this type. That quarter (311 people) nevertheless makes up 46 per cent of the total number (678 people) who say they have been aware of, or influenced by a presence or power. Therefore we cannot say that because someone claims these experiences they will necessarily have anything to do with traditional religious institutions.

It is quite striking, too, to note that the Princeton Religion Research Center made some very similar findings in the United States in 1978. In a comparison of 'churched' and 'unchurched' Americans[31] (defined in almost exactly the same way as our non-attenders) they discovered that only 43 per cent of 'churched' Americans claimed to have had a religious experience; 24 per cent of the 'unchurched' group claimed that they had.

Finally, a piece of evidence from the study of Nottingham post-graduate students I mentioned earlier. They follow a rather typical pattern for university graduates,[32] in that most of them think of themselves as having been brought up within a religious tradition, but few of them wish to be thought of as belonging to a church. From my random sample of 100, out of a total of sixty-five people reporting experience, only eleven were happy to be called church members. That is, a majority of five to one had either repudiated their formal religious up-bringing or had never had one.

Formal and informal religion

In 1965 Glock and Stark commented on a curious statistic on religious adherence in the United States. Whilst the proportions of people belonging to the churches in America (as in Britain) increase as you move up the educational scale, this trend is reversed at the level of university graduate students, who 'exhibit an unusually large proportion of persons who claim no religious identification as compared with a cross-sectional sample of the United States population'.[33] They interpreted this as a good example of the powerful secularizing effects of a university education, particularly if this has been in a scientific discipline.

Now if secularization means something like 'the churches have lost their grip on the graduates', the postgraduate figures for our research probably support that view. If on the other hand we make a distinction between belonging to a religious institution on the one hand and *being* religious on the other, the assertion becomes less certain. On the grounds of report of religious experience postgraduates could possibly be *more* religious than other people. This fits in with other research findings. The more educated people are, the more likely they are to go to church, with the exception we have just been looking at. But the more educated churchgoers are also the most likely to hold unorthodox views.[34] So postgraduate absence from the churches could simply be another step along the path of unorthodoxy.

There is another small clue that comes from people's attitudes to the 'spiritual side of life'. This is a very vague phrase which could mean all sorts of things. Some use it to refer simply to being cultured and sensitive. However, it could also be one of the few terms left which someone who dislikes formal religion can use to describe the area of human experience traditionally called 'religious'. In our national survey, we asked about people's attitude to the spiritual side of life and found that, of the measures we used, it was by far the best predictor of report of religious experience (Table 9). Approximately

three quarters of those who felt that the spiritual side of life
was 'very important' also claimed to have had a religious experience, compared with only 11 per cent of those who
thought it was 'not important'.

TABLE 9: *'Have you ever been aware of or influenced by a presence
or a power . . .?': importance of spiritual experience*

Very important	74%
Fairly important	40%
Slightly important	26%
Not important	11%

Though it seems an obvious distinction to make, it is not
often pointed out that there is a difference between being a
churchgoer on the one hand and being a religious person on
the other. When someone says they can worship God in the
open air as easily as in church, or more easily, they could be
expressing perfectly well what their own experience is.
Though no doubt the majority of people who go to church are
sincere about their religion, there are insincere reasons for
church attendance; for example, social conformity. There are
also reasons for church attendance which, though sincere, are
not religious, such as a fondness for the aesthetics of ritual or
church music. There are also reasons why genuinely religious
people do not attend church. They may find the teachings of
the churches implausible, or dislike ritual (or the lack of it), or
be repelled by the alliance of the church with the political
establishment.

There is no reason to suppose that people who are in touch
with the experiential dimension of religion will necessarily be
churchgoers. Nevertheless, coming from a background that
has words and traditions that respect this area of human experience perhaps allows people to be open to it. This could
explain the correlations we have been looking at in this
chapter.

10

Putting Experience into Words

'Gentle must my fingers be
And pitiful my heart
Since I must bind in human form
A living power so great,
A living impulse great and wild
That cries about my house.'

KATHLEEN RAINE[1]

Collecting words

It is a curious process, expressing experience in words. What we feel to be private and individual becomes transmuted, via phrases and concepts we have learned from others, into something public. In the next stage of our research we needed to go into that, because in matters of personal experience people have to speak for themselves. What do they have in mind when they tell an N.O.P. or Gallup interviewer on the doorstep that, yes, they have been aware of or influenced by a presence or a power? The Religious Experience Research Unit in Oxford had been collecting replies to that question for several years. Some time ago I spent a summer finding out the kinds of things a cross-section of postgraduate students would say.[2] But we needed to collect descriptions from a random sample of the general public if we were to get a true picture of the normal range of experience.

Nottingham was unlikely to be the most fruitful hunting ground for these experiences. It is a large industrial city and it lies in the heart of the English East Midlands, which our national survey had shown had an average positive response rate of only 30 per cent. However, Nottingham was where we were, so we chose to concentrate our efforts there. We spent several months planning the sorts of question we would like to ask. Then we tried them out on a sample of people in a nearby suburb, improving them until they were as clear as possible. The end-product was a lengthy twenty-seven-page questionnaire. It opened with three pages of short inquiries about attitudes to life, designed to help both the interviewer and the person interviewed to relax. Questions followed about the experience of being aware of or influenced by a presence or power, what the experience had been like, when it had happened, what it had meant to the person, and so on.

The next part was more nerve-racking. From the latest electoral rolls for Nottingham and district we had to select a random sample of local people whom we could try to interview. Sampling is more sophisticated than simply letting a pin come down at random on a race card, but the principle is the same: a random group of electoral districts is chosen, then in each district a random group of electors. On the basis of the national survey, we expected to have to visit about 300 people if we were to get a minimum of 100 people claiming experience – enough to give us a reasonable set of examples. By the time we had made 172 visits we had collected 124 positive responses, or 72 per cent of the total.[3] This was something we hadn't expected. We decided that seventeen of these 'yeses' had come from people who either didn't seem to have understood the question properly or who couldn't actually describe the experience they claimed. So we ignored those replies. That left us with 107 people, 62 per cent, who claimed to have had an experience of this type, more than double what we had predicted on the basis of the national survey.

What had happened? Had we drawn a very biased sample of the Nottingham population, or had people not been telling us the truth? When we compared the proportions of people from the different social groups in the Nottingham sample with the national sample, they were very similar. So it was not a case of overloading with middle-class or elderly people; and the proportion of men in our Nottingham survey was a good deal higher than for the national. Allowing for the fact that our sample was small, and for that reason possibly not truly representative, working-class people, young people and men were almost as likely to claim that they had been aware of a presence or power as anybody else. Were they misleading us, perhaps giving us the kind of answers they thought we wanted? The evidence does not point that way. First, everybody who said 'yes' had to go on to give a description of an experience and it was possible to check it for consistency. Second, we had inserted questions throughout the survey which allowed us to cross-check earlier answers. Third, we included what is called a 'social desirability' measure. This is a way of checking whether people are trying to say things they think will please the interviewer, or being frank. We would have to be suspicious of our 'yes' respondents if they scored highly on this scale. Their average score was lower than other people's. If anything, they were being more honest with us than others.

The probability that what was happening was the breaking of a taboo, is further supported by the results of an in-depth survey completed in 1986 by Dr David Lewis[4] of the Alister Hardy Research Centre as the Religious Experience Research Unit has now been removed. He found that in a random sample of nurses drawn from two large Leeds hospitals, sixty-six per cent of them reported experience of this kind.

So our explanation, for the time being, is similar to Back and Bourque's for their American survey. We spend perhaps an hour, and sometimes much longer, talking with people in their homes. We have a chance to build up a trusting relationship so that people feel free to talk of matters about which they feel very shy or have a taboo.[5] It is therefore much easier for us to explore a topic in depth, than it is for an opinion pollster with a mixed bag of questions and limited time.

The descriptions themselves

Words are not the only way we have of conveying meaning. In a conversation, all sorts of non-verbal cues are going back and forth between the people involved. This is very important for research interviewers: they have to try not to imply by tone of voice or bodily gestures that they are expecting a particular kind of answer to their questions. But non-verbal communication is mentioned here because of its importance in conveying meanings on the part of the people we interviewed.

During many conversations, the people we spoke to were deeply moved, at times to the extent of being in tears as they recalled their experiences. I owe it to them to state as accurately as possible what they intended to express, but unfortunately I have nothing more than their words at my disposal. Written accounts sent into the Alister Hardy Research Centre quite often have a polished literary quality which makes them attractive to read. It is important to realize that the extracts below, which make no pretentions to polish, and may have a laconic quality to the reader, were usually delivered with great intensity of emotion.

The examples I have chosen are designed to give a feeling for the range of experiences described. At my disposal were descriptions collected from a random sample of Nottingham citizens, the fruit of our most recent survey. Also available were accounts given by the random sample of 100 postgraduate students mentioned earlier. There are some differences in the types of experiences reported by the two groups. For example, cases of 'conversion' and mystical experiences 'in contact with nature' were mentioned by some of the students but not by any of the Nottingham citizens. Similarly, 'visits from the dead' were described only by people in the 'citizens' group. I have felt free to present a mixed selection of examples from both sets of descriptions. It will be clear from the context to which group each account belongs.

The presence of God

The largest group of experiences was those referring simply to an awareness of the presence of God. About a quarter of all descriptions fell into this category. The first example, from a middle-aged man, is very typical in that it relates to a time of considerable personal distress:

> It's just a feeling I had at a very acute time of my wife's illness. I did feel at that time – things looked very grim – there was some consolation. The knowledge that there was something else there which didn't make death so final.

The next description, by a woman, involves the resolution of a personal difficulty. Perception is apparently involved:

Something woke me up. There was something or
somebody by my bed; I wasn't frightened. Within ten
minutes the torment I'd felt, for some strange reason left
me. I think I had more peace then than I'd had for a very
long time . . . I have enough knowledge to know that
there's somebody there, to know that I need never be so
alone again . . . he decided I needed help.

When asked who 'he' was, the respondent said, 'Jesus, I
suppose'.

An English graduate describes what to him was the
presence of God during the performance of Hatha Yoga:

At this time, if I'm lucky [during yoga exercises], I
seem to latch on to something akin to a pure emotional
state. A sense of happiness. There is definitely some sort
of power there which seems to greet me, to embrace.

Someone else illustrates how a particular cultural tradition
directed his awareness towards this kind of experience:

I've been interested in God and what it meant since
my teens, and during the study of Victorian poetry, particularly Tennyson and Browning and their searchings
for God, I thought about their problems which seemed
relevant to me. I began praying, not really sure that
there was a God. At one particular time there was [after
a great deal of thought] – a great relaxation came upon
my mind and everything fitted together. It only lasted for
a moment, perhaps four to five seconds . . . I really felt
God was communicating with me.

Christians speak of prayer as a kind of focusing of awareness, a 'raising of the heart and mind to God', and the boundary between prayer and simple awareness, as in the previous
example, is very blurred. The final example in this category
also relates to prayer at a formal religious service. Though in
an environment where you might expect them, accounts of experiences at public worship were very few. The description
below therefore takes on interest simply because it was so
unusual:

It was memorial Sunday [in the church]. I just felt the
whole thing fitted together. There was a hush, a sense of

presence of God . . . I felt the overall guidance of God in pulling the threads of these lives together . . . I think it's all to do with God. I believe it's my encounter with God.

Answered prayer
The legitimacy of separating off this group from the first is a little doubtful, but the idea of petitioning God is rather more strongly expressed in these extracts. There is also the idea of prayer as a regularly carried-out routine, as in the first example, from a female graduate:

> When I pray . . . I am not praying in a vacuum; there is a response and I feel that at the time of praying, otherwise I think I'd eventually give up.

A woman describes a time spent in desperate petitionary prayer:

> When my husband had been told not to have too much hope [of her daughter's recovery] I spent most of the day on my knees, praying. I felt this presence and I knew she'd be all right . . . I never gave too much thought to things like that before; I took things for granted I suppose, but after that, there is somebody up there and he will help. I've turned a bit more to religion now I think.

In similar circumstances, a working-class woman gives a down-to-earth theological explanation of her experience:

> Well, you know how y'pray, well I prayed and he was all right. I was here on my own, he was on the operating table . . . I prayed for him to get better, I'd got nothing else . . . It has given me faith, really. I know God is good after that. I pray, and God acts.

Next, a thoughtful account from a young history graduate whose present religious position is one of very firm agnosticism.

> When I was thirteen, and my father became ill, I began to feel as though I needed something else in life, and seemed to find the answer in prayer . . . for about

two years this whole experience seemed very real to me, and my belief in this 'something', which I called God at the time, was very strong. It was a very personal feeling, just between me and 'God', and I never made any attempt to tell others of my beliefs. But I think it did give me comfort, even if what I was ultimately asking for was not granted. I think it probably meant more to me then than it does now, my memory being coloured by my present attitudes [of agnosticism].

Finally an account of an out-of-the-body experience, of which there were one or two in the reports given to us. This one is interesting as it is couched in metaphors which are familiar to the individual because of his wife's profession. His defensive remark 'I'm a human being' also illustrates the common expectation that these descriptions will be met with scepticism or derision:

> I was seriously ill; they thought I was dying, but I was up there and I was here. I could see a cord, like an umbilical cord; myself was up there in the corner, I could see myself. I prayed the cord wouldn't snap and it didn't . . . Things weren't going very well – I was relying on God and religion – I'm a human being . . . The fact that my wife was a midwife meant that I saw the symbol of the umbilical cord for both life and death.

A presence not named

In this next large category are those cases where our respondents were either unable or unwilling to put a name to the presence or power which they experienced. Quite often people spoke in ways which indicated that they felt they were being acted upon or guided, as in this first example from a young graduate:

> I believe there is something there, and it is very important to me that it is there, but this has no relation with official Christianity . . . something I feel inside me, which I feel seems to be guiding me, yes.

A middle-aged man recalls the experience of having a decision forcefully contradicted. The incident occurred on a battlefield:

They started shelling and I was caught; I ran towards the new shelter . . . Something seemed to push me not to the new one, to the old one. I charged in. All of a sudden the new dug-out was hit – that was where I was going to head for. Something most decidedly told me to go to the other one . . . I felt that I was being looked after . . . I can't explain [the experience]. My people said they were praying for me. I link that with it, but it's still a question for me.

Another example of the tendency to make a somewhat equivocal link with religion is also present in an account of a faith healing:

I once had a lump in my neck. My mother thought I had cancer. She took me to a faith healer. I felt, while he was working, the presence of something else, and I felt detached from myself.

Had the experience altered his outlook?

It just made me aware or sensitive to extrasensory matters. There's more to life than just what you see. I'm certainly not an atheist.

The next example illustrates how, typically, the presence, though not named, is perceived as benevolent:

It was just about dark and I was looking out of the library window over —. I was aware of everything going on around me – and I felt very alone. But at the same time I was aware of something that was giving me strength and keeping me going . . . protecting me.

Another man remembers the experience of almost drowning when he was a boy, after being trapped underwater in the river Trent:

I slowly drowned (as I thought) and it took three to four hours to get me back to consciousness. Under water I imagined myself floating away – I knew I was going to drown, but I felt no fear. I just thought in a flash it was the end. This lack of fear seems to be because there was somebody to assist me.

Nature-mysticism
Here is an example of nature-mysticism at its simplest:

> Frequently I have a very simple awareness of a presence which is engendered in everything around me.

The next account also contains the quality of 'encounter' with a presence, which is associated with numinous experience, yet resembles the nature-mysticism celebrated by Wordsworth. The man who told me of this experience was moved by it to cease attending church, which, after the immediacy of 'this immensely powerful benign force', seemed, at best, second hand:

> About five years ago, sitting on a mountain top in the middle of Dartmoor, I was waiting for some people, and had been there for several hours. I felt that I wasn't alone, but I felt very content although I had to wait all these hours. It came quite suddenly and went on for at least an hour until the others arrived.

These experiences shade into others which fit more accurately the definition of mystical experience I have been using, that is, an experience of the unity of all things. This next account seems to stand astride the boundary:

> I'd say it was an intoxication with the sights, sounds and forces of nature. A feeling of power coming through my body from internal and external sources . . . I can't distinguish what is divine and what is temporal. It's nothing to do with the Christian God.

A philosophy graduate struggles with the inadequacy of language to express what his mystical experience was:

> It's like losing your particular sense of identity and it's just like, say, looking at a tree. You see certain things happening to the tree and you have words to describe it. There's nothing between us, the tree and me.

One of the small number of people we came across who was following a disciplined programme of meditation describes what happens sometimes during transcendental meditation:

I've been doing some TM recently and I find occasionally as my thoughts become more and more refined,
there's a feeling of being a part of a whole. It's a very
physical awareness of myself as an organism which
relates to a greater organism.

The presence of the dead

This was a category for which we were unprepared, yet a
total of twenty-three accounts occurred out of a set of positive responses of 107 in our Nottingham city sample. Quite
often the experiences were integrated into an orthodox
theological framework, as in the following instance which
occurred subsequent to the break-up of a marriage:

I had rather an emotional crisis some years ago . . . I
felt a presence somehow, in my bedroom, and I thought
it was my old grandmother who'd been dead for some
years. I could have sworn I saw her there and I spoke to
her in Welsh. She said, 'You are in trouble my son and I
may be able to help you.'

The man who told me of this experience interpreted the
presence as an act of God:

I believe there's a God and the power of God can overcome anything. My grandmother appeared through the
power of God.

Another example of an attempt to link the presence of a
dead person with Christian orthodoxy occurs in an account of
a holiday in Ireland:

When I got to the boat I felt the presence of my
mother. It gave me a saintly feeling, it's hard to explain
. . . to me it was very, very real . . . almost as if she were
at my shoulder all the time, as if I was walking on air, a
wonderful experience.

Asked what it meant to her,

You seem to come nearer the Lord don't you, really?
To me it seemed like a miracle; actually you can't put it

into words really, very deep rooted peace of mind . . .
When there's arguments about religion, when they scoff,
that's when I'd like to tell then, but then they'd think
there's something wrong with you.

The various explanations were not all orthodox. A woman
says,

I would imagine life goes on around us in another form.
He [my uncle] is separated from us by a veil.

Finally those inclined to a 'down-to-earth' explanation
found that this led them to question the reality of their experience and to have conflicting feelings:

It was quite unbelievable; even to this day I don't
know whether it was real, whether I was dreaming,
whether I'd woken up and had an optical illusion; it mys-
tifies me. I think it was real – to me it was – probably to
anyone else they'd think I was barmy.

Premonitions

These differ from the other kinds of experience we have been
examining so far, in that their immediate effect is usually to in-
duce feelings of disturbance and agitation. Because they are
taken as advance warnings however, they are commonly seen
in a positive light. The first example illustrates a religious interpretation of a premonition:

I had a dream and woke up screaming. She'd had an
accident. [I saw] exactly the same place as she'd had it.
I'd had a feeling all the morning . . . I don't know what it
was that put it into my mind; there was something . . .
[It's] made me believe there is something more in life, a
warning to me, I think from God . . . I'm a believer;
that's my explanation, God being involved and caring.

The second example comes from a young English graduate
who gives a straight account without offering an explanation:

It was a Friday. I had lectures from about 10.00 a.m.
to 3.00 p.m. Three hall mates had gone to London the
day before. I didn't know when they were coming back. I
attended the first two lectures and then at 12 I had a very

strong desire to go back to hall, ran out of the university
building. A bus turned up instantly (I was in quite a
worried state actually) and I went back to hall. Just as I
entered the corridor, the telephone rang. Another bloke
answered it and told me that my friends had been involved in a car crash the previous evening.

Explanations of premonitions, when given, were not usually
religious. A man was driving fast, late at night:

The cats-eyes turned red. I couldn't understand. I
looked round to see what the reflection was of. I slowed
down for interest, wondered what was going on. As I
came round the next bend there was a tractor and a cart.
The cart was on its side right across the bend. If I'd not
slowed down, I'd have hit it.

His interpretations are based on telepathy:

I have one or two alternatives. [First] it was a sort of
telepathy from the couple of lads round the tractor.
Because telepathy is unusual, the brain can't put it into
words that I would understand and therefore at a sub-
conscious level it transfers the warning to something I
can understand, i.e. the red light. [Second], similar, but
without people; if you like, remains of an atrophied sixth
sense.

Meaningful patterning of events
In a few cases we were given accounts of a sequence of events
in the life of an individual which was experienced as the operation of a supernatural power. These examples differ from those
under the heading 'A presence not named', (p. 141) in that
what is being referred to is a long series of apparent coinci-
dences, not a single incident. Thus,

I believe in fate. A professional musician lives on a
thin wire. I always come out on top. For some reason
things always seem to work out. It's just something I
became aware of; it's difficult to define. I don't believe in
much, but I believe in fate. I'm not a greatly religious
person but I'm not an atheist . . . I don't disbelieve in
God and it's probably tied up in some way.

In fact a majority of the examples in this small group contain the notion of God-ordained fate:

> When you look back it's the feeling that you were being influenced in some way . . . could be a series of coincidences, but it was real enough at the time . . . I do believe a life force is running through the whole of the universe to which you can attune yourself.

Conversion

This was a very small category. Accounts of a 'conversion' experience yielded only four examples. It is mentioned because of the historical importance of this type of report in the scientific study of religious experience. All four accounts came from students. The first extract has a formal and traditional ring to it and comes from a chemistry graduate:

> Over approximately two years, both through the reading of the Bible and through the faithful preaching of the same, I came under a conviction of my own sin and was brought to faith in the Lord Jesus Christ. It's a God-given thing – not at all the work of man.

The other brief account, both ecstatic and gentle, is from a woman with a joint mathematics and physics degree:

> In adolescence after receiving instruction for confirmation, one day in church I prayed for Christ to come into my life. A sense of relief, the peace of God, something fantastic.

Evil powers

The last category for which I would like to give examples differs from all the others in that it belongs to the negative aspects of human experience. All the accounts in this small group refer to unpleasant or frightening events. The first example involves the use of a ouija board, and one or two other cases also related to its use. My informant was a biochemistry graduate:

> I've experienced evil. We were asking questions and testing in a seance with a ouija board. It was a purely

experimental situation, where the answers that were given had, to us, a logical explanation. On one occasion answers were not given, so we asked why. The answer spelt out CHRYSTOS and the glass ended opposite a person wearing a crucifix. At this point, I opted out.

Next, a classics graduate describes madness, experienced as the presence of evil forces:

I had the experience of being the prey of powerful forces which could destroy me and cast me out. Madness led me to see significance [signs?] of their power in things I experienced and read.

And, finally, a late-night experience in the Sussex countryside:

I was out one night in Sussex, near —, and when I came to a ruined building, I felt the presence of something evil, which made me feel extremely uncomfortable and frightened . . . on no other occasion in my life have I had such an overpowering feeling of the presence of evil . . .

Detecting patterns

The task of selecting these examples has reminded me how vivid and unique most people found their experiences. As in the case of the national sample, for many they were once or twice in a lifetime events, and they were like nothing that had happened before or since. In spite of their intensity, most experiences were very brief (Table 10), a majority of them being over in a matter of seconds or minutes. For this type of

*TABLE 10: *'Approximately how long did the experience last?'*

A few seconds/Ten minutes	51%
Up to a day	23%
Up to a month	9%
Up to a year or longer	6%
Unclassified	10%

* All tables in this chapter refer to the positive respondents from the Nottingham city survey, with the exception of Table 14.

experience there seemed to be no way to switch it on or volun-
tarily to return to it; it came and went unpredictably. The other
kind of experience, a more or less continuous awareness which,
as it were, could be turned to at will, was far less common, and
had a quieter, less ecstatic mood associated with it.

In spite of the unique quality of most of these experiences in
the lives of individuals, when we look at large groups it is
possible to see relatively clear patterns. As we have just seen,
they could be classified into recognizable types. When we
compared our collection with the 3,000 accounts which had
already been analysed at the Alister Hardy Research Centre,[6]
we found that they fell into the commonest categories sent to
Oxford, with the possible exception of experiences of the
presence of the dead.

We were interested in Marghanita Laski's[7] idea that experiences of this type have 'triggers', that is, special circumstances
which have something to do with causing them. When asked,
a small number mentioned prayer, a particular physical event,
or some sort of stress, but nearly three quarters (73 per cent)
said they could think of nothing. So I am not entirely happy
with the idea of the 'trigger', because it implies a causal relationship that most people don't seem to make. However,
when we inquired about people's state of mind before the experience occurred, one particular circumstance did stand out
(Table 11): 50 per cent reported that they were distressed or ill
at ease. As my examples show, the distress was often about the
severest of human predicaments, such as the possible impend-
ing death of oneself or a close relative, severe damage to the
body or the loss of a livelihood. Problems like these have not
changed since the appearance of our species on the planet.

TABLE 11: *'What was your state of mind before you had the
experience?'*

Distressed or ill at ease	50%
Confused	6%
Curious or searching	5%
Praying or concentrating	5%
Nothing special	34%

A second characteristic circumstance was that people were usually alone (Table 12). Not far short of two thirds of our positive respondents in the Nottingham sample were completely alone when their experience occurred. In the 1986 Gallup survey which I mention below, we similarly found that the great majority of people reported the experience as happening when they were alone.

TABLE 12: *'Were you alone or in the company of other people at the time?'*

Completely alone	61%
Alone, but in a public place	9%
With one or two uninvolved friends	9%
With one or two involved friends	13%
In a communal setting	7%

Some were with one or two friends who might or might not be aware of what their companion was experiencing. Only 7 per cent of accounts came from people who were taking part in a social gathering such as a religious service.

After the experience was over, the most typical report was of a dramatic change in state of mind towards positive feelings such as peace, restoration, happiness, elation, being uplifted or awestruck (Table 13). In almost all cases there was no alteration whatever in the outward physical circumstances, to account for the change in mood. The way people expressed it

TABLE 13: *'How would you describe your state of mind after the experience left you?'*

At peace or restored	41%	
Happy/elated	14%	61%
Uplifted/awestruck	6%	
Exhausted/numb		7%
Confused		12%
Alarmed/troubled		15%
Normal/no change		7%

implied that they had 'perceived' a presence or power and this in itself had resulted in a radical alteration in their state of mind. A small group of 7 per cent felt the power of what they had been through to be so great that the main effect was exhaustion or numbness. Some, who were unable to interpret satisfactorily for themselves what had happened, felt confused. The 15 per cent who were alarmed or troubled had either experienced an unnerving premonition or felt the presence of an evil power. Only 7 per cent felt there had been no change in their state of mind.

So the overall pattern is roughly as follows. Most experiences occur over a relatively short period of time, perhaps only a matter of seconds. A small group of people say their experience is more or less continuous. The briefer experiences are commonly associated with being either alone or in a state of distress, and when they happen they usually change people's state of mind in a positive direction. This finding for our sample of Nottingham adults is more or less duplicated in three other pieces of research. I found virtually the same pattern amongst the postgraduate group from which I drew some examples to illustrate this chapter. In addition, Eileen Barker of the London School of Economics[8] used some of our questions in a study of the moonies, a modern religious sect. To see how the sect compared with other people she put the same questions to a sample of 107 people unselected for religious adherence. This latter group again resembled our Nottingham adults very closely. Finally, in David Lewis' study of nurses in Leeds the nurses very often reported their experiences as beginning to appear for the first time in relation to the stress they encountered in caring for patients who were suffering or dying.

Addendum: 1987

In 1986 Gordon Heald, the director of Gallup Poll London, and myself, prepared some questions for use in a British national survey.[9] They gave us for the first time an indication of the proportions of people reporting the major types of experience which we already knew about from our 'in-depth' work. These are summarized in Table 14. We also found that using a broader range of questions increased the total positive rate to nearly 50%.

TABLE 14: *National frequency of report of different types of experience*

Total positive response	48%
Types:	
Patterning of events	29%
Awareness of the presence of God	27%
Awareness of receiving help in prayer	25%
Awareness of a guiding presence not called God	22%
Awareness of the presence of the dead	18%
Awareness of a sacred presence in nature	16%
Awareness of an evil presence	12%
Experiencing that all things are 'One'	5%

What the statistics confirm is that the Western monotheistic tradition is still deeply present in the British consciousness. Although the biggest single group is the 'patterning of events', the majority of reports fall into what is, broadly speaking, the numinous category. 'Monistic' mysticism is relatively uncommon, being reported by only 5 per cent of the population, though 'nature mysticism' which is enshrined in the English Romantic tradition, is reported a good deal more commonly. The hint about frequency of report of the presence of the dead which we had picked up in our Nottingham survey was confirmed, with 18 per cent of the sample claiming such experience. Finally, the report of awareness of an 'evil presence' by 12 per cent of the sample is a good deal higher than we would have expected on the basis of previous work.

There is not much doubt that people are telling us about something that is real in their experience, even if it has extraordinary features. So far, I have been calling this sort of experience 'religious', but this is somewhat loose usage. Some of the examples I have presented may not appear to the reader to be at all religious, and to fall more suitably into some such category as the 'paranormal'. Those who report the experiences, as we have seen, have a variety of ways of making sense of what has happened to them. It is now time to explore how people make interpretations and to describe the sorts of influences that affect the way they make their judgements.

11

Responding to Experience

'I never knew a voice,
Man, beast, or bird, better than this. I told
The naturalists; but neither had they heard
Anything like the notes that did so haunt me,
I had them clear by heart and have them still.
Four years, or five, have made no difference.'

EDWARD THOMAS[1]

Making sense

In the early 1950s, a young national serviceman was trying to survive the institutionalized drudgery of two years in the R.A.F. Whenever he could, he got away from the station, by himself. Once,

> I'd been walking in the woods alone and it was on coming out of the woods and looking towards the fields over a gate that I had a sort of visual image of everything being brighter and larger than life and at the same time I had this feeling of understanding and being a part of it . . . I didn't think I would tell you about it.

A quarter of a century later, in the 1970s, he told me how, still,

> I always recall this experience on seeing similar geographical details but I have never again felt the sensation I have described.

He felt privileged, as though he had been 'permitted a glimpse of something special', and over the years had kept his eyes and ears open for an explanation of what had happened to him. The writings of the nature mystic Richard Jefferies[2] had seemed

153

as helpful as any. Jefferies, like himself, was not conventionally religious and he did not think the word 'religious' an appropriate one to describe his experience. How long had his experience lasted? 'A fraction of a second.'

This brief experience of insight and its aftermath illustrates
several of the points I want to discuss in this chapter. First of
all, the use of the word 'religious' as a blanket term for the experiences we have been studying is, at the very least, controversial. Our question about 'being aware of or influenced
by a presence or power' was certainly designed to collect
examples of religious experience. But as a matter of deliberate
choice, the term 'religious' does not appear in the question
itself. The very proviso, 'whether you call it God or not', is an
encouragement to mention experiences which do not fall into
the conventional mould of Western religion. The man whose
experience I have just been describing did not want it to be
given any kind of religious label, and this was true of a number
of those we interviewed. So having tried to prescribe a
universe of human experience, within which lies what is
commonly called 'religious' experience, we were curious to
know whether that was the way people defined their experience for themselves.

We saw in the last chapter that a whole range of experience
was described. Depending on the type of experience, people
were more or less inclined to define it as religious (Table 15).*
Overall, almost exactly two thirds of both the Nottingham city
adults and the postgraduate student group who claimed experience interpreted it this way, a finding which has been
duplicated by Eileen Barker with her London sample.[3] In
other words, somewhat over 40 per cent of all those interviewed believe they have had an experience of being aware of
or influenced by a presence or power, which they further
define for themselves as being 'religious'.

In most cases these experiences were self-evidently religious
to those who reported them. Our question 'Why was your experience religious?', which followed if they had so defined it,

* Amongst the student group, all conversion experiences, two
thirds of the nature mysticism accounts, and half the experiences of
an evil power were interpreted religiously.

TABLE 15: 'Was your experience religious?'

The presence of God	100%
Answered prayer	100%
Meaningful patterning of events	73%
Presence of the dead	55%
A presence not named	43%
Premonitions	36%

was often seen as stupid or irritating. For these people, the very awareness of a presence seemed to carry with it a knowledge of who the presence was. A parallel may be the way that, when we meet a person familiar to us, there is no gap between seeing them and knowing who they are. One person's reply to our question was typical:

Because it was Jesus.

Other people made attempts to qualify their answer, though in effect merely confirming a recognition:

Because it falls within my set idea of religion; to do with Christ.

A thirty-three-year-old working-class woman recognizes where the words which she uses to express her experience come from:

When you're brought up that way, you just see things that way.

The experience itself almost always has the perceptual quality which was noted in the previous chapter. There is however, a gradation from what is experienced as immediate recognition towards more reflective ways of interpretation. Asked why his experience was religious, one man says,

Probably because religion to me is a way of life which is influenced by a spiritual awareness.

For someone else,

* Tables refer to responses from the Nottingham city survey, with the exception of Table 17.

It makes you feel there is a power you can call God or the Life Force.

Uncertainty about the orthodoxy of the experience comes through in the following comment:

When I think of religion, I think of Jesus and the God that you read about in the Bible. I don't really know if what is guiding us is that God.

The label 'religious' continues to be used by many whose interpretations would certainly not be considered as Christian orthodoxy, though familiar enough in Indian religion:

You're apparently making contact with something other than yourself, or with a deeper part of your own nature that you don't know about.

A woman who still calls her experience religious says:

In a very very loose definition, yes. Certainly I do believe it's myself, but I don't think it's my ordinary everyday self.

Finally amongst those who called their experiences religious, a very small group did so by elimination: 'It can't be explained in any other way.' The infrequency of this interpretation suggests that criticisms of the 'God of the gaps' have made a very deep impression.

For the group of people who rejected the label 'religious' as a description of their experience, the commonest reason was that it did not fit with what they understood by the word. Several accounts sounded very much as if they fell into the traditional category of religious experience, but not as defined by our informants. For example:

No! [This was personal] To me religion means a Churchianity study.

And,

I've never been very interested in religion. I suppose religion implies belief, and this was pure experience.

Or,

I don't believe in God; I disapprove of religions.

Premonitions, encounters with the dead and encounters with an evil presence were often ruled out of the category 'religious' on the grounds that they did not fit with the Christian picture as it had been taught. A surprisingly small number of people offered an explanation of their experience in naturalistic terms. Telepathy, which has a somewhat dubious status within orthodox science, was drawn upon, or simply 'psychology'. Thus,

> I believe it was a psychological process. At the time possibly I thought it was a god.

And,

> I'm fairly sure it's completely to do with upbringing.

Practical effects

One of Joachim Wach's ideas which we looked at previously was that 'genuine' religious experience has some kind of effect on the individual's behaviour. This is no doubt based on the biblical injunction 'By their fruits shall ye know them', and one of the criticisms of Wach as a student of religion was his failure to take a detached view of the phenomenon.[4] Nevertheless, religious people themselves do make claims about discerning genuine religion by its fruits. So we were curious about how people saw experiences of this sort affecting their lives. It was not possible to observe changes in behaviour, of course, but we asked everyone who reported an experience whether it had altered their outlook in any way.

TABLE 16: *'Has your experience altered your outlook on life?'*

Confirmed or intensified my beliefs	24%
Made me more optimistic	22%
Given me more insight into life	16%
Encouraged moral behaviour	10%
Can't state the effect	4%
I'm avoiding this area of life	1%
No difference	24%

The replies (Table 16) showed that approximately three quarters of those reporting experience felt that it had changed their outlook to some degree. Again, somewhat more than three quarters of the postgraduate group made a similar claim, and the results of the L.S.E. study are closely parallel. The range of effects varies from 'shattering' to 'none at all', with the largest single group being those who have had what was previously a theoretical belief confirmed or intensified by what they believe to be practical evidence. A young married woman says:

I feel God's always with me; it's confirmed and strengthened the things I've been brought up to know; given me the will-power to go on.

A young man whose experience gave him relief from personal anguish remembers:

If you can smile inwardly – I was doing that . . . It's made me happier for most of the time. Although I get sceptical feelings now and again, they don't matter because now I know.

An increase in optimism is very typical. A skilled tradesman expresses this practically:

It gives you that bit more experience so that next time a problem arises you've got this information in your mind so as you can solve it.

A factory charge-hand claims:

Well I've certainly been a lot happier. I've been able to mix with people more. More at ease with life.

Several people, particularly in academic life, spoke about insight. Someone expresses

Amazement . . . I just stood there and let it happen. I'm more aware of things around me. I now consciously look around me . . . Science tells me there isn't anything out there, but I wonder.

A twenty-four-year-old graduate says:

It completely changed my viewpoint, my philosophy of living. Instead of thinking that everything could be decided on the basis of reason, I realized that the deeper things were intuitive . . .

Others referred to a moral effect. A retired packer in a factory says:

I behave better; it touches the conscience.

And another postgraduate,

I now have far more respect for physical surroundings as well as fellow humans . . . I don't think they were important to me before.

About a quarter of those describing an experience felt it had not affected their outlook on life; usually their experience was not defined as religious either. Only one person we came across felt he wished to make a negative comment about his experience, and that referred to an occult experience which made him decide to avoid the area in future.

Differences between social groups

Even individual accounts hint at the importance of a person's social group in forming the way he will express his experience. A skilled craftsman thinks of his experience as giving him a further skill; an academic uses words like 'insight'. There's evidence too, on a larger scale, that different types of experience tend to be reported by different sub-groups in the community. For example, the experience most commonly named by regular churchgoers, not surprisingly, was the presence of God. However, 90 per cent of the reports relating to prayer, or premonitions, or a presence not labelled 'God', came from people who seldom or never went to church. All cases of report of a meaningful patterning of events came from people who, though they claimed religious belief, never went to church.

Apart from the differences between churchgoers and non-churchgoers there are some hints of other sorts of social link. For example, the majority of accounts of meaningful patterning of events came from men. Most of the examples of contact

with the dead came from working-class women who have had
a minimum of formal education. When David Lewis split his
1986 sample of Leeds nurses into two groups, one highly
educated and the other less well educated, he found that the
less well educated group were much more likely to report encounters with the dead.

Amongst working-class people there is quite a range of experience reported which has little to do with Christian
orthodoxy, and which one can imagine might be looked on
with some horror by the institution. Thus, one of our informants described experiences connected with witchcraft and
himself claimed to be a witch. Another ascribed his experience
to the influence of flying saucers, and several people seemed to
have a religion which concentrated its interest on contact with
the spirits of the dead, either directly or via a medium.

Alongside their disaffection from official religion in the sixteenth and seventeenth centuries, the English peasantry, as
Keith Thomas[5] has shown, maintained a wide variety of folk
beliefs. It may be this unofficial folk-religion that we are un-
covering here, with UFOs being a modern variant. Robert
Towler notes the strength of this kind of religion:

> The fact that popular religion, or common religion as
> we prefer to call it here, lies outside the confines of official
> religion makes it no less significant. It has greater signifi-
> cance if anything, since it survives only because of its
> continued ability to express the transcendent element in
> people's experience, and to bestow meaning on what
> would otherwise be perplexing. Common religion has no
> . . . organizational props. If it survives, it does so because
> it remains credible.[6]

Something parallel could be happening in the graduate groups
that have been studied. While the doctrines of the churches
may be unattractive or implausible to them, they have other
explanatory resources available to them amongst the nineteenth century nature mystics and poets, and also, more
recently, via Asian religious philosophy.

Sometimes it is possible to see in conversation with people
how a shift from one community to another alters their interpretation of their experience, or even extinguishes the

experience itself. A young woman with a degree in biology described the effect of her sixth-form studies as follows:

> At the age of fourteen I had a definite feeling that there was something there, but at the age of sixteen or seventeen this feeling stopped. At that time acquiring new knowledge, especially scientific knowledge, seemed to make such a thing untenable, and in a short time I stopped having this kind of feeling.

It is as if there were rules governing what can be accepted as real, and once those rules were themselves accepted, her experience simply ceased to occur.

In another example, a member of a Marxist revolutionary group illustrated the effects of commitment to a belief system which rejects religion as false consciousness. His refusal of even the possibility of religious experience is based on a moral revulsion:

> At times of selfishness, I stumble into otherworldliness, when I feel the need to lean on some emotional peg (I suppose some people would call it prayer). But when I catch myself, I stop it by saying 'There is no power that can help me' . . . The aspect of subservience disgusts me.

It so happened that on the day this interview took place I also spoke to a deeply committed member of the Church of England. His reflections on his religious experience show a striking contrast in value judgement:

> It's something that is there all the time. One's awareness is limited by one's willingness to submit to it. Very often it demands an unconditional giving which is not as easy as shutting ourselves off. This experience is the true end of man.

Invisible religion

One way people can respond to their experiences is to keep quiet about them. In spite of the frankness of many of the people from whom I have quoted, there is much evidence of reticence. The 1976 survey seemed to show that people who are young, male, poorly educated or working-class simply don't have these experiences as commonly as others. That may indeed be true, but there are other possibilities.

First, there is the question of articulacy. Putting words to religious experience is notoriously difficult. William James's first 'mark' of mystical experience was 'ineffability', the impossibility of expressing it adequately in ordinary language. People without fully developed linguistic skills are therefore doubly handicapped. During the piloting of our Nottingham survey, I interviewed someone in his late teens who had left school without qualifications of any kind and who was having difficulty finding a job. Our conversation was going pretty badly, because, although he said 'yes' to the question whether he was aware of a presence or power, he was totally unable to launch into a description. Nor did he seem to grasp the meaning of most of the other questions until I asked whether his experience had had any effect on his outlook on life. His immediate reply was, 'Of course; I know there's a God.' At that point we seemed to have struck a patch where our use of language coincided and we understood each other.

Another reason for reticence could be the taboo which Ann Morisy and I felt we detected during our Nottingham survey. As I mentioned, the differences in proportions of positive responses between social groups which appeared on the national survey were greatly reduced in the local study. However, there were plenty of indications that we were treading on sensitive ground: prefaces to descriptions like 'Well, this is rather embarrassing' and difficulties in articulating certain words like 'God' and 'prayer'. The most striking evidence, though, was the number of people who said they had never told anyone about their experiences. A quarter of all the accounts we were given had never been disclosed to anyone at all before the interview. This figure rises to one third if partly disclosed experiences are included; that is, those which had in the past only been hinted at. Experiences related to prayer were particularly taboo, half of them remaining completely private. Those occasions which were spoken of freely were usually regarded as trivial or without religious significance, except in the case of people belonging to religious sects which commend public testimony.

One of the questions that Gordon Heald and I put into our Summer 1986 survey, enquired about the privacy of these experiences. The national figures show that, if anything, I had been under-estimating the taboo (Table 17).

TABLE 17: *'Have you told anyone else about this experience? Percentage saying "No"'*

Awareness of a sacred presence in nature	44%
Awareness that you are receiving help in answer to prayer	42%
Experiencing in an extraordinary way that all things are one	40%
Awareness of a kindly presence looking after you	39%
Awareness of the presence of God	38%
A patterning of events in your life	33%
Awareness that you are in the presence of someone who has died	28%
Awareness of an evil presence	28%

When we asked why people were not prepared to tell others about their experience, the great majority said that they feared ridicule, or that they would be classed as mentally unbalanced. Some characteristic responses to our question are:

No, you're the first person. It's a thing I should keep to myself.

An eighteen-year-old youth working in a shop:

Never! Just laugh at me; well they'd probably listen but they wouldn't understand.

A middle-aged factory worker:

No, I've not told anyone. For the simple reason, there's such a lot of disbelievers about, and they'd ridicule you, like.

Another worker:

I'd tell the wife. I don't tell me mates, otherwise they'd think I'd gone barmy.

A churchgoer, on whether she would talk about her experience:

> Probably not . . . but on the understanding that they
> know I like to go to church and believe in God . . . I
> wouldn't like people to turn round and laugh at me.

A woman of forty:

> I think I told my son . . . because we were discussing
> religion for his work at school and I tried to put this over
> to him.

The mood of these accounts is very reminiscent of that
which used to surround the public discussion of intimate
sexual matters. There is the same feeling of tentativeness, followed by rapid retreat if no response or an insensitive one is
detected. One person mentioned an isolated attempt to broach
the subject with a visiting clergyman, only to get the feeling
that he didn't know what she was talking about. Even professional representatives of the sacred are not exempt from the
suspicion that they will not understand.

There seems to be a feeling that 'society' in some way does
not give permission for these experiences to be integrated into
ordinary life. This is illustrated by the replies to one of our
questions. We asked everybody to say what sort of person they
thought would report, and the sort of person who would not
report, these experiences. From this we were able to build up a
set of stereotypes, the most interesting one of which was how
people reporting experience pictured those who did not. Their
view of non-experiencers was overwhelmingly negative; only
6 per cent of those questioned felt able to say something positive, whereas 65 per cent had a critical view. The list of pejora-
tive terms was so startling that we sorted the commonest ones
to illustrate a catalogue of extraordinary vehemence. People
who don't report these experiences were said to be:

> Apathetic, bitter, conformists, cowards, dull, emotion-
> less, hard, ignorant, insecure, insensitive, know-alls,
> lacking capacity, liars, materialists, mean, miserable,
> morally lax, narrow-minded, overcontrolled, sceptics,
> self-centred, sneerers, superficial, too busy, unaware, un-
> imaginative, unintelligent, unpleasant and weak.

It is hardly necessary for me to add that during our interviews we came across no evidence whatever to sustain the belief that people not reporting experiences were particularly worthy of this set of epithets. I do think, however, that its intensity is evidence of strong feelings among people who are aware of experiences in their lives which are of importance to them. They fear that 'society', that great anonymous object of our rage, will not permit them to own the significance of their inner perceptions.

Should these experiences be called religious? Most of the descriptions we have collected are not particularly spectacular in comparison with the numinous and mystical occurrences presented by writers like Rudolf Otto or W. T. Stace. But their examples are drawn on the whole from classics of the major religious traditions, where you might expect to meet accounts of experience at its most powerful. They are taken from the lives of religious heroes who, even within a formally religious context, are people of extraordinary personality and commitment. However, there is enough family likeness between the descriptions I have been giving and the more formal accounts from the religious classics to make it possible for an unbiased observer to agree that they belong to the same universe of discourse.

The qualities of the experiences we have been examining compare well with the criteria proposed by Joachim Wach. Their 'given-ness' often amounts to surprise, because they come without warning. One person said, 'What frustrates me is I have absolutely no control over these experiences. They come unasked.' And we have seen that more often than not they occur outside an obviously religious context such as a church service. The majority of experiences are also totally involving; it is impossible to remain a detached observer. In most cases, too, there is a feeling of vivid reality. One of the things we might have measured, but didn't, was this phenomenon. The phrase 'it was more real than me talking to you now' is representative of the view of many of those we spoke to. This feeling, that the experience was more 'real' than everyday reality, is very curious, given that it is normally brief in duration and unpredictable. Finally, these experiences usually have an effect in altering people's outlook on life.

The range of experience presented is a good deal wider than that encompassed by a strict definition of 'numinous' or 'mystical'. Accounts of a presence, whether named as God or not, only occasionally have the staggering or overwhelming quality which Otto defined as one of the marks of numinous experience. On the whole, descriptions speak of a peaceful or perhaps elated mood, though containing the element of surprise. This is not unknown amongst classical accounts of Christian religious experience, for example in the poetry of St John of the Cross:

Upon a lucky night
In secrecy, inscrutable to sight,
I went without discerning
And with no other light
Except for that which in my heart was burning.

It lit and led me through
More certain than the light of noonday clear
To where One waited near
Whose presence well I knew,
There where no other presence might appear.[7]

Other kinds of experience such as premonitions, visions of the dead, the meaningful patterning of events, or experiences of the presence of an evil power are even more remote from the definitions of Otto or Stace. Nevertheless, the criteria which people seem to use in judging whether the occasion was religious correspond closely to those of Wach, that is to say, given-ness, reality, total involvement, effect on behaviour. Where one or other of these criteria was absent, the experience was not usually called religious. The curious category of 'religious experiences of evil' seemed to qualify on the basis that they were negative manifestations of a non-everyday reality.

On the basis of what people have said to us, then, I feel that 'religious experience' is not quite the right term for what we have been describing. It would be more correct to say that it is a type of experience which is commonly given a religious interpretation. For reasons of shorthand I intend to continue to use the word 'religious' while recognizing that this is only one way of looking at it. Those who dislike religion or reject it on intellectual grounds are unlikely to be willing to label any human experience, unless perhaps it is pathological, as religious. Here is the fury of a clergyman's son:

> One thing I detest more than anything is to go inside a church. Man is in charge.

A mathematics graduate says:

> I'm a realist – things that religion tries to explain can often be explained another way. When everything that the Christian religion stands for can be explained it will be discarded.

The mood and the attitudes expressed in these two quotations have been fairly central to the last 200 years of European thought. Yet the vividness and reality of religious experience demands that it be given some sort of interpretation. It is therefore time to return to some of the explanations we looked at earlier in this book.

12

Doubts About the Despisers

'Men are burning the gorse on the down's shoulder;
A drift of smoke
Glitters with fire and hangs, and the skies smoulder,
And the lungs choke.

Once the tribe did thus on the downs, on these downs burning
Men in the frame,
Crying to the gods of the downs till their brains were turning
And the gods came.'

JOHN MASEFIELD[1]

Religion and madness

There is a theory that heart disease has something to do with the hardness of drinking water. It was in following this idea that George W. Comstock, a medical scientist working at Johns Hopkins University in Baltimore in 1971, made a rather odd discovery.[2] He had available to him the results of a huge census conducted in Washington County in western Maryland. Over 90,000 people had answered a questionnaire on a wide variety of subjects important in public health. There were figures for quality of housing, number in the family, history of diseases and so on, and in addition there was information about people in the sample who had died during the period in which the census was going on. Comstock decided to check on all those people who had died from arteriosclerotic heart disease and see if there was any association with the hardness of the domestic water supply to the areas where deaths had occurred.

He didn't find any connection, but as a matter of course he ran a cross-check through the computer to see if there were

168

links with any of the other census data. To his surprise, he
found that by far the best predictor of death from heart disease
was that the person had not been a regular churchgoer. People
who went to church on a weekly basis were only half as likely
to die of heart disease as those who didn't. He attempted to
correct for possible causes of distortion, like the fact that
maybe people with heart disease couldn't get to church very
easily, even if they wanted to. But the differences still remained. Encouraged by this result to search further, he did a
follow-up study[3] and found that churchgoers were also far less
likely to die from pulmonary emphysema and cirrhosis of the
liver, and were less likely to commit suicide.

It appears that Comstock's earlier interpretations were
somewhat hasty.[4] In addition, quite apart from a possible mis-
interpretation of the data, the concept of 'religiosity' is one of
great complexity, as was made clear in Chapter 5. Yet in large
scale surveys it tends to be measured by a single item, usually
asking whether a person attends church or not.

Nevertheless, it is tantalizing to speculate on whether membership of a church group does or does not give people
psychological support. Or are people of a particularly un-
stressed personality attracted to church membership? Or
could it be that religious faith mediates peace of mind and
release of tensions? Recent research on the effect of the mind
on pulse and blood pressure, makes that last speculation not
as ridiculous as it might have appeared a few years ago. The
idea that religion provides both physical and mental therapy
is, of course, very ancient indeed, and one to which Freud was
prepared to grant some substance. But, as we have seen, he
believed that what it offered, was a 'crooked cure' via a socially acceptable neurosis.

However, in recent decades the argument about whether
religion is an illness or a cure for an illness has come to seem
far too simple. The American psychologist of religion Bernard
Spilka[5] has pointed out how religion can function in all sorts of
ways in relation to mental states. For example, it could be used as
an outlet and even an encouragement to mental aberration.
No doubt the average churchgoer in western Maryland has some
pretty staid and predictable religious ideas; but sometimes religious beliefs can be highly unconventional, to the extent that

they might provide a handy vehicle for the symptomatic expression of a disordered mind. Examples are the mass suicides of the followers of Jim Jones in Guyana, or the ritual killings associated with Charles Manson in California. The idea of human sacrifice as a religious rite strikes a particularly horrifying chord, as is well known to the more lurid branches of the modern film industry. But 'ritual' killings have a very long and widespread history,[6] even lying at the root of Western religion – the Hebrew patriach Abraham almost sacrificed his own son, Isaac, on the altar.

Nearer home, human sacrifice probably featured in the religion of the ancient Celtic peoples of Britain[7] and was officiated at by the druids. In his account of the Gallic wars, Julius Caesar left what may be an eye-witness account of human sacrifice amongst the Celts of Gaul. At a great festival which took place every five years, huge wickerwork frames were built in the shape of a man. Live victims, usually condemned criminals or prisoners of war, were placed in the frames along with cattle and other animals, and the whole thing was set on fire, it is thought as a burnt offering to ensure the fertility of the land. Remoteness from these grisly events makes them somehow less appalling than ritual death in modern California, but no doubt Caesar sent his report back to Rome as an illustration of the barbarity of the peoples he was sent to subdue.

Long before Caesar's day, for reasons of political expediency, a bizarre form of religion had made its appearance in Rome itself. Towards the end of the third century B.C. the Romans were at war with Hannibal. At that time,

> The principal instrument of senatorial policy was the so-called Sybilline books;[8] its object the distraction of the commons; its procedure the introduction of deities and practices from Greece and the East. It was in accordance with this policy that in 205 B.C. when the tide of Hannibal's war had now turned, the senate discovered a convenient prophecy that an alien invader would be driven from Italy if the great mother from Ida were brought to Rome.[9]

It was thus that a delegation was sent to Pessinus, near Mount Ida in Asia Minor, and the Mother Goddess Cybele, in the form of a sacred black meteorite, was brought home to Rome and placed in the Temple of Victory. Cybele seemed to do the trick, for Hannibal's reverses continued until he was finally defeated.

However, the citizens were in for a shock. Arriving with Cybele was an attendant retinue of Asian priests whose attitude to religion flabbergasted the local population:

> They were shocked by the Eastern rites, with their loud ululations and wild dances, with their entrancing rhythms, which by pipe and tambourine whipped up the people into ecstasies of bloody self-flagellation and self-injury.[10]

The most upsetting feature was that the *galli* or priests, as part of their initiation, drove themselves into an orgiastic frenzy. At its height they seized a sharp stone, or potsherd or knife, and castrated themselves. Thereafter they took the title of *gallus*, or 'cock', wore clothing of a gaudy and extravagant style, affected the appearance and mannerisms of women, and apparently spent much of their time wandering the streets begging, followed by crowds of enthusiasts. The authorities interpreted all this as nothing short of insanity and forbade Roman citizens to become *galli*, but some eventually did, and the cult survived and even prospered at times.

The poet Catullus, whose father was a friend of Julius Caesar, wrote a poem in the first century B.C. expressing a sophisticated man's disgust at the continuing popularity of the cult, ending with the sardonic lines:

> Great Goddess, Goddess who guards Mount Dindymus
> May your furies all fall far from my house.
> Make other men mad, but have mercy on me.[11]

Yet the religion prospered in Rome up to the fourth century A.D., when St Augustine, who as a young man had witnessed its rituals in Carthage, attacked those who mutilated themselves 'at a whim' and who 'nowadays in Rome serve the mother, not of the gods, but of the daemons'.[12]

That sort of religious cult, which was widespread and longstanding in the Roman Empire and which struck sophisticated Romans as a kind of popular insanity, is by no means unique.

Instances of self-castration are occasionally discussed in psychiatric journals today, and they are usually interpreted in a similar manner, as the behaviour of ignorant and unbalanced people. In 1967, the psychiatrist A. W. Kushner[13] reported the cases of two men who had emasculated themselves, each case being associated with what were described as bizarre religious ideas. The justification given by both men was the verse in St Matthew's Gospel which reads, 'And there be eunuchs which have made themselves eunuchs for the kingdom of heaven's sake'.[14] On the face of it, the self-castrations had parallels with those of the *galli* in ancient Rome, in that they had taken place as an extreme sacrifice in devotion to the highest known good. The psychiatric diagnosis was that both men were suffering from paranoid schizophrenia and they were treated either with drugs or electroconvulsive therapy in a mental hospital. After treatment, both were able to survive, precariously, in the outside world, with the assistance of further drugs and psychotherapy. Interestingly, Kushner records that the psychotherapy involved accepting the version of reality held by the patients and using it to manipulate them into socially acceptable behaviour.

But where does the boundary lie between craziness and what might be called 'intensity of commitment'? A decision about that may depend on what version of reality one accepts. Bodhidharma, the legendary first Zen patriarch, is said to have paid no attention to the young Hui K'o in his pleas for instruction until the latter, as a demonstration of his agonized sincerity, finally cut off his left arm and presented it to the master. Today, Hui K'o is revered as the second Zen patriarch.

Another controversial example is given by the Irish psychiatrist M. O'Connor Drury.[15] One morning at mass, an elderly retired civil servant heard the following words of the gospel read out: 'Go and sell all that thou hast and give to the poor and thou shalt have treasure in heaven, and come and follow me.' The man heard these words as a direct personal command, left the church, leaving all the money he had in his pockets in the poor box, and set out to walk 135 miles to the pilgrimage centre at Lough Derg. His family became worried when he didn't arrive home, and eventually he was traced by the police, examined by a doctor and placed in a mental hospital. He understood clearly what had happened to him and accepted it as God's will. With some difficulty, the hospital authorities were able to get his wife to agree to his discharge, since she was convinced he was suffering from an illness called 'religious mania'. As Drury comments, St Anthony the Hermit heard the same words read out in a church in Alexandria, 1,600 years ago. He responded identically, and walked out into the desert to found the Christian eremitical tradition. He was not certified, but canonized.

Religious experience and sanity

The range of human behaviour illustrated above all purports to be a response to a religious stimulus. Most people looking from the context of contemporary European culture would agree that it represents a spectrum spreading from horrifying and totally unacceptable behaviour through to what might be considered alarming but hardly more than eccentric activity. This spectrum by no means exhausts the ways in which people express themselves religiously. Nevertheless it is perhaps what makes people circumspect when admitting to their own religious experience. They commonly fear that they will be thought of as falling into the same general category and be dismissed as mentally disturbed. It is interesting therefore to note that the consensus of opinion amongst all those we interviewed, whether they claimed experience or not, was strongly against this view. We asked everybody to respond to the proposition that such experiences were possibly due to mental instability, and 75 per cent said they strongly disagreed. Only two people strongly agreed, and it may be significant that one of those was a professional psychiatrist. They, too, have their preconceptions.

We have several pieces of evidence about the psychological state of those reporting religious experience in contemporary society. In our national survey in Great Britain, we included a measure of 'psychological well-being' developed by Norman M. Bradburn of the National Opinion Research Center in Chicago.[16] Our finding was that, on average, people reporting religious experiences had a significantly higher level of psychological well-being than other people. Greeley and McCready[17] used the same scale with their national sample of American 'mystics' and found that they got the highest average score for well-being of any group ever measured with this widely used scale.

To say that someone scores highly on a scale of psychological well-being does not necessarily mean that they are sane by some other criterion. But the scale probably relates closely to the criteria clinicians use to assess mental health. Paul Berkman of the California Department of Public Health reported the results of a large-scale survey made in Almeda County in 1971,[18] using Bradburn's scale. The results suggest that the scale is a good indicator of mental health. In addition, the psychologist Ralph Hood has been working for a number of years at the University of Tennessee on the personality of those reporting mystical experience. On almost all the measures of psychological adequacy he has used, they score more highly than other people.[19]

Obviously more research needs to be done before it is possible to speak with confidence in this area; but all the evidence to date suggests that those reporting religious experience are, if anything, more adequate psychologically than other people. Psychiatrists are currently involved in a very wide-ranging debate on the appropriate criteria to use in assessing someone's psychological state.[20] It is not possible to enter into that here, except to say that differences of opinion on the status of religious experience depend largely on the beliefs of those involved in the argument. Experiences of this type, as we have seen, are certainly not abnormal in the sense of being uncommon; on the contrary, they are widespread. In terms of their capacity to adjust to their personal situation, those claiming religious experience state that it has aided them to behave more competently than before. They are, on average, happier and more optimistic about life than other people.

This is in agreement with Freud's observation that religious people, because they suffer from the universal neurosis, save themselves the trouble of constructing an individual neurosis. But there is something strange about the view that someone who in every other respect is above average in psychological competence is a neurotic with temporary psychotic hallucinations, because he claims to have had a religious experience. It depends for its cogency on the prior belief that religion is nonsensical, and though this is widely argued, the very continuance of the argument shows that it is not a settled issue.

Religion and social injustice

The discussion so far has tried to show that, while religions can be the vehicles for the expression of insane or unacceptable behaviour, they need not be limited to this function. Any public institution, whether religious or secular, can be a vehicle for bizarre behaviour. The use of a particular institution as an outlet of this type may depend as much on availability as anything else. The psychiatrist O. S. Walters,[21] writing in 1964, remarked on the relative decline in 'religious' as opposed to 'secular' delusions amongst patients in mental hospitals over the years, and associated it with the declining presence of an obvious religious institution.

But while it may not be possible to dismiss religions as vehicles for insanity, perhaps it is not so easy to dismiss the charge that they can be used as instruments to perpetuate social injustice. An illustration of this can be found in Santiago, the capital of Chile, which was founded by Pedro de Valdivia, conquistador and fellow countryman of Cortes, in 1541. In the centre of the city, on the site of a shrine set up by Don Pedro, stands Chile's oldest building, the church of San Francisco. Today the cloisters of the church house a remarkable collection of Spanish colonial art, mostly paintings, sculpture and furnishings. The pictures are of conventional religious subjects, but what strikes the visitor from northwestern Europe is the large sprinkling of representations of self-abasement and suffering. One picture shows a Franciscan friar practising humility by allowing his brethren to walk on him while he lies on the ground. A statue of St Peter of Alcantara, one of the people to whom St Teresa of Avila turned for wisdom, depicts him grey and emaciated, a living skeleton, just like the representation of severe malnutrition seen in films of starving refugee or concentration camp victims. The sculptor's knowledge must have come from direct contact.

Images like these are part of the religious heritage of the
million or so people who crowd the shanty areas surrounding
modern Santiago. They project an ideal, wittingly or unwittingly, of the appropriate attitude to life as one of resignation to and acceptance of suffering, and offer the patience of
the saints as a sacred example. As John Plamenatz has
remarked,

> Often it [religion] may do little or nothing to attach
> the exploited and socially inferior to the established
> order, and yet may so affect them that they are resigned
> to it as something they are powerless to change. In that
> sense it may quite often be what Marx called it, *the opium
> of the people.*[22]

Marx could see this happening in his native Rhineland, and it
was this that made him turn with such vehemence on the local
political/religious   establishment   when   they   mouthed
platitudes about the social principles of Christianity:

> The social principles of Christianity preach cowardice,
> self-contempt, abasement, submission, dejection, in a
> word, all the qualities of the *canaille*; and the proletariat,
> not wishing to be treated as *canaille*, needs its courage, its
> self-feeling, its pride and its sense of independence more
> than its bread.[23]

One of the ways that religion could function as a crooked
therapy in a situation of injustice is by suppressing the
symptoms of social disorder. A religion with rigid rules might
be an agency for crushing deviant feelings. It could also provide a haven from stresses in life which would otherwise
become intolerable and lead to physical revolution or mental
breakdown. This relates to one of the more dubious ways of
assessing psychological normality, namely, by how well the individual is adjusted to his situation. It is not clear, for
example, how sane we would consider someone who was well
adjusted to his job in an extermination camp. Or what would
be the significance of a finding, which seems not improbable,
that churchgoers in the Soviet Union are more neurotic than
other people, since such activity runs counter to the national
ideology?

Evidence that there is a certain personality type which finds relief in rigidity and the maintenance of the status quo was given massive empirical support by the German social scientist T. W. Adorno in 1950.[24] Towards the end of the Second World War the scale of the Nazi holocaust was becoming obvious to everyone. Adorno and his colleagues, exiled in the United States, were financed to try to find out what kinds of people were attracted to fascism and to account for their particular type of personality. He and his fellow-workers thought they had identified a type which they called the 'authoritarian personality' who would hold views not unlike those of the Nazis. People like this, they felt, were inclined to be over-concerned with correct or conventional behaviour, they were rigid in their thinking, over-submissive to people in authority, loudly in favour of stern punishment for people whose behaviour or appearance deviated from the normal, and prejudiced against outsiders such as people of a different race or religion. In view of the precepts in the gospel concerning brotherly love, it was a bit of a blow to churchmen when Adorno presented evidence that churchgoers were, on the whole, more authoritarian in personality than non-churchgoers. This was a characteristic they shared with, amongst others, prisoners in San Quentin prison and members of modern fascist-style political parties.[25]

There was something so disturbing and yet so richly ironic about Adorno's claims that they stimulated a flurry of repeat studies which seemed to confirm what he and his colleagues had asserted. It is certainly possible to call to mind the stereotype of a strict churchman, tight-lipped, grim-faced, unbending in conservatism, suspicious and condemnatory of all those outside the house of faith. Such people loom large in the history of literary and political satire, perhaps reminding us of the popular image of Ulster Orangemen, or the band of businessmen who organized affairs to their liking in the Wuppertal of Engels' youth. If true, Adorno's discoveries would most certainly give support to Marx and Engels's view of religion as the ideology of the ruling class – a suitable tool for those whose interest it is to maintain the status quo.

Religious experience and justice

However, these stereotypes do not tell the whole story about Western religion. The gospels describe a different set of images presented by Jesus at the commencement of his mission. He is said to have stood up in the synagogue in Capernaum and opened the scriptures at the Book of Isaiah, the Old Testament prophet whose vision in the temple is almost the archetype of numinous experience. The passage Jesus chose to read was the following:

> The spirit of the Lord has been given to me,
> for he has anointed me.
> He has sent me to bring the good news to the poor
> to proclaim liberty to captives
> and to the blind new sight
> to set the downtrodden free,
> to proclaim the Lord's year of favour.[26]

Having returned the book to the assistant, he stated this as the programme on which his mission was to be based. In a sense he was claiming that the moment had come for the ending of man's alienation from his God-given powers. A parallel passage from Marx takes it that the criticism of religion is the first step in the ending of human self-alienation:

> The criticism of religion ends with the doctrine that man is the supreme being for man. It ends therefore with the categorical imperative to overthrow all those conditions in which man is an abased, enslaved, abandoned, contemptible being.[27]

The evidence that we have been gathering about religious experience, however, shows that it is associated with the overcoming of feelings of abasement and worthlessness. After such experiences, people state that they are better able to cope with their problems, and feel an increase in self-esteem. In Robert Wuthnow's survey in the San Francisco Bay area,[28] people claiming contact with the sacred were more likely than others to find life meaningful, to have a purpose and to be self-assured. Almost by definition, mystical experience involves a reduction in alienation in the sense that someone who hitherto has felt cut off from the rest of the world and his fellow-men finds a new experience of solidarity with them.

Clearly this loss of dejection and isolation, and its replacement by a feeling of unity with the rest of mankind, can be dismissed as a false resolution. In that case, religious experience would be performing its classic Marxist function by making people reconciled to continuing 'objective' alienation in the form of economic and political injustice. Even so, as John Plamenatz[29] has written of religious doctrines and myths, the outcome of religious experience may still have constructive value in an 'objective' sense. In the following passage, which describes a situation where the power of the oppressive sectors of society is still too great to be effectively opposed, I have substituted 'religious experience' for 'religious doctrines'.

> . . . [religious experience] might sustain the self-respect of believers, their sense of their own worth as rational and moral beings. It might satisfy, at least to some extent, some of the deepest and most persistent needs of a self-conscious 'species being'. Engels and Marx took little account of this possibility though they were not committed to neglecting it by their conception of man. If [religious experience] did this for believers, even the exploited among them, we could say it favoured their interests positively by keeping alive in them feelings which men must have if they are ever to challenge the social order. It would maintain in them the self-esteem without which they could never become effective reformers or revolutionaries.[30]

As regards people reporting religious experience, whatever the economic position in which they find themselves in society, the picture suggested by their outlook on life is that they are probably more prepared than others to be involved in the movement to attack the 'objective' causes of alienation. Members of this group, according to Greeley and McCready's study, are more optimistic, less racist and probably less authoritarian than other people. Robert Wuthnow found that people reporting 'peak experiences'[31] (a category that includes religious experience) were less materialistic, less status-conscious and showed more concern with issues of social justice than others.

In the continent of South America, so replete with images of religious passivity and the acceptance of suffering as man's earthly lot, alternative religious images have begun to appear. They are more in accordance with the programme of his mission presented by Jesus, and with the religious experience which has been reported to us in our research. In the working-out of the Latin American theologies of liberation,[32] apathy and resignation to social injustice are presented as being false to man's deepest religious experience, so that religion becomes a vehicle for the ending of both physical and spiritual alienation.

Religion as 'Means', 'End', or 'Quest'?

We have seen how religion can be an outlet for mental aberration, a suppressor of discontent or a haven for the inadequate. We have also seen, however, that people reporting religious experience don't fit very comfortably into those categories, on the whole. Perhaps they fit more appropriately into Bernard Spilka's fourth type of religion. Spilka points out that, apart from being a vehicle for negative processes in society, religion can also provide the occasion for the constructive handling of the stresses and dilemmas inherent in life, so allowing people to use their personal capabilities and broaden their perspectives.

It was because there was something contrary to common-sense in the findings of Adorno and others following him that Spilka decided to explore the odd claim that church members were less likely to behave in ways recommended by the gospels than other people. He believed he was able to show in a long series of research studies[33] that it is possible to identify two broad styles of religion. Firstly there is a large group of people who are religious for instrumental reasons; that is to say, they find religion useful because it helps them to achieve other, non-religious purposes such as a measure of social stability, or reduction of stress, or, perhaps more cynically, as a means to achieving power or status. This type of religion Spilka calls 'consensual'. The second type he refers to as 'committed';

people in this group are religious because they find it gives meaning and value to existence. We are not here comparing people who are 'less religious' with those who are 'more religious', necessarily. Rather, two types of religion are being distinguished. Nevertheless, Spilka and his colleagues believe they have been able to show that those belonging to the 'committed' group are higher in self-esteem, lower in prejudice, less concerned with materialistic goals like money, power or status and more concerned with helping their fellow-men than the 'consensual' group.

The position was complicated in 1982 by the publication of *The Religious Experience* by Daniel Batson and Larry Ventis. In spite of the title of the book, it is not about religious experience as I have been expounding it. Nevertheless the outcome of the debate on their work will affect the argument I am presenting in this chapter. This is because much of their discussion centres round 'born again' Christians, possibly fundamentalists, and therefore, presumably, people who have gone through some kind of religious conversion.

They claim to identify three religious orientations: the 'means' orientation corresponding approximately to Spilka's consensual religion; the 'end' orientation corresponding roughly to Spilka's committed religion; finally, a new orientation called 'quest', which corresponds to an undogmatic but religiously oriented search.[34]

They claim to provide evidence that those people falling into the 'means' orientation are more likely to be mentally unhealthy, lacking in compassion and more prejudiced than other people. Those for whom religion is an 'end', while anxious to present themselves as healthy, compassionate and unprejudiced, appear, when allowance is made for their wish to give socially desirable responses, to be in the same category as the extrinsic. It is this latter category which Batson and Ventis associate with evangelical, 'born again' religion. Only those within their final, 'quest' orientation seem to fit the positive characteristics that religions tend to claim for their adherents.

In a concluding chapter on whether religion is 'on our side', Batson and Ventis decide that it is not, with the exception of people belonging to the 'quest' orientation. At the time of writing, this claim is under intense academic debate,[35] and it is too early to make a pronouncement on it.

In my view it is certainly possible to imagine and identify people of rigid personality who might use not simply religion, but religious experience, as part of a psychological defence mechanism. Nevertheless, on reviewing the data which I have assembled in this book, I conclude that the overwhelming weight of evidence suggests that those personally in touch with the experiential dimension of religion typically find something different. On the whole their experience shifts their personality and behaviour away from rigidity and defensiveness and towards greater constructiveness and concern for others. Furthermore, this link seems to be maintained among people who, though they claim religious experience, have little or no formal connection with the churches.

Those who attempt the criticism of religion on scientific grounds seldom assert that science 'disproves' the truth of religious claims. More usually they take the view that, in the absence of empirical data, scientific research cannot help to settle the matter either way. This does not prevent them from making a negative judgement of religion on 'functional' grounds. That is to say, they believe it is destructive of human welfare. Convinced atheists like Marx and Freud certainly felt they had explained religion away, yet their criticisms, too, are primarily functional: religion is false consciousness, or a neurosis, and leads to the diminishment of man.

It is certainly not possible to argue with the fact that religion has been used as a vehicle for unjust and insane human purposes many times during history. But the evidence collected over the past two decades suggests that these attacks, partly determined by a nineteenth century positivism which had already dismissed religion before examining it in detail, were too sweeping. All recent studies which look directly at the 'experiential' dimension of religion show that it is typically associated with personal integration, a sense of meaningfulness in life, and concern for social justice. In the next two chapters I want to go on to suggest that religious experience is something biologically natural to man.

13

'How Did You Know?'

'The prophets Isaiah and Ezekiel dined with me, and I asked them how they dared so roundly to assert that God spoke to them; and whether they did not think at the time that they would be misunderstood, and so be the cause of imposition.

'Isaiah answer'd: "I saw no God, nor heard any, in a finite organical perception; but my senses discovered the infinite in everything . . ."'

WILLIAM BLAKE[1]

Feeling

Sociologists sometimes speak as if religious experience were socially generated, and I can see what they mean. Take the rhetoric of an evangelical revival meeting, with its close-packed crowds, its hymn singing and its fiery preaching. It seems specifically designed to build up a mood of emotional excitement to the point where it needs to boil over. Thus, an enthusiastic brother in a New York camp meeting at the end of the nineteenth century: 'Brethren, I feel – I feel – I feel – I feel – I feel – I can't tell you how I feel, but Oh, I feel! I feel!'[2] Religious gatherings of this sort are a colourful example of what some people have in mind when they say that religion lies in the realm of the emotions. It could be that, in the very experience of emotional arousal, the members of the congregation believe that they encounter the presence of something divine. As we saw in the last chapter, in certain forms of religion it is accepted that the gods appear when one is in a state of frenzy.

There is some evidence that the way we label our emotions depends at least in part on the context in which they occur. In 1962 the psychologists Stanley Schachter and J. E. Singer[3]

183

published a report of a now famous inquiry. Volunteers were asked to take part in an experiment which purported to be concerned with the effects of a vitamin injection on visual acuity. The injections they were given were actually of adrenalin, a hormone which creates a state of physiological arousal. Unaware of this fact, individuals were asked to stay in a waiting room to give the 'vitamin injection' time to take effect. Also in the waiting room was a confederate of Schachter's, who on some occasions would start to behave in a wildly euphoric manner, throwing paper aeroplanes around the room, screwing up sheets of paper and practising basketball shots into a waste-bin. With other subjects there was a requirement, during the period of waiting, to fill in a questionnaire which included insulting questions like:

With how many men (other than your father) has your mother had extramarital relations?

> 4 (and under)
> 5 through 9
> 10 and over

Here the confederate behaved as if he were getting angrier and angrier, eventually tearing the questionnaire in pieces and stamping out of the room.

The unsuspecting subjects themselves tended to follow the behaviour of their partner in the waiting room, and accordingly became euphoric or angry. The curious twist to the experiment was that another group of people were also given an adrenalin injection, but told what to expect in terms of physiological arousal, before they went into the waiting room. In their case, there was no evidence of being tempted to join in the antics of the other person present. They either waited peacefully or filled out the questionnaire while ignoring the excesses of Schachter's confederate. It seemed that because they knew the source of their arousal, they had no need to cast around in the environment for cues to give a label to their feelings.

Suppose someone felt otherwise unaccountable emotions in a religious setting; perhaps Schachter's experiment would explain why they might label such feelings as a religious experience. The following example,[4] taken from William James, seems to fit rather well. James quotes an account of the experience of Stephen Bradley, which occurred shortly after Bradley had returned from attending a revival meeting, impressed by what he had heard but not apparently emotionally moved:

> I retired to rest soon after I got home, and felt indifferent to the things of religion until I began to be exercised by the Holy Spirit, which began in about five minutes after, in the following manner:
> At first I began to feel my heart beat very quick all of a sudden, which made me at first think that something is going to ail me, though I was not alarmed, for I felt no pain. My heart increased in its beating, which soon convinced me that it was the Holy Spirit from the effect it had on me. I began to feel exceedingly happy and humble . . . In the meantime while thus exercised, a thought rose in my mind, what can it mean? . . . and it appeared to me just as if the New Testament was placed open before me, eighth chapter of Romans . . . and I read these words 'The Spirit helpeth our infirmities with groanings which cannot be uttered'. And all the time that my heart was a-beating, it made me groan like a person in distress . . .

The sequence of emotional arousal without apparent reason, followed by attribution to the action of the Holy Spirit, is more or less what Schachter would predict, since Bradley's recent attendance at the revival meeting provided the explanation nearest at hand. Within that context, it might be argued, a further search for scriptural authority gave him a satisfactory explanation of the fact of his groaning, which was real enough to cause his brother to come in from another room to see if he was all right.

This explanation of the identification of certain kinds of feelings as religious has a lot of plausibility. Perhaps in the excitement of revival meetings or in a delayed aftermath, people are inclined to label their feelings as 'religious'. The suggestion resembles quite closely that of Durkheim, who attributed religious experience to the 'effervescence' generated at large cultic meetings. Nor is this necessarily an explaining away, unless you have a prior disbelief in the reality of religion. In everyday life we are constantly identifying the source of our emotions on the basis of an appraisal of the situation, such as the presence of a lover or a hated rival, but we do not therefore dismiss the emotions as spurious.

However, there is very little evidence, from the accounts of religious experience which we have collected, that this explanation would hold water for the people describing them. Very few cases can be attributed to group effervescence in the Durkheimian manner. Very few indeed took place in the context of, or following upon, a religious gathering, or for that matter any kind of gathering. The typical situation in which experiences take place is one of solitude or silence. Many years ago the anthropologist Bronislaw Malinowski[5] made the same objection to Durkheim's identification of religious experience with the excitement generated in group rituals. Reflecting on his own experience, and appraising the available anthropological evidence, he came to the conclusion that 'the strongest religious moments come in solitude'. Our evidence suggests that this continues to be true for most people in modern industrial society.

Perception

Nevertheless, religious experience is often spoken of as if it were a feeling. The theologian Friedrich Schleiermacher, who temporarily caught the interest of Engels before he made his final break with religion, thought it was rooted in a 'feeling of absolute dependence'.[6] A century later, Freud, though claiming no personal acquaintance with mysticism, equated it with 'oceanic feeling', implying that it was primarily emotional.

The trouble with the word 'feeling' is that it is ambiguous. Apart from 'emotion' it can also mean 'perception', and this is much more like the connotation to be found in the descriptions we have collected. Sometimes this is stated directly, though seldom in the extreme manner of one person who said: 'There's no emotion attached; it's a perception.' However, the strong emotions which are often associated with religious experience seem much more like a consequence of the experience, rather than the thing in itself.

An aspect of these experiences which also makes one think of perception is the immediacy of recognition. A high proportion of people in our survey claimed that they knew at once

who or what was present to them. In these cases there did not
seem to be a gap between the first moment of awareness and a
time when, for example, after some deduction, the presence
was concluded to be God. This quality of immediate recognition came out most obviously when we pursued the reasons for
people labelling their experience as 'religious'. A typical remark might be something like 'Well, because it was to do with
God', accompanied by a puzzled look as if we had asked a
stupid question. If we persisted and asked how they knew it
was God, the question tended to be received with incom-
prehension, rather as if we had asked how they knew we were
sitting there. Occasionally, somebody used to discussing questions like 'How do I know that what I see exists?' might make
a stab at a further explanation, but it seldom involved claiming physically to see or hear something; more usually they
spoke of an intensely real but unseen presence.

This insistence on the experience as perceptual has also
been noticed by the Swedish psychologist of religion Johan
Unger,[7] in a study of reports of religious experience amongst
his students at the University of Uppsala, published in 1976.
Again the absence of perception via the normal 'five senses'
gives a paradoxical quality to many of the accounts. A representative quotation from one of Unger's students is, 'I saw the
Resurrected without seeing with my eyes.'[8] Experiences of this
type, where there is claimed to be a perception which does not
register on the normal sense organs, are of course very well
known in the annals of Western mysticism. St Teresa of Avila
classified them as 'intellectual visions'.[9]

The similarity of all these claims is intriguing, because, as
Feuerbach remarked, there is no obvious 'organ of religious
perception'. Nevertheless, it would be too hasty to dismiss
such experiences as having nothing at all to do with natural
perception. We certainly have no idea of the physiological
condition of people who spontaneously come across a religious
experience; but there is information available nowadays about
what happens to those who attempt formally to put themselves into a state of what they believe to be religious awareness. Many studies have been made of the physiological
changes that go on in someone's body when they sit down to
meditate. Some of the earlier claims made for the uniqueness

of the states achieved in, for example, transcendental meditation now seem to have been over-enthusiastic[10] but people practising a variety of meditation techniques do appear to exhibit distinctive brain-wave patterns.

Subjectively, the experience of meditating is of putting oneself into a state of profoundly relaxed alertness, so that awareness is greatly heightened. It depends on the technique used, but usually the consciousness is directed to an aspect of the 'here-and-now' situation of the meditator, such as a chosen object in the environment. Thus, the American psychiatrist Arthur J. Deikman gave a group of volunteers a meditation instruction adapted from a classical yoga exercise. They were required to concentrate their attention on a blue vase:

> By concentration I do not mean analysing the different parts of the vase, or thinking a series of thoughts about the vase; but rather trying to see the vase as it exists in itself, without any connections to other things. Exclude all other thoughts, or feelings, or sounds or body sensations. Do not let them distract you, but keep them out so that you can concentrate all your attention, all your awareness on the vase itself. Let the perception of the vase fill your entire mind.[11]

During ten half-hour sessions, spread over a month, Deikman's volunteers attempted the task and described their experiences to him after each occasion. He noticed that there were striking changes in their perceptions which were rather reminiscent of descriptions of mystical experience, even though the experiment was thoroughly 'secular' and of relatively brief duration. People perceived that

> (1) There was an increase in the vividness and richness of the vase image (e.g. they described it as 'luminous', 'more vivid'). (2) The vase seemed to acquire a life of its own, to be animated. (3) There was a decrease in the subject's sense of being separate from the vase, occurring especially in those subjects who continued longest in the experiment (e.g. 'I really began to feel, you know, almost as though the blue and I were merging or that the vase and I were one. It was as though everything was sort of merging'). (4) A fusing of perceptual modes (e.g. 'When

the vase changes shape, I feel this in my body' and 'I
began to feel this light going back and forth').[12]

Deikman felt that these experiences could be explained as the
result of what he called 'de-automatization' of perception.
Most of our time in adult life is spent in relatively forceful
manipulation of the world. When we are busy operating a
machine, hurrying from one place to another, thinking what to
do next, or performing any well-established example of behaviour, our movements are automatic. Our perceptual
awareness becomes much less intense, and this is very useful
to us, because in the world of aggressive action it conserves
our energy. But the cost to us in terms of perception is a profound dulling of awareness and isolation from the immediate
reality of our environment. In meditation, thinks Deikman,
there is a deliberate attempt to de-automatize our perception,
so that by remaining passively open to an incoming stimulus
we can be much more vividly aware of it. Similarly the respondents to our surveys in Nottingham contend that spontaneous
religious experiences often have a quality of extraordinary
vividness, as might be associated with heightened perception,
and this is something that Abraham Maslow noted about
'peak experiences'.

Knowing who or what it is

But if, in most cases, people don't physically hear or see something during their religious experience, how do they know who
or what it is? Even in the strange territory of religious awareness, surely there must be something that is recognized and
named? In the world of ordinary perception there seems to be
no problem. Suppose, for example, that I am wandering
through the streets of a strange city, one that I have never
been to before, when suddenly I am confronted by an old
friend walking towards me. I may feel surprise or shock, but
even out of his normal context, immediately on seeing him I
recognize him. He has certain distinctive features which make
him quite unmistakable, including details of his complexion,
hair, physical build and manner of walking. These incoming
data enable me to recognize him, and are what some

psychologists call the 'data-driven' aspect of perception.[13] Without this input, any supposed sighting of my friend would have to be dismissed as an hallucination.

There is more to it than that, though. However powerful and undeniable the impact of all this on my senses, there is no way I could possibly recognize my friend unless I already knew what he looked like. Recognition of the features of our environment requires a great deal of learned information if we are to distinguish them in the first place. Even looking directly at the contents of a microscope slide through a microscope, children are notoriously unable to see anything at first, except a vague mush. Only after a teacher guides their awareness do they become able to discriminate the cells, nuclei and so on which are apparent to the trained biologist. Young student nurses and doctors, after being given lectures on the signs and symptoms of various conditions, are known to sit on buses observing examples of the disease in the people around them. Physical data which had always been there become obvious for the first time. If I am bird-watching in a summer woodland and hear the haunting voice of a bird, sometimes a naturalist can help me by identifying the song and pointing out from where it is coming.

In the same way, it could be suggested, learned concepts enter into the perception involved in religious experience. Most people's religious experience turns up spontaneously, out of the blue, as a once or twice in a lifetime occurrence. Yet they do not come to it entirely naïve, because, whether believers or not, they belong to a culture with a long religious history.

It seems reasonable to assume that spontaneous experiences of this type have occurred in the lives of some people ever since man appeared on the face of the earth. We can imagine that our ancient ancestors investigated these experiences as they would any others, and over the millenia developed a variety of explanatory traditions, some of which have come down to us today via the great religious cultures. Along with intense concern about these experiences as moments of communication with a sacred reality, there would develop a tradition of practical instruction for people who wished to lay themselves open to its presence.

Whether it is due to separate discovery, or the diffusion of one idea, the best-known mystical traditions right across the Euro-Asian land mass seem to have come to rather similar conclusions on the most appropriate instructions to give. They all require the novice to silence the discursive, grasping aspect of consciousness and maintain awareness of the 'here-and-now'. Thus, a beginner's instruction in 'one-minute Zazen' from Japan says:

> With your eyes wide open, stare at, say, the corner of a building outside the window, or at a point on a hill, or a tree or a hedgerow, or even at a picture on the wall. Stare at a fixed part of the object and do not allow your eyes to move. At the same time stop, or nearly stop, breathing, and with your attention concentrated on that one point try to prevent ideas coming into your mind.[14]

Formal Zazen usually begins with concentration or inhalation and exhalation during breathing. In the Russian Orthodox tradition there is the same instruction to still the thoughts and concentrate on the breathing. St Simeon the New Theologian writes:

> Sit down alone and in silence. Lower your head, shut your eyes, breathe out gently and imagine yourself looking into your own heart. Carry your mind, i.e. your thoughts, from your head to your heart. As you breathe out, say, 'Lord Jesus Christ have mercy on me.' Say it moving your lips gently or simply say it in your mind. Try to put all other thoughts aside. Be calm, be patient, and repeat the process very frequently.[15]

The use of a regularly repeated word or phrase as a 'mantra' is well-nigh universal. Here, from the English East Midlands, where we collected our modern accounts of religious experience, the anonymous fourteenth century author of the *Cloud of Unknowing* advises:

> The shorter the word the better, being more like the working of the spirit! A word like 'God' or 'Love'. Choose which you like, or perhaps some other, so long as it is of one syllable. And fix this word fast to your heart, so that

it is always there, come what may . . . With this word you
will suppress all thought under the cloud of forgetting.[16]

Instructions like these, so similar in certain ways, are
nevertheless of limited use to the novice, unless he already belongs to a religious tradition, at least if he is to advance very
far. This is why people engaged in a programme of meditation
need a teacher or spiritual director, or at the very least a
textbook, to help them to fit their practical experience into a
context.

The practical instructions may be similar, but they are
placed within very different interpretative traditions. For
example, the young student of Zen will derive much of his language and conceptual framework from the Sutras of the
Mahayana Canon. For a Westerner following the *Cloud of
Unknowing*, a major influence on his language and concepts
will be the Judaeo-Christian scriptures. Here, if you like, is the
distinction between the 'data-driven' aspect of religion –
meditative awareness – and what some psychologists call
'concept-driven' perception – learning what to expect through
a tradition.

Though most of the examples of religious experience in this
book seem to have been spontaneous, those reporting them
have been brought up with at least some contact with a religious tradition. They know what God is like because they
were told about him as children, or they may have read parts
of the Bible. Often it must be on the basis of this that they
have the experience of an immediate recognition of who is involved when they have a transcendental encounter. Some
people, of course, having severe doubts about the plausibility
of the religious system in which they were reared, will not go
beyond referring to a 'benign presence'. Others who adhere to
small religious or semi-religious sub-groups, such as UFO enthusiasts, may use the labels of that system for their experiences of awareness. Some may leave it an open question. One
of our respondents says, 'What the forces are and why they
made themselves known to me remains a mystery for which I
am actively seeking an explanation.'

Finally, of course, some people absolutely refuse to accept
the reality of such experience and take steps to ignore it.

Scientific investigation

A few years ago the physicist and theologian Ian Barbour[17] made out a case for saying that the way investigations are made in religious matters is really surprisingly like the way they are made in science. For him, science is a much more subjective affair and religion a more objective affair than most of us suppose.

When it comes to religious experience there may be something in what he says. Take the focusing of awareness which people are trained for in religious meditation. Most of us are inducted into a rather similar tradition of disciplined attention to reality when we learn science in school. The data which are used are almost always very obvious features of our everyday environment which in the past we have not noticed or only observed sporadically. Here is a well-known example.[18]

A science teacher in a junior secondary school class places a small drop of ether on a watch-glass on the front bench and asks the class members what they notice. After a short time, those nearest the front begin to be able to smell the ether, and as time passes more and more people notice it, until it can be smelt all over the room. A science teacher properly conversant with the contemporary tradition in science teaching will probably now ask the members of the class if they can think of an explanation for this phenomenon. Amongst the usual suggestions are that the ether is rather like an endlessly extensible blob of matter which can spread out over a great distance, or that it breaks up into minute particles which somehow move through the air, away from the watch-glass. On the basis of suggestions like this, the teacher will gradually move towards the 'particulate' theory as the most plausible, backing it up with further experiment and discussion. Eventually it will be decided to accept the theory that ether is made up of molecules.

Once we reach adult life, most of us who have been through this system forget there was ever a time when we didn't 'know' that matter is made up of particles. Yet no secondary school child has ever 'seen' a molecule of ether, nor have his teachers, nor have the university teachers and research workers who in turn taught them. Most of us believe in the particulate nature of matter, not on the basis of our own primary observations, but because those observations seem plausibly explained to us on the basis of a highly complex system of scientific inference and experiment. Without a teacher or a textbook to induct us into the system, it is most probable that our understanding would be primitive, confused or bewildered. Most of the knowledge even of professional scientists is at second-hand and depends on accepting the authority of numerous text-books which they have to regurgitate to pass exams. However, the vast majority of humankind has an even remoter connection with the disciplined world of first-hand scientific investigation. For an explanation of what they are experiencing in the world of empirical phenomena they depend on what they have been told by a small professional elite.

While this tends to make people rather superstitious about the power of science, on the whole the system seems to work to most people's satisfaction. At least that is so if the criterion is the extent to which science has increased our power to manipulate the material environment. But in science, as in every other human endeavour, from time to time human considerations blur the clear perception of data. The historian of science Thomas Kuhn[19] has shown how the large-scale pictures of reality, or 'paradigms', held by a culture can render most people blind to important features of the world which conflict with their preconceptions. Kuhn illustrates the blinkering effect of our prior 'knowledge' by quoting an experiment done nearly forty years ago by the psychologists Jerome Bruner and Leo Postman.[20]

They asked subjects to identify a set of playing cards on very short exposure, using a machine called a tachistoscope. Most of the cards they displayed were normal, but some had been intentionally altered to make them differ from normal expectation. For example they might introduce a red six of spades or a black four of hearts. Single cards were shown for gradually increasing periods of time and people were asked to identify them, which most managed to do, even on very brief exposures. With normal cards they were usually right, but the incongruous cards were also identified very quickly, without apparent confusion, as normal.

> The black four of hearts might, for example, be identified as the four of either spades or hearts. Without any

awareness of trouble it was immediately fitted to one of
the conceptual categories prepared by prior experience.
One would not even like to say that the subjects had seen
something different from what they had identified. With
a further increase of exposure to the anomalous cards,
subjects did begin to hesitate and to display awareness of
anomaly. Exposed, for example, to the red six of spades,
some would say. That's the six of spades, but there's
something wrong with it – the black has a red border.
Further increase of exposure resulted in still more hesitation and confusion until finally, and sometimes quite
suddenly, most subjects would produce the correct identification without hesitation . . . A few subjects, however,
were never able to make the requisite adjustment to their
categories.[21]

Kuhn goes on to show that misperceptions of this kind have
been a continual hazard in the history of science, and there is
no reason to suppose that human psychology has altered in
this respect during our own time.

At times a scientific preconception may lead people to
refuse to consider even the possibility that something is right.
Probably the most famous example in Western scientific history was the occasion on which Galileo's friend Cesare
Cremonini refused to look through his telescope, because what
Galileo claimed to see conflicted with the Aristotelian
paradigm. The episode is recorded in a conversation between
Cremonini and Paolo Gualdo, who later reported it to Galileo
in a letter:

Not long ago I was at Dr Cremonini's house, and com-
mencing to discuss you, I said to him, jokingly, 'Signor
Galileo is anxious to know what is coming out in your
book.' He replied, 'He has no reason for anxiety, because
I make no mention whatever of these observations of his.'
I answered, 'Probably it is enough for you to hold the
exact opposite of what he does.' 'Oh, yes indeed, since I
do not want to endorse things of which I have no knowledge whatever, and have not seen.' 'That,' I said, 'is
what has annoyed Signor Galileo – that you have not
wanted to see them.' He replied, 'I believe that no one

but Galileo has seen them; and besides, looking through
those spectacles gives me a headache.'[22]

Cremonini's objections were not religious, since he was in-
different to such matters. But perhaps the very thought of
having to undergo a personal revolution in his thinking was
enough to bring on a headache.

The case of Galileo is often cited because of its connections
with religious obscurantism. When people reporting religious
experience couch it in the language and conceptions of a formal religious tradition, as many of our respondents do, critics
are entitled to inquire whether preconceptions are not affecting their perceptions; whether they are making an inaccurate
appraisal of what is there. The critics may be right, but of
course this sort of criticism cuts both ways. As Kuhn has
shown, this is always a problem with powerful traditions of
knowledge, whether they are political, religious or scientific. It
could be argued that the popular paradigm of science, with its
nineteenth century positivist flavour, simply will not allow
people to admit that experiences such as we have been
examining can exist as anything more than hallucinations or
the errors of cranks.

Active investigation of the world is central to the scientific
endeavour. But perhaps to proceed rationally it needs to be
based on data gathered in a relatively contemplative or
meditative frame of mind, if distortion due to preconception is
to be minimized. The French phenomenologist and student of
perception Maurice Merleau-Ponty pointed out:

> The whole universe of science is built upon the world
> as directly experienced, and if we want to subject science
> itself to rigorous scrutiny and arrive at a precise assess-
> ment of its meaning and scope, we must begin by re-
> awakening the basic experience of the world of which
> science is the second-order expression.[23]

In a way, that is what traditional meditation programmes are
about. The very quality of the instruction, which advises the
meditator how to cease discursive thought and be passive
before the reality of the 'here-and-now', seems designed to
provide some protection against 'concept-driven' distortions
of the basic data. Instructions like 'God cannot be thought' or

'trample on the Buddha' sound a warning against bringing in any kind of preconception.

In both science and religion, there comes a time for reflection on practice, and it is here that tradition is built up. In the same way that we look to what we have learned in science to give us a framework of understanding when we are grappling with the material world, so people seem to use the religious traditions to make sense of their experiences of transcendence.

It is precisely the similarities between people's descriptions of their experiences which call to mind the world of science. There is a slightly unnerving moment for someone who, for the first time, examines a large number of accounts of apparently spontaneous religious experience. It is when the realization dawns that they are not simply random descriptions. They can be classified satisfactorily[24] and it is possible to detect patterned relationships with other phenomena. Though at the individual level religious experiences have unique and even paradoxical features, when studied as a group they exhibit a considerable degree of uniformity, consistency and comparability. Patterning of this sort is what we expect when we come across a phenomenon which is part of the real, objective world of scientific investigation. In the next chapter I shall explain why religious awareness is probably natural to the species and has evolved by natural selection.

14

The Resilience of Religious Experience

'Modern man is free to despise mythologies and theologies, but that will not prevent his continuing to feed upon decayed myths and degraded images.'

MIRCEA ELIADE[1]

Man and nature

Even after a battering from a sceptically-minded friend, urging us to doubt the evidence of our senses, most of us, darting glances hither and thither at the world around us, come to the conclusion that it is really there. At a slightly less exalted level of debate, it seems obvious that, however inaccurate our perceptions are in detail, broadly speaking our picture of the world is right. If it was not, we would fail to survive, making way for a species with a perceptual apparatus rather better-tailored to reality.

It is in the light of this fact that the universality of report of religious experience is inclined from time to time to make the biologist sit up and take notice. As Sir Alister Hardy pointed out,[2] if accounts of such experience are so widespread and become part of the central meaning systems of practically every culture, it takes more than a sophisticated sneer to dismiss it all as illusion. Writing about the 'sacred' in human evolution, the anthropologist Roy A. Rappaport states,

> It is both plausible and prudent to assume, at least initially, that anything which is universal to human culture is likely to contribute to human survival. Phenomena that are merely incidental, or peripheral, or epiphenomenal to the mechanisms of survival are hardly likely to become universal, nor to remain so, if they do.[3]

The necessity to make sense of existence at an ultimate level, to get in touch with the presumed sacred foundations of reality, seems to be the concern of at least some people in any large community of the species *Homo sapiens*. Indeed, loss of ultimate meaning because a traditional belief system comes to seem implausible leads some into a state of despair and even to lose the wish to survive. Religious 'angst' was almost a popular motif in Victorian times when old religious certainties were crumbling fast. But destruction of *any* culture can empty life of its meaning. The anthropologist Ruth Benedict quotes the sorrow of Ramon, an elderly Californian Digger Indian, remembering what was gone for good:

> . . . when he talked of the shamans who had transformed themselves into bears before his eyes in the bear dance, his hands trembled and his voice broke with excitement . . . One day without transition, Ramon broke in upon his descriptions of grinding mesquite and preparing acorn soup. 'In the begining,' he said, 'God gave to every people a cup, a cup of clay, and from this cup they drank their life . . . they all dipped in the water . . . but their cups were different. Our cup is broken now. It has passed away.'[4]

Benedict remarks that he didn't mean there was any question of the extinction of his people, but he wept at the loss of something that had as much value as life, the 'whole fabric of his people's standards and beliefs', which of course *could* lead, in certain circumstances, to a loss of the will to survive.

Ramon could equally well have been talking about the loss of contact with the sacred. When a culture is destroyed, the traditional routeways for interchange between man and his gods lose plausibility and are taken away. Though these ways are multiple, they are not unrecognizable for what they are, even across chasms like that which separated the sixteenth century Spaniards from the Aztecs. The variations are the stuff of human cultural adaptation. The following comment from the ethologist Irenäus Eibl-Eibesfeldt could be expanded to include the universality of report of encounter with the sacred:

Exploring Inner Space

One may take as a starting point that man's tendency is to vary culturally whatever can be modified. In New Guinea alone, several hundred dialects are spoken. This is bound up with the tendency of human beings to isolate themselves into small groups . . . but if one finds in spite of this, in certain situations, such as in greeting, or in the behaviour of the mother towards her child, the same behaviour patterns recur repeatedly and among the most different peoples, then it is highly probable that they are innate behaviour patterns.[5]

To a biologist like Hardy, it seemed highly probable that religious awareness is something innate, both because of its universality and its survival value. It was Émile Durkheim who expressed most forcefully an observation which has been made repeatedly by anthropologists:

The believer who has communicated with his God . . . is a man who is *stronger*. He feels within him more force, either to endure the trials of existence, or to conquer them. It is as though he were raised above the miseries of the world.[6]

Even Marx's reference to religion as 'opium' is a backhanded recognition of its survival value.

Most of the examples already cited from our research programme suggest that people in contemporary Britain evaluate their religious experience as life-giving and enhancing their ability to survive. Further quotations will illustrate this. A young man says:

I think I've got a far greater emotional and spiritual strength so that I can cope with the various stresses laid upon me which I couldn't have faced before.

A woman recalls moments of mystical communion with nature:

I can remember the emotions of these experiences after they have finished and they represent a secure fixed point in my life.

Finally, a thoughtful description from someone who had been in hospital for surgery because of a detached retina:

At certain times I was acutely aware of a presence or power . . . I was very aware of being on the verge of the possibility of understanding profound things, which were life-giving in so far as they released me from rather negative emotions and created a feeling of ease, well-being, confidence and led me very quickly back into normal contact with people, rather than isolation.

The impression one gets, on the basis of recent research, is of a perfectly natural kind of human awareness, differing certainly in many respects from everyday sensory awareness, but having valued outcomes which enhance people's ability to survive. Such characteristics, if ascribed to any other biological phenomenon, would undoubtedly be attributed to evolution. Natural selection favours those features which are most likely to ensure the survival of the species.

Biology and culture

If religious awareness is natural, why doesn't everybody have it? Well, to suggest that religious awareness is natural to man is not the same thing as saying that all people are religiously aware. An example which may have some parallels is the claim that aggression is a biological attribute of the human species. I believe this claim to be correct, and that, if sufficiently provoked, almost everybody is capable of behaving aggressively. However, it is also an obvious fact that some people and some societies are notably unaggressive. I do not think therefore that they do not have the capacity to be aggressive, but that their personal psychology or the culture to which they belong has instilled into them the idea that under no circumstances should it be displayed.[7] In a similar way, it could be suggested, cultural and psychological factors affect whether religious awareness expresses itself.

Biologically speaking, we are subjected to a well-nigh infinite number of incoming stimuli from our environment. The number is so large that we cannot cope consciously with all of it. Psychologists have concluded that there must be some sort of filtering mechanism which selects those incoming messages which are important to us. For example, if you have been able to read this chapter so far with relative ease, it has been at the expense of cutting out of awareness all sorts of stimuli coming from your own body, other people, or other parts of your surroundings. Usually it is assumed that the filtering mechanism works by causing us to attend to stimuli which are of biological importance for our survival. Hence, we are normally able to attend selectively to the traffic ahead of us when out driving, so that we do not collide with it. Occasionally there may be a problem of deciding on the hierarchy of importance of incoming stimuli. Some male drivers, finding themselves attending selectively to a pretty woman, fail to notice the traffic in the same visual field, with predictable and catastrophic results.

Religious awareness, I suggest, could be a potential in the species which either is or is not attended to. The question then becomes, 'What causes us to choose certain stimuli and ignore others?' At the level of the detailed psychology of selective attention, this is simply too difficult and complex a question to go into.[8] However, at a more general level it is possible to make a few suggestions.

Firstly, there is the question of being psychologically open or closed. The psychologist Abraham Maslow has already been cited in connection with 'peak experiences'. He included religious experiences as a major element among the ecstatic moments of life. These 'peak experiences' he also found were very commonly reported by those he interviewed.[9] In fact after having questioned a considerable number of people about peak experience, he found himself expecting people to report them rather than not. This made him begin to concentrate on the personality of those he called 'non-peakers', people who didn't seem ever to have had these experiences. Gradually he built up a subjective picture of someone who 'suppresses, denies, turns away from, or forgets "core-religious or transcendent" experience':

> Any person whose character structure (or *Weltan-schauung*, or way of life) forces him to try to be extremely rational or 'materialistic' or mechanistic tends to become a non-peaker . . . The person who is afraid of going insane and who is, therefore, desperately hanging on to

stability, control, reality etc., seems to be frightened by peak experiences and tends to fight them off. For the compulsive obsessive person, who organizes his life around the denying and controlling of emotion, the fear of being overwhelmed by an emotion (which is interpreted as a loss of control) is enough for him to mobilize all his stamping-out and defensive activities against the peak experience.[10]

Maslow's reflections, written in 1964, are given support by the recent research reported in this book. People claiming religious experience do seem to be less defensive psychologically than others.

A second reason for the non-appearance of religious awareness could be the damaging effects of chronic stress on sensitivity. Marianne Frankenhaeuser of the University of Stockholm has noted recently the effects, biologically speaking, of bombardment with too many, too strong or too frequent stimuli – as happens in the multi-media world of the modern city. One of the effects is that the nervous system adapts by gradually failing to respond:

> The physiological stress effects become less intense and feelings of aversion and discomfort fade. But so do feelings such as involvement, understanding, consideration and sympathy . . . the mechanism of habituation involves a blunting of emotions, a reduction of sensitivity and reactivity.[11]

This could be one of the factors behind the finding that the larger a city is, the less frequently is religious experience reported in it. In the same publication, Frankenhaeuser comments that in a consumer society where there is manifest social inequality and a sensory overload from advertising media, if the poor subscribe to the consumer ideology they automatically suffer more stress than others:

> The poor are exposed to the same offers as the rich, but their freedom of choice is severely circumscribed. Being excluded from the possibilities presented so stridently may generate feelings of impotence, failure and anger.[12]

Marx felt that the poor clung to religion as a pain-killer in an unjust world. Pain-killer or not, if anything the poor are less likely to admit to religious experience than others. If Frankenhaeuser is right, the stress of being caught in the grip of naked economic forces for years on end could be what is blunting natural religious awareness. That is, the absence of religious experience could be like every other impoverishment, an alienation of people's natural powers.

The social control of religious experience

Nevertheless, Marx's conviction that any aspect of religion whatever is indicative of man's alienated condition is wholeheartedly accepted in the Soviet Union. The decay of religion is taken to be a sign of hope. What happens, then, to religious awareness (supposing it to be natural) in that kind of environment?

The anthropologist Clifford Geertz notes that nowadays when people try to understand a culture:

> The focus is . . . neither on subjective life as such, nor on outward behaviour as such, but on the socially available systems of significance – beliefs, rites, meaningful objects – in terms of which subjective life is ordered and outward behaviour guided.[13]

Whatever our experience as biological organisms is, simply by the fact that we never exist outside a culture, we make sense of it in terms of symbols that culture gives us. So suppose I am born into Soviet society; from my earliest moments of awareness I am being inducted into a world interpreted for me by Marxist/Leninist beliefs, symbols and rituals of meaning. This has got nothing to do with brainwashing – it happens inevitably to anyone in any society, simply by virtue of belonging to it. However, because of the values admired in the Soviet Union, I will have my attention directed to those aspects of reality most in keeping with them. On the other hand, I will not be given any kind of symbol system to make sense of my religious experience.

On the contrary, when religion cannot be ignored altogether, attempts will be made to discredit traditional systems of religious understanding. As we have seen, this is done by a combination of instruction in the historical role of religious institutions as the tool of the ruling classes, in the function of surviving religion as a backwater of bourgeois consciousness, and by the illustration of faulty reasoning in religious arguments. In addition there seems to be evidence of ridicule and social discrimination against believers,[14] though this is not officially sanctioned.

Growing up inside this kind of culture, my initial selection of possibilities within the world of sensory awareness is not likely to be religious. Even if I should spontaneously come across such experience, my learned hierarchy of values will tend to make me ignore it. In any case the experience may be well-nigh inchoate because I have no systematic language at my disposal with which to engage it. However, via elderly relatives, classical Russian literature or small groups of religious enthusiasts I may find a way of expressing my experience. Even then, I have to consider the pressure of a society which casts a disapproving and at times punitive eye on anyone who becomes interested in that realm of life. Convictions which survive these hurdles are likely to be of considerable importance to the believer, and there is of course some evidence that strong religious beliefs do survive in the Soviet Union.

It is interesting to note the comments of the Leningrad student of religion, V. R. Bukin, writing in a Soviet philosophical journal in 1969. While naturally enough dismissing religion as belonging to the world of the fantastic, Bukin admits that, in a sense, religious experiences are real enough:

> Religious emotions make a specific contribution to the development of religious consciousness. They develop into a system of religious experiences on the basis of which there take shape corresponding interests, volitional processes and requirements.

For him, all this is of course a manifestation of alienation; yet religious experiences

> perform the function of a coordinating centre in the psychic life of believers. Religious requirements help to

transform the psychic world of a believer into a self-organizing system with autonomous control.[15]

Wisely (from his point of view), Bukin's advice on dealing with this problem is not to argue with believers, but to try to steer people away from contact with religious meaning systems and occupy their minds with

> that fund of experiences . . . which has not yet taken on a religious cast and which under proper direction can crowd out religious experiences.[16]

In certain corners of Soviet life, notably 'rites of passage', religious rituals until recently retained some prominence and were a source of contact with the world of the sacred. In agreement with Bukin's advice, however, secular rituals for occasions like birth, marriage and death have been developed, and in recent years have been meeting with considerable success.[17] The social and psychological cost to those who continue to give value to their religious experience is thus likely to become even greater.

Suppose, on the other hand, that I have been brought up in a society where there is a welcoming of the religious aspect of the human consciousness. In this case, the chances are that from the moment I have been able to comprehend the speech of my fellows, I will have been imbibing the symbols and rituals which give public expression to the inner experiences of religion. Anyone growing to maturity within, for example, a traditionally Christian community has in their consciousness a multitude of images and metaphors for God, his dealings with man, and how people have become aware of the divine presence. This rich conceptual framework means that should what I have been calling religious experience appear, with all its strangeness, it has a familiarity which has been built up since infancy. In addition, religious specialists will be on hand to instruct in the ways of laying myself open to the divine, whether through public ritual or private meditation. Because of the esteem in which religion is held there will be strong social support for any inclination I may have to search in that particular direction.

The evidence we have from comparative religion is that literally anything or any occasion can be associated with a sudden moment of religious awareness or 'hierophany'. There are records of such moments during childbirth, at the point of death, during sexual intercourse, at a meal, during fasting, in a cathedral, on a rubbish dump, on a mountain top, in a slum; in association with a particular plant, stone, fish, mammal, bird and so on *ad infinitum*. However, our culture does tend to teach us to associate transcendental experience with particular occasions and places. That is why there is some substance in Marghanita Laski's suggestion that there are special 'triggers' for mystical experience.[18] In the context of an old church, or beautiful scenery, or listening to music we may lay ourselves open to these experiences; though it is worth repeating that there seems to be no way of 'switching them on' by such means.

Religious rituals, doctrines and scriptures often enshrine the remembrance of the most intense and powerful experiences, and for this reason they tend to be clung to with fierce conservatism. We see this in the way that the scriptures of several of the major religions are still read in a language which has long ceased to be that of everyday life. J. B. Pratt recounts a curious example of highly conservative behaviour from Denmark:

> In a Danish village church the custom of bowing when passing a certain spot in the wall was maintained into the nineteenth century, but no one knew the reason for this until, on the whitewash being scraped away, a picture of the Madonna was found on the wall; thus the custom had outlived the Catholicism which prompted it, by 300 years.[19]

It is because of this conservatism in relation to the sacred that people are likely to become confused should they belong to a traditionally religious community which comes in contact with vigorous secular ideas. On the one hand, the religious institution is likely to be insistent on clinging to unchanged sacred traditions, because they are thought to reflect the unchangeability of the divine. On the other hand, alongside this, most people are spending their daily lives making sense of their experience in ways that have little or no connection with traditional religion. From their perspective, formal religion can only appear as a more and more implausible backwater. It may be this combination of circumstances in contemporary Britain which leads to our finding that very few reports of religious experience are connected with church services. Even allowing that the "most powerful religious moments come in solitude', the fact that the formal purpose of a service is the worship of God would lead us to give at least some credence to Durkheim's claim that the religious assembly is an important source of religious experience.

But it is not, for most of those we interviewed. And there may be another twist to this. Well-meaning church people sometimes attempt to remedy the religious–secular disjunction by updating ritual and doctrine so that they fit better with secular interpretations of reality. On the whole, from the religious point of view, this would seem an eminently sensible thing to do. But the reformers sometimes appear not to believe in the value of their own contribution to human well-being, that is, the mediation of the sacred to mankind via powerful, many-layered symbols. The result is that at times modern church services have about as much feeling for the numinous as the average bus-station.

Yet, even in a period when the tattered remains of an ancient interpretative system are all that is left to most people, it is clear that religious experience still appears with extraordinary frequency. It is revealing to note the kinds of occasions when it breaks through with particular force. First, as we have seen, people are more likely to report a religious encounter when they have been alone. It is when we are by ourselves that we are least under pressure to conform to the expectations of our fellows, or to fit in with the accepted and approved knowledge system of our society. We are, as it were, free from censorship. It is arguable that, in these circumstances, whatever is natural to us, but is normally suppressed by social pressure, has the chance to express itself; in this case, an openness to religious experience. While religions give us the symbols and language in which to clothe our experience, they themselves typically enjoin upon us that we should seek the divine in solitude, or at least in silence. This is so well known that only a couple of examples need be given as illustrations. Thus, in yoga:

> Day after day, let the yogi practise harmony of soul: in
> a secret place, in deep solitude, master of his mind,
> hoping for nothing, desiring nothing.[20]

And in Christianity,

> But when you pray, go to your private room and, when
> you have shut your door, pray to your Father who is in
> that secret place.[21]

In these circumstances there is no one to posture for, nothing
to hide, unless our personal neurosis requires us to hide from
ourselves. As we have seen, the data suggest that neurotic
people seldom report religious experience.

A second common occasion on which religious awareness
breaks through is in states of severe distress. This is not the
long-drawn-out chronic distress in which, as Frankenhaeuser
believes, there may be a defensive withdrawal into apathy and
sensory dulling. Almost always, people are referring to a temporary state of acute upset. In these moments it may be that
people find that their everyday secular knowledge system no
longer helps them and ceases to have plausibility. It does a
bad job of making sense of suffering, or of the kind of existential crisis when people are faced starkly with problems of ultimate meaning. When things have reached such a pass that it
no longer matters what the generality of mankind thinks, then
perhaps alternative forms of consciousness once more become
available.

This is not the kind of interpretation which will be made by
observers living in the knowledge system so lately proved inadequate for the person in distress. For them, he may be
labelled as driven to distraction by his condition, no longer
able to be rational, open to delusion and so on. There may not
be any dispute about the reality of the experience to the person
in distress. The argument is basically over how to interpret it.

The third occasion on which religious experience commonly
manifests itself is in contact with nature. There may be a connection with traditional expectations here, as expressed in the
phrase that nature (even heavily interfered with by man) is
'God's handiwork'. Furthermore, as several of those we interviewed mentioned, there is a strong literary tradition of nature
mysticism, which may allow people to be more open to it as a

source of hierophany than in more strictly ecclesiastical settings.

Very large numbers of people undoubtedly do come across these experiences. They then have the problem of coping with something which they nevertheless feel may be confined to an atypical minority of the general population. The sociologist Peter Berger has shown that belonging to a 'cognitive minority' has its difficulty[22] and that people use a variety of strategies to handle it.

Most of us feel uneasy if we find that we hold an opinion or belief that differs from that of the people around us. In a well-known experiment, the psychologist Solomon Asch[23] showed that a surprisingly large number of people (approximately a third of those tested) will not stand by their own *correct* judgement about the relative lengths of three straight lines, if (on the prior instruction of Asch) they are unanimously contradicted by the other people in a small group. When questioned later why they collapsed in the face of group pressure they are inclined to say that they feared they would look stupid or be thought crazy. This is reminiscent of the explanation for their secrecy given to us by those who had told no one of their religious experience.

Another way of coping with religious experience might simply be to repress it out of consciousness altogether, because it conflicts too violently with our social or moral convictions. We have no direct evidence of this in our research, though some hints of suppression were mentioned in Chapter 10. The notion of a sort of Freudian repression of religious experience is nevertheless intriguing and somewhat ironic. It is interesting that in his book *Freud and the Jewish Mystical Tradition* the psychologist David Bakan[24] implies something very like this in the case of Freud himself. In a lively article, Peter Berger has speculated that there may be some evidence for a widespread repression of religious experience in Western society:

> Let me then state a simple hypothesis: *The current occult wave (including its devil component) is to be understood as resulting from the repression of transcendence in modern consciousness.* This repression is socially and culturally institutionalized – in the schools, in the communications media,

even in the language of everyday life (in which, for example, curses have become domesticated as merely emotional expletives). In other words, it is institutionalized secularity that is playing the role of censor. If this is so, we can learn a useful lesson from Freud: repressed contents have a way of coming back, often in bizarre forms.[25]

In parentheses, is it not slightly odd that so much energy is poured into the study of ESP in the Soviet Union, while it is the subject of a fair amount of well-bred scepticism in the West?

A third way of coping with religious experience could be to join an intellectual 'ghetto'. It might be possible to protect the reality and importance of the experience by cutting oneself off from the mainstream of surrounding thought and living in a closed community which shares a belief system which gives a valued place to such experience. Many of the 'new religious movements' which have sprung up in the sixties and seventies, including Christian fundamentalist groups like the 'Jesus Freaks', might fall into this category. During our research, we came across one or two examples of this.

However, the commonest way of responding to this kind of experience was to accept its reality and give it importance; it seemed too powerful and its effects were too positive to allow it to be ignored. Quite a number of these respondents had some kind of link with the major Western religious traditions, though they often felt themselves to be unorthodox, or somewhat at odds with the institution. Nevertheless they found the religious interpretations of their experiences to be plausible and in certain respects self-evident to them. Certainly current models of the world which simply explained away their experience were not felt to have much validity.

On the other hand there was no real evidence of a discarding of contemporary scientific and other presuppositions about the world. To the extent that they thought about this, I assume that this must have left them with many confusing and unanswered questions about how it all made sense. Nevertheless, it may be necessary to live with uncertainty as an alternative to living with a closed mind.

Epilogue

The Future of
Religious Experience

'A rule of thinking which would absolutely prevent me from acknowledging certain kinds of truth, if those kinds of truth were really there, would be an irrational rule.'

WILLIAM JAMES[1]

Surface and depth

Idly exploring, I once crossed over the Menai Straits from Wales into Anglesey. After turning through the town of Beaumaris, I came to the long low spit of land which goes skimming into the Irish Sea to form the easternmost tip of the island. Lying at the end of this peninsula, lonely and exposed to the weather, is Penmon church, on the site of a sixth century Celtic Christian foundation. As I remember it now, for I have never been back, I climbed a flight of steps to get into a garden or churchyard and entered the building by the south door. Inside, all was in good order, brown polished woodwork, rows of pews, prayer books in neat piles, sparkling freshness; a reassuringly familiar Victorian church, the sort that deludes you into thinking all's right with the world.

Then I noticed a glass door at the back of the church, but it wasn't possible to see what lay behind. When I opened it, I walked through into another world. It was like falling out of the ordered, rule-bound surface of everyday life into the realm of powerful forces which lie hidden beneath. At first there was no light, nothing to be seen. Then gradually the shapes of ancient stonework began to emerge, never clearly, but enough to make me realize I was standing in the nave of a Norman church, far older than the chancel from which I had come. The strength of the metaphor was so great that I could do nothing but stand there for a long time, in silence.

Traditional meaning systems, like those of Victorian religion, laid down detailed rules which gave a clear framework to the world, so that it became secure and predictable from cradle to grave, and perhaps beyond. The trouble is that there are deeper streams to our lives which flow along their own unconfined channels beneath the surface, and occasionally, to our great surprise, emerge into consciousness. Freud was the first 'modern' to remind us of that ancient truth. Within this realm, I believe, lies what I have been calling religious experience, and when it manifests itself it tends to alter people's attitudes to the rest of their lives: 'It is as though certain parts of a life's experience were discovered and declared as sacred in order to suggest that the whole of life is, in some final sense, sacred.'[2]

The guardians of religious institutions are not usually unaware of what they are guarding; but by the very fact that they lay down rules to protect the sacred, they tend to make light of its unpredictability. The form that human contact with the sacred must normally take is laid down by the various religious groups, sometimes with great rigidity. For example, in many Christian evangelical sects it has been traditional to hope and pray for a moment of conversion. If historical records speak accurately, this kind of modelling worked very well for millions; the 'trigger' for the hierophany was appropriate.

The difficulty about defining how and when men will come face to face with their gods is that the rules are coercive. Many are the young people brought up in a tightly controlled religious environment who have strained to conform to the proper image of hierophany within their group; to hear the call they are supposed to hear, or see the vision, or speak with tongues, only to fail. Worse still, because the pain of being an outsider is too much, they may mimic the whole thing, even to the point of deceiving themselves. The coercive power of the institution is so great that it destroys the freedom which it claims to celebrate. By laying before us a pattern of expectation, institutions may force us into living the greatest of all lies: a pretended or deluded assent to something that does not correspond with the truth of our personal experience.

The denial of the sacred

At the turn of the century it might have been easier to argue
than it is today that religious experiences were somehow
'generated' by religious institutions. But in contemporary
Western society, the coercive power of religious institutions is,
for most people, fairly small. As far as formal religion is concerned, we can take it or leave it.

Far more powerful, because so seldom questioned, is the
scientific establishment. Our everyday world of meanings is
modelled, not surprisingly, on ways of thinking which give
success in the scientific and technological manipulation of
matter and energy. We volunteer to confine ourselves to those
parts of reality which are clear, distinct, measurable and
therefore examinable by the methods of empirical science. By
sticking to these rules, we have brought ourselves unparalleled
material success, so that they tend to become paramount in
our minds. Indeed they are so powerful that there is a permanent temptation to despise all that is not matter and energy,
or, as in the case of J. B. Watson and consciousness, to deny its
existence.

The pressure to conform is now not simply a matter of
fitting one's deeper experience into a predetermined religious
mould, but to deny utterly its validity or its existence. Gordon
Lawrence of the Foundation for Social Innovation in Paris
points out how deviating from the norms of the institution
may even lead to the risk of being labelled 'mad':

> As people living within the frame of institutions we tell
> each other 'lies' about the institutions and we believe
> them. Not to believe and subscribe to them would be to
> step out from the crowd, from the shared perception, and
> be made a deviant or even 'mad' in social terms. Con-
> sequently, people go along with what is believed. While
> people in institutions like to think they are pragmatic,
> realistic and are effectively pursuing goals, there are
> other reasons for their existence [that is, to give a secure
> sense of reality].[3]

The pretence in our own time is very likely to be to a bland
secularity, which denies or blots out of consciousness the deeper

strands of our experience. The regular admission by our informants that they fear they will be thought mad illustrates the
fact that social pressures are running strongly in this direction.

But scientific rules are simply human rules and certain
phenomena are paramount because we choose to make them
so. The saving grace of science is its built-in possibility for
reform. In spite of, or rather because of, our knowledge of
scientific laws and theories, every now and then we stumble
across phenomena which aren't supposed to be there. We trip
over a bit of reality when we thought the road was charted,
and because of that we have to tear up a few old maps and
start again. In spite of conservatively minded scientists,
science does not remain static. The experiences which we have
been examining in this book fall into the realm of realities
which it is not politic to admit are there, except as a kind of
fantasy or aberration. From a traditional scientific point of
view, they conflict with too many well-established theories.
However, the weight of evidence which has been accumulating over the past fifteen years or so makes that dismissal seem
rather premature.

The return of the depths

On the face of it we are presented here with an extraordinary
phenomenon. Why *should* so many people have religious experience to report? It is not necessarily related to some official
norm of sanctity. Evil and unpleasant people at times believe
they have come face to face with the divine. Sometimes the
supposed encounter turns them from their evil ways, sometimes not, as when the devout murderer described in
Dostoevsky's novel *The Idiot* prays for forgiveness before
slitting his friend's throat. Madmen quite often claim religious
experience and perhaps some are driven mad by it. Holy fools
are proverbial. But all of these are not the norm. Probably a
majority of the more intelligent, saner and socially responsible
people in the Western world even in as secular a nation as
Britain would claim, perhaps rather shyly, to have had these
experiences. They may fear they are in a minority, and will be
thought by most people to be stupid or mentally unbalanced;
but they are merely claiming the kind of contact with ultimate

reality which lies at the heart of Western culture and of every great historical culture.

This book, like other books, is liberally sprinkled with unsupported philosophical assumptions. One assumption that I do *not* make, however, is that somehow or other these experiences 'prove' that there is a God, except perhaps to the satisfaction of the person to whom the experience happened. On the other hand, they, like any other human experiences, are data which ought not to be ignored in making coherent sense of one's world. Most people are struck dumb if they do not use traditional religious language when they try to describe the meaning of their experience. This is evidence of how destitute contemporary models of reality are when it comes to dealing with these deeper aspects of life, not that these deeper aspects do not exist.

As we have seen, it is alleged that religious experience is associated with guilt, sexual frustration, alienation, social deprivation, mental illness, total solitude, distress, scenes of natural beauty and so on. I feel sure that most or all of these claims are true; there is nothing which cannot be the source of hierophany. This neither detracts from nor adds to the validity of these experiences, it merely specifies their context. What is more interesting, in the world of practical affairs, is their outcome. The common testimony of the religious traditions and of those who have spoken to us is that they normally lead in the direction of personal integration and just behaviour towards fellow human beings.

I doubt very much that religion is about to die out. The awareness out of which it grows is too widespread for that. More dangerous, because more likely, is that it may continue to be isolated from the mainstream of modern life. Human realities which are resolutely ignored tend, as Freud pointed out, to return in bizarre and fanatical forms.

We need to attend more openly to our religious awareness, so that at the very least its constructiveness and creativity can be used for the benefit of the species. Everyone knows in theory that we will have to behave unselfishly if we are to deal with problems of massive social and political injustice, depletion of natural resources, overpopulation, threatening nuclear warfare – the familiar catalogue of human ills. Unfortunately, theoretical discussions about these problems remain just that, when, in their heart of hearts, the poor are crushed into accepting their lot rather than organizing the fight for justice. Pious discussions amongst the well-to-do over the plight of the world seldom result in effective action, when, in their heart of hearts, they believe that competitive striving for material wealth is the only way to ensure personal well-being. People who become religiously aware seem to experience *directly* their solidarity with their fellow-human beings and their responsibility towards them. Tasks which had previously appeared impossible begin to look less formidable. They are less inclined to be seduced into the amassing of goods, because they perceive that there are other sources of security. Life gains meaning. These would appear to be advantages of our biological heritage not to be lightly ignored.

Notes

Preface

1. *The Seven Lamps of Architecture*, Allen & Unwin, 1903, p. 142.

Chapter one: **The Religious Animal**

1. Review of Labriola, 'Essais sur la conception matérialiste de l'histoire', *Revue Philosophique*, 44, 1897, pp. 645–51.
2. Fernando Alvarado Tezozomoc was descended from an Aztec prince. In 1598 he wrote the *Cronica Mexicana*, which includes an account of the moment when the Spaniards arrived, as experienced by his countrymen. Extracts from this and other Aztec manuscripts are available in translation in Miguel Leon-Portilla (ed.), *The Broken Spears*, Constable, 1962.
3. The similarities between Mesoamerican artefacts and European and North African ones have led to the suggestion by some that cultural contacts must have been made across the Atlantic at some time in the remote past. However, apart from the Vikings, who appear to have reached North America in early medieval times, the evidence for this view is on the whole very slim. For a review of the question, see Carrol L. Riley, et al., *Man Across the Sea; Problems of Pre-Columbian Contacts*, Austin: University of Texas Press, 1971. For an entertaining account of some of the wilder theories, see Robert Wauchope, *Lost Tribes and Sunken Continents*, University of Chicago Press, 1962.
4. Tezozomoc, op. cit.
5. Florentino Codex. This description of the conquest of Mexico was written by Indian students of the Franciscan Bernardino de Sahagún. It was written in Nahuatl, the language of the Aztecs, and based on first-hand accounts by people who were there. Quoted in Leon-Portilla, op. cit.
6. Bernal Diaz, *The Conquest of New Spain* (trs. J. M. Cohen), Penguin Books, 1963.
7. Hernan Cortes, *Dispatches from the New World* (texts ed. Harry M. Rosen), New York: Grossett & Dunlap, 1962.

218

8. *Burning Water: Thought and Religion in Ancient Mexico*, Thames & Hudson, 1956.
9. Quoted in Marvin Harris, *Cannibals and Kings: The Origins of Cultures*, Fontana, 1978.
10. Sahagún, in Leon-Portilla, op. cit.
11. Florentino Codex, in Leon-Portilla, op. cit.
12. Bartolomé de Las Casas, a Dominican friar and later bishop, is the most prominent of those who attacked the behaviour of the Spaniards towards the Indians during the conquest of America. See his book *The Tears of the Indians* (tr. J. Phillips), New York: Oriole Chapbooks, 18, 1972.
13. From the collection of *Cantares mexicanos* in the National Library of Mexico. Quoted in Leon-Portilla, op. cit.
14. For a readable account of this area by a non-sociologist, see Owen Chadwick, *The Secularisation of the European Mind in the Nineteenth Century*, Cambridge University Press, 1975.
15. The best brief account of theories about the origins of religion is E. E. Evans-Pritchard, *Theories of Primitive Religion*, Oxford University Press, 1965.
16. E. Tylor, *Primitive Culture* (2 vols.), John Murray, 1871.
17. Samuel Baker, *The Albert Nyanza, Great Basin of the Nile and Explorations of the Nile Sources*, Macmillan, 1885.
18. Samuel Baker, 'The Races of the Nile Basin', *Transactions of the Ethnological Society of London*, Vol. 5, 1867, pp. 228–39.
19. See Dorothy Middleton, *Baker of the Nile*, Falcon Press, 1949.
20. Baker, op. cit. (1867).
21. ibid.
22. Baker, op. cit. (1885).
23. ibid.
24. See C. G. Seligman, *Races of Africa*, Oxford University Press, 3rd edn, 1957.
25. E. E. Evans-Prichard, *Nuer Religion*, Oxford University Press, 1956.
26. Godfrey Lienhardt, *Divinity and Experience. The Religion of the Dinka*, Clarendon Press, 1961.
27. Tylor, op. cit.
28. That is not to say that people belonging to traditional cultures were, or are, always attentive to religion. The anthropologist Mary Douglas quotes an example of a 'tribe of Persian nomads who are so lacking in religious feeling that any priest in a smart London parish would find his own congregation fervent by comparison' (see 'Heathen Darkness, Modern Piety', *New Society*, 12 March 1970; and *Natural Symbols*, Penguin Books, 1973). She gives a sociological explanation for variations in interest in public religion,

220 *Notes*

a point I will be taking up in relation to religious experience later in this book.

29. Tylor, op. cit.

30. See, for example, Alexander Carmichael, *Carmina Gadelica – Hymns and Invocations*, Oliver & Boyd (Vols. 1–5); Scottish Academic Press (Vol. 6), 1900–1971.

31. A. Leroi-Gourhan, 'The Flowers Found with Shanidar IV, a Neanderthal Burial in Iraq', *Science*, Vol. 190, 1975, pp. 562–4.

32. From Ralph Solecki, *Shanidar. The First Flower People*, New York: Knopf, 1971.

33. Much of the original work on palaeolithic religion is in French or German. However, there is an account available in Johannes Maringer, *The Gods of Prehistoric Man*, Weidenfeld and Nicolson, 1960. More recently, the status of the palaeolithic bear cult has been reviewed in Mircea Eliade, *A History of Religious Ideas*, Vol. 1, *From the Stone Age to the Eleusinian Mysteries*, University of Chicago Press, 1978.

34. I am not making the traditional sociological distinction between magic and religion. In the real world, as Worsley notes, the differences between the two are very blurred, if present at all. See Peter Worsley, *The Trumpet Shall Sound*, McGibbon & Kee, 1968.

35. See A. I. Hallowell, 'Bear Ceremonialism in the Northern Hemisphere', *American Anthropologist*, Vol. 28, 1926, pp. 1–175.

36. An English translation of this was published in 1704. Quoted in S. Giedion, *The Beginnings of Art*, New York: Pantheon Books, 1962.

37. See N. G. Munro, *Ainu Creed and Cult*, New York: Columbia University Press, 1963.

38. Maringer, op. cit.

39. For example by André Leroi-Gourhan, (husband of Arlette Leroi-Gourhan) in *Les Religions de la Préhistoire: Paléolithique*, Paris: Presses Universitaires de France, 1964.

40. This was the considered view of Professor E. O. James, summing up a lifetime of study of prehistoric religion in *Historia Religionum: Handbook for the History of Religions*, Vol. 1, ed. C. J. Bleeker and G. Widengren, Leiden: Brill, 1969.

41. See G. P. Murdock's paper 'The Common Denominator of Cultures', reprinted in S. L. Washburn and P. C. Jay (eds.), *Perspectives on Human Evolution*, I, New York: Holt, Rinehart & Winston, 1968. In his 'partial list' of the phenomena which occur in 'every culture known to history or ethnography' are included: cosmology, eschatology, funeral rites, magic, mythology, propitiation of supernatural beings, religious ritual, soul concepts.'

42. Evans-Pritchard, op. cit. (1956).

43. Sahagún, in Leon-Portilla, op. cit.

44. For a discussion of definitions of religion, see Roland Robertson,

The Sociological Interpretation of Religion, Oxford: Blackwell, 1969; also
J. Milton Yinger, *The Scientific Study of Religion*, Collier-Macmillan,
1970.
45. Yinger, op. cit.
46. 'The Dharmakaya, which literally means "body or system of
being", is, according to the Mahayanists (Northern Buddhists), the
ultimate reality that underlies all particular phenomena.' Quoted
from D. T. Suzuki, *Outlines of Mahayana Buddhism*, New York:
Schocken Books, 1963.
47. If we decide, as outsiders, what is primary in religion and concentrate on that, we are in danger of ignoring the 'phenomenon' itself, that is, how religion is for the insider.

Chapter two: **Cultured Despisers**

1. From 'Of Germany Since Luther', published in 1834. Quoted in
Henri De Lubac, S.J., *The Drama of Atheist Humanism*, Sheed &
Ward, 1949.
2. In L. N. Mitrokhin, 'Methods of Research into Religion', from G.
V. Osipov (ed.), *Town, Country and People*, Tavistock, 1969.
3. ibid.
4. ibid.
5. ibid.
6. From a letter to Maxim Gorky in 1913. Quoted in V. I. Lenin, *On
Religion*, Moscow: Progress Publishers, 1969.
7. Friedrich Wilhelm Krummacher, *An Autobiography*, T. and T.
Clark, 1869.
8. Marx, Engels, *Collected Works (MECW)* Lawrence & Wishart,
1975, Vol. II, p. 578.
9. ibid. p. 581.
10. ibid., p. 555.
11. ibid., p. 397.
12. ibid., p. 7.
13. Krummacher, op. cit., p. 131.
14. ibid., p. 10.
15. ibid., p. 10. In his autobiography Krummacher notes that his
preaching received the attention of no less a person than Goethe,
whose comments were almost entirely critical. In fact Goethe spoke
of his 'narcotic sermons' as devices to make people forget their
bodily and mental injuries – an interesting forerunner of Marx's jibe
about religion as 'opium'. Cf. Krummacher, op. cit., p. 135.
16. From 'The Child's Companion and Juvenile Instructor', Religious Tract Society, 1854. See also the article by Jennifer Hart,
'Religion and Social Control in the Mid-Nineteenth Century', in

A. P. Donajgrodsi, (ed.), *Social Control in Nineteenth Century Britain*, Croom Helm, 1977.
17. *MECW*, op. cit., p. 426.
18. *The Life of Jesus Critically Examined* (ed. P. C. Hodgson) S.C.M., 1972.
19. See Horton Harris, *David Friedrich Strauss and his Theology*, Cambridge University Press, 1973. It is interesting to note that, as a young man, Strauss had more than a passing interest in mysticism and the writings of Jacob Boehme. Engels also read Boehme.
20. Ibid., p. 41.
21. *MECW*, op. cit., p. 457.
22. ibid., p. 458.
23. ibid., p. 487.
24. In the year Engels went to Berlin, Feuerbach published *The Essence of Christianity* (translation by George Eliot, published with an introductory essay by Karl Barth in Harper Torchbooks, New York, 1957).
25. ibid., p. 73.
26. ibid., p. 140.
27. Written in 1845. Quoted in Marx, Engels, *On Religion*, Moscow: Progress Publishers, 1957.
28. See Helmut Gollwitzer, *The Christian Faith and the Marxist Criticism of Religion*, St. Andrew Press, 1970.
29. See David E. Powell, *Anti-Religious Propaganda in the Soviet Union: A Study of Mass Persuasion*, Cambridge, Massachusetts: M.I.T. Press, 1975.
30. ibid., p. 92.
31. ibid., p. 51.
32. cf. Gollwitzer, op. cit.
33. *The Life and Work of Sigmund Freud*, (3 vols.), Hogarth Press, 1953, 1955, 1957.
34. *Standard Edition*, Vol. IX, Hogarth Press, 1959, p. 115.
35. ibid., p. 120.
36. 'A Religious Experience', published in 1928. Reprinted in *Standard Edition*, Vol. XXI, Hogarth Press, 1961, p. 169.
37. Summary in Theodor Reik, *From Thirty Years with Freud*, New York: Farrar & Rinehart, 1940, p. 140.
38. ibid., p. 147.
39. The 'nothing more than' clause is very characteristic of nineteenth- and early-twentieth-century scientific writing and arises from a belief that complex processes can be 'reduced' in the end to the laws of physics. Very few modern psychoanalysts would take such an outdated view. See Chapter 1 of *Civilisation and its Discontents*, published in 1930, reprinted in *Standard Edition*, Vol. XXI, Hogarth Press, 1961, p. 64.

40. Franz Alexander interpreted Buddhist meditation in this way in his paper 'Buddhistic Training as an Artificial Catatonia' in *Psychoanalysis*, Vol. 19, 1931, pp. 129–45.
41. *In Group Psychology*, first published in 1921. Reprinted in *Standard Edition*, Vol. XVIII, Hogarth Press, 1955, p. 142.
42. *The Psychology of Religious Mysticism*, Kegan Paul, Trench, Trubner, 1929.
43. ibid., p. 141.
44. ibid., p. 200.
45. 'On the Significance of Militant Materialism', from *On Religion*, op. cit., p. 67.
46. Feuerbach, op. cit., p. 89.
47. *On Religion: Speeches to its Cultured Despisers* (tr. J. Oman), New York: Harper & Row, 1958.
48. *Lectures on the Essence of Religion* (tr. Ralph Manheim), New York: Harper & Row, 1967, Twenty-fourth Lecture, p. 218.

Chapter three: **Dreams and Origins**

1. This chapter is heavily indebted to Professor Evans-Prichard's excellent brief account, *Theories of Primitive Religion*, Oxford University Press, 1965.
2. In *Myth and Reality*, New York: Harper & Row, 1963.
3. In *Totem and Taboo*, first published in 1913; tr. James Strachey, Routledge & Kegan Paul, 1950.
4. See Claude Lévi-Strauss, *Le Totémisme aujourd'hui*, tr. R. Needham as *Totemism*, Penguin Books, 1969.
5. *Totem and Taboo*, op. cit., p. 161.
6. Published in London by John Murray, 1859.
7. Two entertaining discussions of Comte are available in, Ronald Fletcher, *Auguste Comte and the Making of Sociology* (Auguste Comte Memorial Trust Lecture 7), Athlone Press, 1966, and E. E. Evans-Pritchard, *The Sociology of Comte: An Appreciation*, Manchester University Press, 1970. Comte's sociology is reviewed in Raymond Aron, *Main Currents of Sociological Thought*, Vol. 1, Penguin Books, 1965.
8. Auguste Comte, *A Discourse on the Positive Spirit* (1844) (tr. Edward Spencer Beesley), William Reeves, 1903.
9. Auguste Comte, *Cours de philosophie positive*, Vol. 1, p. 4. Quoted by Evans-Pritchard, op. cit.
10. Comte got this idea from his fellow Frenchman Charles De Brosses, who published an account of fetishism in 1760.
11. Comte, (*Discourse*), op. cit., p. 7.
12. Evans-Pritchard, op. cit., p. 1. The woman was Clothilde de Vaux.

13. E. Tylor, *Primitive Culture* (2 vols.), John Murray, 1871.
14. ibid., 6th edn (1920), Vol. 1, p. vii.
15. ibid., p. 433.
16. ibid., p. 437.
17. ibid., p. 436.
18. ibid., Vol. II, p. 246.
19. Émile Durkheim, *The Elementary Forms of the Religious Life* (1912), tr. J. W. Swain, Allen & Unwin, 1915.
20. A. A. Goldenweiser, review in *American Anthropologist*, Vol. 17, 1915, pp. 719–35. Sociologists nowadays tend to find Durkheim's emphasis on crowd-psychology rather dated, and are much more interested in the cognitive aspect of his sociology (cf. Steven Lukes, note 21, below). Nevertheless it is the former theme I am emphasizing, because it is there that Durkheim places the experience on the basis of which religions are constructed.
21. In Steven Lukes, *Émile Durkheim: His Life and Work*, Allen Lane, 1973, p. 64.
22. From the introduction to Anthony Giddens, *Émile Durkheim – Selected Writings*, Cambridge University Press, 1972.
23. Durkheim, op. cit., p. 417. New translation in W. S. F. Pickering, *Durkheim on Religion*, Routledge & Kegan Paul, 1975.
24. ibid., p. 210; tr. Giddens, op. cit.
25. Giddens, op. cit., p. 20.
26. Matthew, v. 6.
27. Durkheim, op. cit., Book III, Chapter 2; tr. Giddens, op. cit.
28. Comte (*Discourse*), op. cit., p. 3.
29. See Andrew Lang, *The Making of Religion*, Longmans, Green, 1898.
30. See Wilhelm Schmidt, *The Origin and Growth of Religion* (tr. H. J. Rose), Methuen, 1931.
31. See Ernest Jones, *The Life and Work of Sigmund Freud* (one-Volume abridged edition), Penguin Books, 1964, p. 622.
32. Joseph Ernest Renan (1823–92), French rationalist. Best known for his *Life of Jesus*, published in 1863.
33. Schmidt, op. cit., p. 6.
34. The German student of religion K. T. Preuss described its beginnings as rooted in '*Urdummheit*', roughly translatable as 'primeval stupidity'.
35. Cambridge scholar and author of a famous twelve-volume work on magic and religion, *The Golden Bough*, finally completed in 1915. In 1922 he produced an abridged version, published by Macmillan.
36. See F. Max-Müller, *Lectures on the Origin and Growth of Religion*, Longmans, Green, 1878.

37. From *The Life and Letters of the Right Honourable Friedrich Max-Müller* (edited by his wife), Longmans, Green, 1902, p. 3.
38. ibid., p. 173.
39. See Roger Lancelyn Green, *Andrew Lang*, Edmund Ward, 1946.
40. ibid., p. 71.
41. Lang, op. cit., p. 331.
42. ibid., p. 3.

Chapter four: **Disappearing Symbols**

1. Quoted in Allen Andrews, *The Life of L. S. Lowry, 1887–1976*, Jupiter Books, 1977, p. 69.
2. See Titus Burckhardt, *Siena, City of the Virgin*, Oxford University Press, 1960.
3. Quoted in S. S. Acquaviva, *The Decline of the Sacred in Industrial Society*, Oxford: Blackwell, 1979, p. 124.
4. Guiseppe Parenti, quoted by Acquaviva, op. cit., p. 128.
5. ibid., p. 128.
6. ibid., p. 129.
7. ibid., p. 127.
8. ibid., p. 131.
9. Quoted in Stuart Woolf, *A History of Italy 1700–1860*, Methuen, 1979, p. 150.
10. Quoted from Emmanuel Le Roy Ladurie, *Montaillou: Cathars and Catholics in a French Village 1294–1324*, Scolar Press, 1978; Penguin Books, 1980.
11. Acquaviva, op. cit., p. 130.
12. Keith Thomas, *Religion and the Decline of Magic*, Penguin Books, 1973, p. 179.
13. ibid., p. 180.
14. ibid., p. 191.
15. ibid., p. 192.
16. ibid., p. 201.
17. ibid., p. 193.
18. Quoted in K. S. Inglis, *Churches and the Working Classes in Victorian England*, Routledge & Kegan Paul, 1963.
19. In Hugh McLeod, *Class and Religion in the Late Victorian City*, Croom Helm, 1974, p. 56.
20. ibid., Chapter 3.
21. ibid.
22. Inglis, op. cit., p. 1.
23. See Robert Currie, Alan Gilbert and Lee Horsley, *Churches and Churchgoers: Patterns of Church Growth in the British Isles since 1700*, Clarendon Press, 1978.

226 *Notes*

24. ibid., p. 25.
25. Michael P. Hornsby-Smith and Raymond M. Lee, *Roman Catholic Opinion*, University of Surrey, 1979.
26. Currie, Gilbert and Horsley, op. cit., p. 158.
27. *A Church of Daylight*, Geoffrey Chapman, 1973.
28. ibid., p. 178.
29. The relative resilience of Roman Catholicism in Ireland (in spite of a declining number of vocations to the religious life) is sometimes used to explain the better showing of Catholics in Great Britain, since most of them are of Irish origin. Variations in patterns of resilience or decline of the Christian institution are explored in David Martin, *A General Theory of Secularisation*, Oxford: Blackwell, 1978.
30. The huge and complex debate about secularization is beyond the scope of this book. Some key works dealing with the subject, apart from Martin, op. cit., are Bryan Wilson, *Religion in Secular Society*, Watts, 1966; David Martin, *The Religious and the Secular*, Routledge & Kegan Paul, 1969; Richard Fenn, *A Theory of Secularisation*, Society for the Scientific Study of Religion Monographs, No. 1, 1978.
31. Cited in *Religion in America – The Gallup Opinion Index 1977–78*, American Institute of Public Opinion, Princeton, 1978, p. 27.
32. In *The Sign of Jonas*, Hollis & Carter, 1953.
33. Quoted in Peter Berger, *Facing Up to Modernity*, Penguin Books, 1979.
34. ibid.
35. *Gallup Opinion Index 1977–78*, op. cit., p. 27.
36. For a forceful argument against the secularization thesis for the United States, see Andrew M. Greeley, *Unsecular Man*, New York: Schocken Books, 1972.
37. Acquaviva, op. cit., p. 130.
38. Andrews, op. cit.
39. See Robert Currie, *Methodism Divided*, Faber & Faber, 1968.
40. Berger, op. cit., p. 203.
41. By the English comedian the late Dick Emery.
42. See Clifford Geertz, *The Interpretation of Cultures*, New York: Basic Books, 1973.

Chapter five: **Religion: Public and Invisible**

1. Joachim Wach, *Sociology of Religion*, University of Chicago Press, 1962.
2. Quite often the answer was 'No'. Robert Kaiser, in his entertaining book *Inside the Council*, Burns Oates, 1963, describes how prelates would interview reporters after the sessions to find out what had been going on.

3. Quoted in H. H. Gerth and C. Wright Mills (eds), *From Max Weber*, Routledge & Kegan Paul, 1948, p. 204.
4. ibid., p. 226.
5. Quoted in Dom Cuthbert Butler, *The Vatican Council 1869–70*, Fontana, 1962, p. 344.
6. ibid., Chapter 20.
7. ibid., p. 339.
8. Gerth and Mills, op. cit., p. 299.
9. Kaiser, op. cit., p. 9.
10. Dogmatic Constitution on the Church 'Lumen Gentium' ('Light of all Nations'), in Walter M. Abbott, (ed.), *The Documents of Vatican II*, Geoffrey Chapman, 1966, p. 14–96.
11. cf. Charles Y. Glock, 'The Dimensions of Religious Commitment', from C. Y. Glock (ed.), *Religion in Sociological Perspective*, Belmont: Wadsworth Publishing Co., 1973. Glock proposes five dimensions: the experiential, the ritualistic, the ideological, the intellectual and the consequential. Some attempts have been made to measure these and related dimensions in population samples, with varying success. For purposes of coherent exposition, however, I find Ninian Smart's proposals more helpful.
12. Ninian Smart, *The Religious Experience of Mankind*, Fontana, 1971.
13. Cf. Kaiser, op. cit. Also the four volumes by Xavier Rynne, *Letters from Vatican City; The Second Session; The Third Session; The Fourth Session*, Faber & Faber, 1963–6.
14. Abbott (ed.), op. cit.
15. For example, Matthew xvi, 18: 'You are Peter and on this rock I will build my church.'
16. 'Lumen Gentium', Chapter 3.
17. Acts ii.
18. Illustrated by the continuing difficulties of the Catholic theologian Hans Küng, author of *Infallible?*, Fontana, 1972.
19. Quoted in Trevor Ling, *A History of Religion East and West*, Macmillan, 1968, p. 316.
20. For a marvellous collection of religious texts and mythologies from all the main traditions except Judaism and Christianity, see Mircea Eliade, *From Primitives to Zen*, Collins, 1967.
21. See Gustavo Gutierrez, *A Theology of Liberation*, S.C.M., 1974.
22. My usage is based on that of the anthropologist Bronislaw Malinowski, who calls myths 'statements of reality, products of a living faith'. See his article 'Myth in Primitive Society' in *Magic, Science and Religion*, Souvenir Press, 1974.
23. Smart, op. cit., p. 106.
24. See George Every, *The Mass*, Dublin: Gill & Macmillan, 1978.
25. In *Ritual in Industrial Society*, Allen & Unwin, 1974, p. 37.

26. The standard work is J. A. Jungmann, *The Mass of the Roman Rite: Its Origins and Development* (2 vols.), New York: Benziger Brothers, 1951, 1955.

27. A good brief review of 'rites of passage' is given in, Lucy Mair, *An Introduction to Social Anthropology*, Clarendon Press, 1965, Chapter 14.

28. In *Mythologies*, Paladin Books, 1973. Many of Barthes' examples are 'actings-out' or ritual expressions of mythologies. His contemptuous view of bourgeois mythology does not detract from the fact that it exists as a secular reality. Barthes uses a more restricted meaning for myth than I have chosen to do, since he limits it to 'false-consciousness'.

29. This view is most fully developed in Wach, op. cit.

30. Psalm cxxxviii (cxxxix), 14. 15.

Chapter six: **The New England Connection**

1. *Treatise Concerning Religious Affections*, (edited by John E. Smith), Yale University Press, 1959.

2. *Institutes of the Christian Religion*, 2 vols., (edited by John T. McNeill, translated by Ford Lewis Battles), S.C.M., 1960, p. 79.

3. Max Weber, *The Protestant Ethic and the Spirit of Capitalism*, (translated by Talcott Parsons), George Allen and Unwin, 1930, p. 104.

4. See, Michael Watts, *The Dissenters*, Vol. I, Oxford: Clarendon Press, 1978.

5. ibid.

6. Breward, I. (ed.), *The Work of William Perkins*, The Sutton Courtenay Press, 1970.

7. ibid.

8. Peter Erb, *Pietists: Selected Writings*, (edited with an introduction by Peter C. Erb; preface by F. Ernest Stoeffler), S.P.C.K., (Classics of Western Spirituality Series), 1983, p. 105.

9. Curnock, N. (ed.), *The Journal of the Rev. John Wesley, A.M.*, 8 Vols., London: Robert Culley, 1909, Vol. I, pp. 475–476.

10. For a presentation of Edwards' philosophy, see, Perry Miller, 'Jonathan Edwards on the Sense of the Heart', *Harvard Theological Review*, Vol. 41, 1948, pp. 122–145.

11. See, Patricia J. Tracy, *Jonathan Edwards, Pastor: Religion and Society in Eighteenth Century Northampton*, New York: Hill and Wang, 1980.

12. In, *Studies in New England Transcendentalism*, New York: Columbia University Press, 1908, p. 18.

13. Reproduced in Frederic I. Carpenter, *Ralph Waldo Emerson: representative selections, with introduction, bibliography and notes*, New York: American Book Co., 1934, p. 13.

14. ibid., p. 10.

15. Carpenter, op. cit., p. 43.

16. See E. D., Starbuck, *The Psychology of Religion*, New York: Walter Scott, 1899.

17. *Collected Letters*, Vol. II, Boston: Atlantic Monthly Press, 1920, p. 108.

18. Quoted in, Ralph Barton Perry, *The Thought and Character of William James*, 2 vols, Boston: Little, Brown & Co., 1935, Vol. I, p. 165.

19. *Letters*, op. cit., Vol. 1, p. 310.

20. ibid., Vol. II, p. 127.

21. A. C. Bouquet, in, 'Soter: A consideration of some fundamentals of Christian Theology', *The Modern Churchman*, Vol. 12, 1969, p. 267–279.

22. *Letters*, op. cit., Vol. II, pp. 76–77.

23. See, Cushing Strout, 'The pluralistic identity of William James', *American Quarterly*, Vol. 23, 1971, pp. 135–152.

Chapter seven: **Strange and Difficult to Describe**

1. Quoted in Rudolf Otto, *The Idea of the Holy*, Oxford University Press (2nd edn), 1950, p. 191.

2. In Mircea Eliade, *From Primitives to Zen*, Collins, 1967, p. 483.

3. Mark i, 10–12.

4. In *Jesus and the Spirit*, S.C.M., 1975.

5. ibid., p. 65.

6. Quoted in D. T. Suzuki, *Outlines of Mahayana Buddhism*, New York: Schocken Books, 1963.

7. See *The Science of Religion and the Sociology of Knowledge*, Princeton University Press, 1973.

8. Description by John Harvey in the introduction to the English edition of Otto, op. cit., p. xii.

9. Otto, op. cit.

10. The example comes from Harold W. Turner's very helpful commentary on *The Idea of the Holy*, produced by the Department of Religious Studies at Aberdeen University.

11. Otto, op. cit., p. 8.

12. ibid., p. 60.

13. Isaiah vi, 1–6.

14. Isaiah vi, 6–7.

15. Otto, op. cit.

16. See W. T. Stace, *Mysticism and Philosophy*, Philadelphia: J. B. Lippincott, 1960.

17. This quotation comes from the Indian Buddhist philosopher

Nagarjuna (*c* A.D. 200). See Alan Watts, *The Way of Zen*, Penguin Books, 1962, p. 83.

18. Quoted in Philip Kapleau, *The Three Pillars of Zen*, Boston: Beacon Press, 1967.

19. Eliade, op. cit., p. 526.

20. Quoted by Stace, op. cit., p. 63.

21. ibid.

22. Quoted by R. F. Gombrich, *Precept and Practice: Traditional Buddhism in the Rural Highlands of Ceylon*, Clarendon Press, 1971.

23. Eliade, op. cit., p. 41.

24. Aldous Huxley, *The Perennial Philosophy*, Chatto & Windus, 1946.

25. Raymond Pannikar, *The Unknown Christ of Hinduism*, Darton, Longman & Todd, 1965.

26. From Steven T. Katz, 'Language, Epistemology and Mysticism', in the book edited by the author, *Mysticism and Philosophical Analysis*, New York: Oxford University Press, 1978, p. 34.

27. ibid., p. 38.

28. See Dom Aelred Graham, *The End of Religion*, New York: Harcourt-Brace Jovanovich, 1971.

29. See William Johnston, *Silent Music*, Fontana, 1976.

30. Personal communication from A. D. Wooster.

31. See J. K. Kadowaki, *Zen and the Bible*, Routledge & Kegan Paul, 1980.

32. Johnston, op. cit., p. 36.

33. From Ludwig Von Bertalanffy, *General System Theory*, Allen Lane, 1971, p. 240.

34. From Huston Smith, 'Do Drugs Have Religious Import?' *Journal of Philosophy*, Vol. 61 (18), 1964, pp. 517–30. The first account comes from an article on 'consciousness-expanding' drugs in *Main Currents in Modern Thought*, 20 (1), 1963, pp. 10–11; the second comes from R. M. Bucke, quoted by William James in *The Varieties of Religious Experience*. The first experience was drug-induced, the second was not. When Smith tried it on his students, twice as many chose wrongly as chose correctly.

35. In *The Comparative Study of Religions*, New York: Columbia University Press, 1958, p. 31.

36. In *The Varieties of Religious Experience*, Fontana, 1960, p. 73.

37. Jeremiah xx, 8–9.

38. Bertalanffy, op. cit., p. 244.

39. For example it was only with the invention of modern detection equipment that we became aware of the existence of a vast range of electromagnetic radiation, varying from tiny gamma rays to huge radio signals.

40. Bertalanffy, op. cit., p. 253.

41. See R. D. Laing and A. Esterson, *Sanity, Madness and the Family*, Vol. 1, *Families of Schizophrenics*, Tavistock, 1964.

Chapter eight: **Entering the World of Personal Experience**

1. In *Exploring Mysticism*, Penguin Books, 1975, p. 107.
2. See *The Psychology of Religion*, New York: Walter Scott, 1899.
3. ibid., pp. 22–3.
4. See *Adolescence: its Psychology*, New York: Appleton, 1904, p. 281.
5. Preached by Edwards on 8 July 1741 at Enfield, Connecticut, during a time of highly charged revival in the district. See E. O. Winslow (ed.), *Jonathan Edwards: Basic Writings*, New York: New American Library, 1966, p. 150.
6. Dorothy, Ross, *G. Stanley Hall: The Psychologist as Prophet*, University of Chicago Press, 1972.
7. William James, *The Varieties of Religious Experience*, Fontana, 1960, Lecture 1.
8. Starbuck, *Psychology of Religion*, p. 77.
9. ibid., p. 148.
10. *Varieties*, op. cit., p. 204.
11. Ibid., p. 487.
12, 13, 14. ibid., p. 490.
15. ibid., p. ix.
16. Abraham Cronbach, 'The Psychology of Religion: A Bibliographical Survey', *Psychological Bulletin*, Vol. 30 (5), 1933, pp. 327–61.
17. In 'Religion as a Cultural System', reprinted in Clifford Geertz, *The Interpretation of Cultures*, New York: Basic Books, 1973.
18. See Joseph Maréchal, *Études sur la psychologie des mystiques*, 1924; English translation, *Studies in the Psychology of the Mystics*, Burns Oates & Washbourne, 1927.
19. See *The Graces of Interior Prayer*, Kegan Paul, Trench, Trubner, 1912. Poulain gathered together a very interesting set of descriptions of religious experience in this book and analysed them with great care. However, some theological critics were unhappy with the psychological emphasis Poulain and others gave to contemplative prayer. See, for example, Anselm Stolz, *The Doctrine of Spiritual Perfection*, St Louis: B. Herder Book Co., 1938.
20. Maréchal, op. cit., p. 226.
21. J. H. Leuba, 'Recent French Books on Religious Mysticism', *Psychological Bulletin*, Vol. 23, 1926, p. 723.
22. Paul Creelan, 'Religion, Language and Sexuality in J. B. Watson', *Journal of Humanistic Psychology*, Vol. 15 (4), 1975, pp. 55–78.

23. In *The Future of an Illusion*, Hogarth Press, 1928, p. 56.

24. See L. L. Thurstone and E. J. Chave, *The Measurement of Attitude*, University of Chicago Press, 1929.

25. From Aron Gurwitsch, *Phenomenology and the Theory of Science*, Evanston: North-Western University Press, 1974. For an excellent review of the problem of bias in the scientific study of religion see Ninian Smart, *The Science of Religion and the Sociology of Knowledge*, Princeton University Press, 1973.

26. See Alfred C. Kinsey, W. B. Pomeroy and C. E. Martin, *Sexual Behavior in the Human Male*, Philadelphia: W. B. Saunders, 1948.

27. ibid., p. 36.

28. The Gifford Lectures for 1965 were delivered by Hardy at Aberdeen University and Volume 2 was published as *The Divine Flame*, Collins, 1966 (republished 1978, by R.E.R.U., Manchester College, Oxford). This book describes the ideas which led to the foundation of the Religious Experience Research Unit at Manchester College. See also by Sir Alister Hardy, *The Biology of God*, Jonathan Cape, 1975, and *The Spiritual Nature of Man*, Clarendon Press, 1979. Hardy's final book, *Darwin and the Spirit of Man*, was published by Collins in 1984. Studies based on the records collected by the R.E.R.U. include two volumes by Edward Robinson, one on the religious experiences of childhood, *The Original Vision*, (1977) and another on the growth of religious experience during life, *Living the Questions* (1978). Timothy Beardsworth has published a study of quasi-sensory experience, *A Sense of Presence* (1977).

29. Hardy, op. cit. (1979), Chapter 2.

30. In *Religious Thinking from Childhood to Adolescence*. Routledge & Kegan Paul, 1964.

31. *Ecstasy*, Cresset Press, 1961.

32. See Bradburn's book *The Structure of Psychological Wellbeing*, Chicago: Aldine Press, 1969.

33. Reported in Andrew M. Greeley, *The Sociology of the Paranormal: A Reconnaissance*, Sage Research Papers in the Social Sciences (Studies in Religion and Ethnicity Series No. 90–023), Beverley Hills/London: Sage Publications, 1975.

Chapter nine: **The Common Experience**

1. The title of a book by J. M. Cohen and J.-F. Phipps (Rider, 1979). It is concerned with experiences of enlightenment and draws heavily from the files of the Alister Hardy Research Centre in Oxford.

2. From the poem 'After May', in Cavanagh's *Collected Poems*, New York: Devin-Adair, 1964.

3. See Charles Y. Glock and Rodney Stark, *Religion and Society in Tension*, Chicago: Rand McNally, 1965, Chapter 8, 'Social Contexts of Religious Experience'.
4. ibid., p. 158.
5. Kurt Back and Linda Brookover Bourque, 'Can Feelings Be Enumerated?', *Behavioral Science*, Vol. 15, 1970, pp. 487–96.
6. ibid., p. 489.
7. Quoted in Theodore Roszak, *The Making of a Counterculture*, Faber & Faber, 1970, p. 124.
8. See *Religion in America – The Gallup Opinion Index 1977–78*, Report No. 145, p. 54.
9. See David Hay and Ann Morisy, 'Reports of Ecstatic, Paranormal or Religious Experience in Great Britain and the United States – A Comparison of Trends', *Journal for the Scientific Study of Religion*, Vol. 17 (3), 1978, pp. 255–68.
10. Unpublished data provided by Gallup Poll, London.
11. Reported in A. M. Greeley, *The Sociology of the Paranormal*, Beverley Hills/London: Sage Publications, 1975.
12. By courtesy of George Gallup, Jr. Very similar figures have been found in a recent unpublished survey in Australia.
13. Cited in Michael Argyle and Benjamin Beit-Hallahmi, *The Social Psychology of Religion*, Routledge & Kegan Paul, 1975, p. 71.
14. ibid., p. 75.
15. Greeley, op. cit., p. 60.
16. Argyle and Beit-Hallahmi, op. cit., p. 68.
17. Greeley, op. cit., p. 54.
18. *Religion in America*, op. cit., p. 54.
19. Greeley, op. cit., p. 60; *Religion in America*, op. cit., p. 54.
20. See Robert Wuthnow, *Peak Experiences: Some Empirical Tests*, mimeographed publication # A161 of the Survey Research Center, University of California, Berkeley, 1976.
21. See David Hay 'Religious Experience Amongst a Group of Postgraduate Students: A Qualitative Study', *Journal for the Scientific Study of Religion*, Vol. 18 (2), 1979, pp. 164–82. Eileen Barker of the London School of Economics used some of our questions in her research. In a group of young people, two thirds of whom were students, she obtained a positive response rate of 63 per cent (personal communcation).
22. See, for example, V. Lanternari, *The Religions of the Oppressed: a Study of Modern Messianic Cults*, New York: Knopf, 1963; Also I. M. Lewis, *Ecstatic Religion*, Penguin Books, 1971.
23. See Gustav Jahoda, *The Psychology of Superstition*, Penguin Books, 1970, p. 140.
24. *Religion in America*, op. cit., p. 54.

25. The 1985 Gallup Poll in the United States, conducted for the Alister Hardy Research Centre, used Hardy's question for the first time in the U.S.A. There was a consistent rise in positive response to the question, moving from non-high school graduates up to college graduates. It may be that the wording of the Hardy question is more easily handleable by educated people.
26. Back and Bourque, op. cit., p. 493.
27. Argyle and Beit-Hallahmi, op. cit., pp. 33–4.
28. See Back and Bourque, op. cit., *Religion in America*, op. cit.
29. ibid.
30. *Religion in America*, op. cit., p. 54.
31. Dr Michael Mason of the Yarra Theological Union, Australia.
32. See *The Unchurched American*, Princeton Religion Research Center and the Gallup Organization, 1978.
33. Hay, op. cit. (1979), p. 178.
34. Glock and Stark, op. cit., p. 269.
35. Argyle and Beit-Hallahmi, op. cit., pp. 33–4.

Chapter ten: **Putting Experience into Words**

1. 'Northumbrian Sequence IV', from *The Collected Poems of Kathleen Raine*, Hamish Hamilton, 1965.
2. David Hay, 'Religious Experience Amongst a Group of Post-graduate Students: A Qualitative Study', *Journal for the Scientific Study of Religion*, Vol. 18 (2), 1979, pp. 164–82.
3. See David Hay and Ann Morisy, 'Secular Society Religious Meanings: A Contemporary Paradox', *Review of Religious Research*, Vol. 26 (3), 1985, p. 213–227.
4. David Lewis, 'All in good faith', *Nursing Times*, March 18–24, 1987, pp. 40–45.
5. See David Hay, 'The Taboo on religion', *The Clergy Review*, Vol. 69 (5), 1984, pp. 157–162. A very recent and as yet unpublished piece of research by Edward Robinson and Michael Jackson of the Alister Hardy Research Centre, suggests the intriguing possibility that the taboo may be losing strength. Robinson and Jackson have given me permission to quote from the results of their project, *Religion and Values at Sixteen Plus* (a joint C.E.M./A.H.R.C. Research Project). They surveyed approximately six and a half thousand young people in Britain and Ireland, aged between fifteen years and nineteen years. 52 per cent of the teenagers said they had experienced a numinous presence at some time in their lives, perhaps in times of difficulty or danger. Even more surprising, 79 per cent claimed to have had some kind of 'nature-mystical' experience. In the United States, Andrew Greeley has recently repeated his 1970s

survey of religious experience, and similarly notes heavy increases in positive responses. Could it be that the earlier reports of widespread experience have 'given permission' for people to claim their experience?

6. Alister C. Hardy, *The Spiritual Nature of Man*, Clarendon Press, 1979.

7. *Ecstasy*, Cresset Press, 1961.

8. Personal communication. See also, Eileen Barker, *The Making of a Moonie*, Basil Blackwell, 1984.

9. David Hay and Gordon Heald, 'Religion is good for you', vol. 80, 17 April, 1987.

Chapter eleven: **Responding to Experience**

1. From 'The Unknown Bird'. See *The Collected Poems of Edward Thomas* (ed. and introduced by R. George Thomas), Clarendon Press, 1978.

2. See Richard Jefferies' spiritual autobiography *The Story of My Heart*, Eyre & Spottiswoode, 1949.

3. Personal communication.

4. For a criticism of the stance adopted by both Wach and Otto, see Ninian Smart's book *The Science of Religion and the Sociology of Knowledge*, Princeton University Press, 1973.

5. *Religion and the Decline of Magic*, Penguin Books, 1973.

6. See, especially, Chapter 8 in Robert Towler, *Homo Religiosus*, Constable, 1974.

7. From 'En una Noche Oscura', translated by Roy Campbell in *The Poems of St John of the Cross*, Harvill Press, 1951. This poem forms a prelude to two of St John's major works, *The Ascent of Mount Carmel* and *The Dark Night*, See Kieran Kavanaugh, O.C.D. and Otilio Rodriguez, O.C.D., *The Collected Works of St John of the Cross*, Washington D.C.: Institute of Carmelite Studies, 1973.

Chapter Twelve: **Doubts About the Despisers**

1. From the poem 'Up on the Downs', reprinted in *The Penguin Book of English Verse*, Penguin Books, 1956.

2. G. W. Comstock, 'Fatal Arteriosclerotic Heart Disease, Water Hardness at Home, and Socio-economic Characteristics', *American Journal of Epidemiology*, Vol. 94 (1), 1971, pp. 1–10.

3. G. W. Comstock and K. B. Partridge, 'Church Attendance and Health', *Journal of Chronic Diseases*, Vol. 25, 1972, pp. 665–72.

4. See Jeffrey S. Levin and Kyriakos S. Markides, 'Religious attendance and subjective health', *Journal for the Scientific Study of Religion*, Vol. 25 (1), 1986, pp. 31–39.

5. See Bernard Spilka and Paul H. Werme, 'Religion and Mental Disorder: A Research Perspective', in Merton P. Strommen (ed.), *Research on Religious Development: A Comprehensive Handbook*, New York: Hawthorn Books, 1971.
6. The classic compendium on this is J. G. Frazer's *The Golden Bough*.
7. See *The Golden Bough* (abridged edition) Macmillan, 1922, Vol. II, p. 855; also, Stuart Piggott, *The Druids*, Thames & Hudson, 1968.
8. The Sybilline Books were a set of prophecies made by the Sybil of Cumae, a priestess of Apollo. They were housed in the temple of Jupiter on the Capitoline Hill in Rome and consulted in times of national emergency.
9. See John Ferguson, *The Religions of the Roman Empire*, Thames & Hudson, 1970, p. 27.
10. See Maarten J. Vermaseren, *Cybele and Attis: The Myth and the Cult*, Thames & Hudson, 1977, p. 96.
11. See *The Poems of Catallus* (tr. James Michie), Rupert Hart-Davis, 1969, p. 125.
12. Vermaseren, op. cit., p. 161.
13. A. W. Kushner, 'Two Cases of Auto-castration Due to Religious Delusions', *British Journal of Medical Psychology*, Vol. 40, 1967, pp. 293–8.
14. Matthew xix, 12.
15. In *The Danger of Words*, Routledge & Kegan Paul, 1973.
16. See Norman M. Bradburn, *The Structure of Psychological Wellbeing*, Chicago: Aldine Press, 1969.
17. Andrew M. Greeley, *The Sociology of the Paranormal*, Beverley Hills/London: Sage Publications, 1975, p. 61.
18. Paul L. Berkman, 'Measurement of Mental Health in a General Population Survey', *American Journal of Epidemiology*, Vol. 94 (2), 1971, pp. 105–11.
19. Ralph Hood, 'Conceptual Criticisms of Regressive Explanations of Mysticism', *Review of Religious Research*, Vol. 17, 1976, pp. 179–88.
20. For a review of the spectrum of opinion see D. Bannister (ed.), *Issues and Approaches in the Psychological Therapies*, London: Wiley, 1975.
21. O. S. Walters, 'Religion and Psychopathology', *Comprehensive Psychiatry*, Vol. 101 (5), 1964, pp. 24–35.
22. In John Plamenatz, *Karl Marx's Philosophy of Man*, Oxford University Press, 1975.
23. In 'The Communism of the Paper *Rheinischer Beobachter*'. Reprinted in Marx and Engels, *On Religion*, Moscow: Progress Publishers, 1957, p. 74.
24. T. W. Adorno, et al., *The Authoritarian Personality*, New York: Harper, 1950.

25. For a good, though now dated, brief review, see Roger Brown, *Social Psychology*, Collier-Macmillan, 1965, Chapter 10.

26. Isaiah lxi, 1–2.

27. In 'Contribution to the Critique of Hegel's Philosophy of Right'. Translation in Plamenatz, op. cit.

28. Robert Wuthnow, *Peak Experience: Some Empirical Tests*, Berkeley: University of California, 1976.

29. Plamenatz, op. cit., p. 246.

30. ibid.

31. Wuthnow, op. cit.

32. For a readable recent review see José Comblin, *The Church and the National Security State*, New York: Orbis Books, 1979. The classic text is Gustavo Gutierrez, *A Theology of Liberation*, S.C.M. Press, 1974.

33. See R. O. Allen and B. Spilka, 'Committed and Consensual Religion: A Specification of Religion–Prejudice Relationships', *Journal for the Scientific Study of Religion*, Vol. 6, 1967, pp. 191–206; and, for a useful overview, Bernard Spilka, ' "The Compleat Person": Some Theoretical Views and Research Findings for a Theological Psychology of Religion', *Journal of Psychology and Theology*, Vol. 4 (1), 1976, pp. 15–24.

34. See C. Daniel Batson and W. Larry Ventis, *The Religious Experience: a social-psychological perspective*, New York: Oxford University Press, 1982.

35. See for example the following papers: Daniel Batson and Lynn Raynor-Prince, 'Religious orientation and complexity of thought about existential concerns', *Journal for the Scientific Study of Religion*, Vol. 22 (1), 1983, pp. 38–50. Also the symposium on religious orientation typologies in Volume 24 (4), 1985, of the *Journal for the Scientific Study of Religion*. And, Gary L. Sapp and Logan Jones, 'Religious orientation and moral judgment', *Journal for the Scientific Study of Religion*, Vol. 25 (2), 1986, pp. 208–214; P. J. Watson, Ronald Morris, James E. Foster and Ralph W. Hood, 'Religiosity and social desirability', *Journal for the Scientific Study of Religion*, Vol. 25 (2), pp. 215–232.

36. Ralph Hood, 'The Construction and Preliminary Validation of a Measure of Reported Religious Experience', *Journal for the Scientific Study of Religion*, Vol. 14, 1975, pp. 29–41. Hood found a strong correlation between reports of religious experience and 'intrinsic religious orientation', a term used by the psychologist G. W. Allport. However, Spilka has shown that 'intrinsic' and 'committed' religion amount to different terms for the same thing. See Spilka, op. cit.

Chapter thirteen: **'How Did You Know?'**

1. 'A memorable fancy' from *The Marriage of Heaven and Hell* (1793). Reprinted in *Poetry and Prose of William Blake* (ed. Geoffrey Keynes), Nonesuch Press, 1927, p. 195.
2. See J. B. Pratt, *The Religious Consciousness: A Psychological Study*, New York: Macmillan, 1923, p. 184.
3. S. Schachter and J. E. Singer, 'Cognitive, Social and Psychological Determinants of Emotional State', *Psychological Review*, Vol. 69, 1962, pp. 379–99.
4. Discussed in an interesting paper, Wayne Proudfoot and Phillip Shaver, 'Attribution Theory and the Psychology of Religion', *Journal for the Scientific Study of Religion*, Vol. 14 (4), 1975, pp. 317–30; See also, Bernard Spilka, Phillip Shaver and Lee A. Kirkpatrick, 'A general attribution theory for the psychology of religion', *Journal for the Scientific Study of Religion*, Vol. 24 (4), 1985, pp. 1–19.
5. See *Magic, Science and Religion and Other Essays*, Souvenir Press, 1974, p. 56.
6. *On Religion: Speeches to its Cultural Despisers* (tr. J. Oman), New York: Harper & Row, 1958.
7. See *On Religious Experience: A Psychological Study*, Stockholm: Almquist and Wiksell, 1976. Unger bases his account of religious perception on the theories of the Swedish psychologist Hjalmar Sundén, none of whose works have been translated into English. I am however indebted to Unger's exposition of those theories.
8. ibid., p. 113.
9. For a description of an 'intellectual vision' see *Complete Works of St Teresa* (tr. and ed. E. Allison Peers), Sheed and Ward, 1975, Vol. 1, Chapter 27.
10. See P. B. C. Fenwick et al., 'Metabolic and EEG Changes During Transcendental Meditation: An Explanation', *Biological Psychology*, Vol. 5, 1977, pp. 101–18.
11. See Arthur J. Deikman, 'Bimodal Consciousness', *Archives of General Psychiatry*, Vol. 25, 1971, pp. 481–9.
12. ibid.
13. See Peter H. Lindsay and Donald A. Norman, *Human Information Processing*, New York: Academic Press, 1977, especially Chapter 7.
14. Katsuki Sekida, *Zen Training: Methods and Philosophy*, New York: Weatherhill, 1975, p. 47.
15. See R. M. French, *The Way of a Pilgrim*, S.P.C.K., 1972, p. 10.
16. See *The Cloud of Unknowing* (tr. Clifton Wolters), Penguin Classics, 1961, p. 61.
17. In *Myths, Models and Paradigms*, S.C.M., 1974.
18. For this and numerous other examples, see *Nuffield Chemistry: The Basic Course, Stages I and II*, Longmans/Penguin Books, 1966.

19. See Thomas Kuhn, *The Structure of Scientific Revolutions* (2nd edn), University of Chicago Press, 1970.
20. J. S. Bruner, and Leo Postman, 'On the Perception of Incongruity: A Paradigm', *Journal of Personality*, Vol. 18, 1949, pp. 206–23.
21. Kuhn, op. cit., p. 63.
22. Quoted in Ludovico Geymonat, *Galileo Galilei: A Biography and Inquiry into his Philosophy of Science*, New York: McGraw-Hill, 1965.
23. In the preface to *Phenomenology of Perception*, Routledge & Kegan Paul, 1962 p. viii.
24. See, Alister C. Hardy, *The Spiritual Nature of Man*, Clarendon Press, 1979. Dr Geoffrey Ahem of A.A.R.C. is currently developing a computer assisted method of classifying religious experience accounts.

Chapter fourteen: **The Resilience of Religious Experience**

1. In *Images and Symbols*, Sheed & Ward, 1969, p. 19.
2. See for example *The Biology of God*, Jonathan Cape, 1975.
3. Roy A. Rappaport, 'The Sacred in Human Evolution', *Annual Review of Ecology and Systematics*, Vol. 2, 1971, 23–44.
4. In *Patterns of Culture*, Routledge & Kegan Paul, 1935, p. 15.
5. In *Love and Hate*, Methuen, 1971, p. 13.
6. *The Elementary Forms of the Religious Life* (tr. J. W. Swain), Allen & Unwin, 1915, p. 416.
7. Mary Midgley has discussed the relationship between biology and culture very interestingly in her fine book, *Beast and Man* (Harvester Press, Hassocks, Sussex, 1979). I first saw the quotations from Benedict's *Patterns of Culture* and Eibl-Eibesfeldt's *Love and Hate* reproduced there.
8. See, for example, William N. Dember and Joel S. Warm, *Psychology of Perception*, New York: Holt, Rinehart & Winston, 1979, Chapter 5.
9. See *Religions, Values and Peak Experiences*, Columbus: Ohio State University Press, 1964.
10. ibid.
11. See *Man in Technological Society: Stress, Adaptation and Tolerance Limits*, Reports from the Psychological Laboratories, University of Stockholm, Supplement No. 26, 1974.
12. ibid.
13. In *Islam Observed*, Yale University Press, 1968.
14. See reports published by Keston College in Kent, which specializes in the study of religious communities in the Soviet Union and Eastern Europe.
15. V. R. Bukin, 'Religious Emotions and the Place They Hold in

Believers' Consciousness', *Voprosii Filosofii*, Vol. 23 (11), 1969, pp. 57–66.

16. ibid.

17. See Christopher Binns, 'The Changing Face of Power: Revolution and Accommodation in the Development of the Soviet Ceremonial System II', *Man*, Vol. 15 (1), 1980, pp. 170–87.

18. *Ecstasy*, Cresset Press, 1961.

19. In *The Religious Consciousness: A Psychological Study*, New York: Macmillan, 1923.

20. From the *Bhagavad Gita*, Chapter 6, v. 10.

21. Matthew vi, 6.

22. For a readable discussion of this see, Peter Berger, *A Rumour of Angels*, Allen Lane, 1961.

23. S. Asch, 'Studies of Independence and Conformity: A Minority Against a Unanimous Majority', *Psychological Monographs*, Vol. 70 (9), 1956 (Whole No. 416).

24. New York: Schocken Books, 1965.

25. In 'The Devil and the Pornography of the Modern Mind', reprinted in Peter Berger, *Facing up to Modernity*, Penguin Books, 1979.

Epilogue: **The Future of Religious Experience**

1. In *The Will to Believe*, Longmans Green, 1904, p. 28.

2. From Vincent Buckley, *Poetry and the Sacred*, Chatto & Windus, 1968.

3. In *Making Life at Work Have Quality*, Tavistock Institute of Human Relations, Document No. 2T281, 1979.

References Cited

Abbott, Walter M. (ed.), *The Documents of Vatican II*, Geoffrey Chapman, 1966.

Acquaviva, S. S., *The Decline of the Sacred in Industrial Society*, Oxford: Blackwell, 1979.

Adorno, T. W., et al., *The Authoritarian Personality*, New York: Harper, 1950.

Alexander, Franz, 'Buddhistic Training as an Artificial Catatonia', *Psychoanalysis*, Vol. 19, 1931, pp. 129–45.

Allen, R. O., and Spilka, B., 'Committed and Consensual Religion: A Specification of Religion – Prejudice Relationships', *Journal for the Scientific Study of Religion*, Vol. 6, 1967, pp. 191–206.

American Institute of Public Opinion, *Religion in America – The Gallup Opinion Index 1977–78*, Princeton, 1978.

Andrews, Allen, *The Life of L. S. Lowry 1887–1976*, Jupiter Books, 1977.

Anonymous, *The Cloud of Unknowing* (tr. Clifton Wolters), Penguin Books, 1961.

Argyle, Michael, and Beit-Hallahmi, Benjamin, *The Social Psychology of Religion*, Routledge & Kegan Paul, 1975.

Aron, Raymond, *Main Currents of Sociological Thought* (2 vols.), Penguin Books, 1965.

Asch, Solomon, 'Studies of Independence and Conformity: A Minority Against a Unanimous Majority', *Psychological Monographs*, Vol. 70 (9), 1956 (Whole No. 416).

Back, Kurt, and Bourque, Linda Brookover, 'Can Feelings be Enumerated?' *Behavioral Science*, Vol. 15, 1970, pp. 487–96.

Bakan, David, *Sigmund Freud and the Jewish Mystical Tradition*, New York, Schocken Books, 1965.

Baker, Samuel, 'The Races of the Nile Basin', *Transactions of the Ethnological Society of London*, Vol. 5, 1867, pp. 228–39.
   The Albert Nyanza, Great Basin of the Nile and Explorations of the Nile Sources, Macmillan, 1885.

Bannister, D. (ed.), *Issues and Approaches in the Psychological Therapies*, Wiley: 1975.

Barbour, Ian, *Myths, Models and Paradigms*, S.C.M., 1974.

Barker, Eileen, *The Making of a Moonie*, Basil Blackwell, 1984.

Barthes, Roland, *Mythologies*, Paladin Books, 1973.

Batson, Daniel and Raynor-Prince, Lynn, 'Religious Orientation and Complexity of Thought about Existential Concerns', *Journal for the Scientific Study of Religion*, Vol. 22 (1), 1983, pp. 38–50.

Batson, Daniel and Ventis, W. Larry, *The Religious Experience: a Social-Psychological Perspective*, New York, Oxford University Press, 1982.

Beardsworth, Timothy, *A Sense of Presence*, Religious Experience Research Unit, Manchester College, Oxford, 1977.

Benedict, Ruth, *Patterns of Culture*, Routledge & Kegan Paul, 1935.

Berger, Peter, *A Rumour of Angels*, Allen Lane, 1969.

Berger, Peter, *Facing Up to Modernity*, Penguin Books, 1979.

Berkman, Paul L., 'Measurement of Mental Health in a General Population Survey' *American Journal of Epidemiology*, Vol. 94 (2), 1971, pp. 105–11.

Bertalanffy, Ludwig Von, *General System Theory*, Allen Lane, 1971.

Binns, Christopher, 'The Changing Face of Power: Revolution and Accommodation in the Development of the Soviet Ceremonial System II', *Man*, Vol. 15 (1), 1980, pp. 170–87.

Blake, William, *The Poetry and Prose of William Blake* (ed. Geoffrey Keynes), Nonesuch Press, 1927.

Bleeker, C. J., and Widengren, G. (eds.), *Historia Religionum: Handbook for the History of Religions*, Vol. 1, Leiden: Brill, 1969.

Bocock, Robert, *Ritual in Industrial Society*, Allen & Unwin, 1974.

Bouquet, A. C., 'Soter: A consideration of some fundamentals of Christian Theology', *The Modern Churchman*, Vol. 12, 1969, pp. 267–279.

Bradburn, Norman M., *The Structure of Psychological Wellbeing*, Chicago: Aldine Press, 1969.

Breward, I. (ed.), *The Work of William Perkins*, The Sutton Courtenay Press, 1970.

Brown, Roger, *Social Psychology*, Collier-Macmillan, 1965.

Bruner, J. S., and Postman, Leo, 'On the Perception of Incongruity: A Paradigm', *Journal of Personality*. Vol. 18, 1949, pp. 206–23.

Buckley, Vincent, *Poetry and the Sacred*, Chatto & Windus, 1968.

Bukin, V. R., 'Religious Emotions and the Place They Hold in Believers' Consciousness', *Voprosii Filosofii*, Vol. 23 (11), 1969, pp. 57–66.

Burckhardt, Titus, *Siena, City of the Virgin*, Oxford University Press, 1960.

Butler, Dom Cuthbert, *The Vatican Council 1869–70*, Fontana, 1962.

Calvin, John, *Institutes of the Christian Religion*, 2 Vols., (edited by John T. McNeill, translated by Ford Lewis Battles), S.C.M., 1960, p. 79.

Carmichael, Alexander, *Carmina Gadelica – Hymns and Invocations*, Oliver & Boyd (Vols. 1–5); Scottish Academic Press (Vol. 6), 1900–1971.

Carpenter, Frederic I., *Ralph Waldo Emerson; representative selections, with introduction, bibliography and notes*, American Book Co., New York, 1934.

Cavanagh, P., *Collected Poems*, New York: Devin-Adair, 1964.

Chadwick, Owen, *The Secularisation of the European Mind in the Nineteenth Century*, Cambridge University Press, 1975.

Cohen, J. M., and Phipps, J.-F., *The Common Experience*, Rider, 1979.

Comblin, José, *The Church and the National Security State*, New York: Orbis Books, 1979.

Comstock, G. W., 'Fatal Arteriosclerotic Heart Disease, Water Hardness at Home, and Socio-economic Characteristics', *American Journal of Epidemiology*, Vol. 94 (1), 1971, pp. 1–10.

Comstock, G. W., and Partridge, K. B., 'Church Attendance and Health', *Journal of Chronic Diseases*, Vol. 25, 1972, pp. 665–72.

Comte, Auguste, *A Discourse on the Positive Spirit* (tr. Edward Spencer Beesley), William Reeves, 1903.

Cortes, Hernan, *Dispatches from the New World* (texts ed. Harry M. Rosen), New York: Grossett & Dunlap, 1962.

Creelan, Paul, 'Religion, Language and Sexuality in J. B. Watson', *Journal of Humanistic Psychology*, Vol. 15 (4), 1975, pp. 55–78.

Cronbach, Abraham, 'The Psychology of Religion: A Bibliographical Survey', *Psychological Bulletin*, Vol. 30 (5), 1933, pp. 327–61.

Curnock, N. (ed.), *The Journal of the Rev. John Wesley, A.M.*, 8 Vols., London: Robert Culley, 1909.

Currie, Robert, *Methodism Divided*, Faber & Faber, 1968.

Currie, Robert, Gilbert, Alan, and Horsley, Lee, *Churches and Churchgoers: Patterns of Church Growth in the British Isles since 1700*, Clarendon Press, 1978.

Darwin, Charles, *The Origin of Species*, John Murray, 1859.

Deikman, Arthur J., 'Bimodal Consciousness', *Archives of General Psychiatry*, Vol. 25, 1971, pp. 481–9.

Dember, William N., and Warm, Joel S., *Psychology of Perception*, New York: Holt, Rinehart & Winston, 1979.

Diaz, Bernal, *The Conquest of New Spain* (tr. J. M. Cohen), Penguin Books, 1963.

Donajgrodski, A. P. (ed.), *Social Control in Nineteenth Century Britain*, Croom Helm, 1977.

Dostoyevsky, Fyodor, *The Idiot* (tr. David Magarshack), Penguin Books, 1955.

Douglas, Mary, 'Heathen Darkness, Modern Piety', *New Society*, 12 March 1970.
Natural Symbols, Penguin Books, 1973.
Drury, M. O'Connor, *The Danger of Words*, Routledge & Kegan Paul, 1973.
Dunn, James D. G., *Jesus and the Spirit*, S.C.M., 1975.
Durkeim, Émile, *The Elementary Forms of the Religious Life* (tr. J. W. Swain), Allen & Unwin, 1915.
Edwards, Jonathan, *Treatise Concerning Religious Affections* (Ed. John E. Smith), Yale University Press, 1959.
Eibl-Eibesfeldt, Irenäus, *Love and Hate*, Methuen, 1971.
Eliade, Mircea, *Myth and Reality*, New York: Harper & Row, 1963.
From Primitives to Zen, Collins, 1967.
Images and Symbols, Sheed & Ward, 1969.
A History of Religious Ideas, Vol. 1, *From the Stone Age to the Eleusinian Mysteries*, University of Chicago Press, 1978.
Erb, Peter, *Pietists: Selected Writings*, (edited with an introduction by Peter C. Erb; preface by F. Ernest Stoeffler), S.P.C.K., (Classics of Western Spirituality Series), 1983.
Evans-Pritchard, E. E., *Nuer Religion*, Oxford University Press, 1956.
Theories of Primitive Religion, Oxford University Press, 1965.
The Sociology of Comte: An Appreciation, Manchester University Press, 1970.
Every, George, *The Mass*, Dublin: Gill & Macmillan, 1978.
Fenn, Richard, *A Theory of Secularisation*, Society for the Scientific Study of Religion Monographs, No. 1, 1978.
Fenwick, P. B. C., et al., 'Metabolic and EEG Changes During Transcendental Meditation: An Explanation', *Biological Psychology*, Vol. 5, 1977, pp. 101–18.
Ferguson, John, *The Religions of the Roman Empire*, Thames & Hudson, 1970.
Feuerbach, Ludwig, *The Essence of Christianity* (tr. George Eliot, and with an introduction by Karl Barth), New York: Harper Torchbooks, 1957.
Lectures on the Essence of Religion (tr. Ralph Manheim) New York: Harper & Row, 1967.
Fletcher, Ronald, *Auguste Comte and the Making of Sociology* (Auguste Comte Memorial Trust Lecture 7), Athlone Press, 1966.
Frankenhaeuser, Marianne, *Man in Technological Society: Stress, Adaptation and Tolerance Limits*, Reports from the Psychological Laboratories, University of Stockholm, Supplement No. 26, 1974.
Frazer, J. G., *The Golden Bough* (abridged edition), Macmillan, 1922.
French, R. M., *The Way of a Pilgrim*, S.P.C.K., 1972.

Freud, Sigmund, 'Obsessive Actions and Religious Practices', reprinted in *Standard Edition*, Vol. IX, p. 115, Hogarth Press, 1959.
'A Religious Experience', reprinted in *Standard Edition*, Vol. XXI, p. 169, Hogarth Press, 1961.
Group Psychology, Hogarth Press, 1921.
The Future of an Illusion, Hogarth Press, 1928.
Civilisation and its Discontents, Hogarth Press, 1930.
Totem and Taboo, Routledge and Kegan Paul, 1950.
Geertz, Clifford, *Islam Observed*, Yale University Press, 1968.
The Interpretation of Cultures, New York: Basic Books, 1973.
Gerth, H. H., and Mills, C. Wright (eds.), *From Max Weber*, Routledge & Kegan Paul, 1948.
Geymonat, Ludovico, *Galileo Galilei: A Biography and Inquiry into his Philosophy of Science*, New York: McGraw-Hill, 1965.
Giddens, Anthony, *Émile Durkheim – Selected Writings*, Cambridge University Press, 1972.
Giedion, S., *The Beginnings of Art*, New York: Pantheon Books, 1962.
Glock, Charles Y., and Stark, Rodney, *Religion and Society in Tension*, Chicago: Rand McNally, 1965.
Glock, Charles Y. (ed.), *Religion in Sociological Perspective*, Belmont: Wadsworth Publishing Co., 1973.
Goddard, H. C., *Studies in New England Transcendentalism*, New York: Columbia University Press, 1908.
Goldenweiser, A. A., review of 'The Elementary Forms of the Religious Life', *American Anthropologist*, Vol. 17, 1915, pp. 719–35.
Goldman, Ronald, *Religious Thinking from Childhood to Adolescence*. Routledge & Kegan Paul, 1964.
Gollwitzer, Helmut, *The Christian Faith and the Marxist Criticism of Religion*, St Andrew Press, 1970.
Gombrich, R. F., *Precept and Practice: Traditional Buddhism in the Rural Highlands of Ceylon*, Clarendon Press, 1971.
Graham, Dom Aelred, *The End of Religion*, New York: Harcourt, Brace Jovanovich, 1971.
Greeley, Andrew M., *Unsecular Man*, New York: Schocken Books, 1972.
The Sociology of the Paranormal: A Reconnaissance, Sage Research Papers in the Social Sciences (Studies in Religion and Ethnicity Series No. 90–023), Beverley Hills/London: Sage Publications, 1975.
Green, Roger Lancelyn, *Andrew Lang*, Edmund Ward, 1946.
Gurwitsch, Aron, *Phenomenology and the Theory of Science*, Evanston: North-Western University Press, 1974.
Gutierrez, Gustavo, *A Theology of Liberation*, S.C.M., 1974.
Hall, G. Stanley, *Adolescence: Its Psychology*, New York: Appleton, 1904.

Hallowell, A. I., 'Bear Ceremonialism in the Northern Hemisphere', *American Anthropologist*, Vol. 28, 1926, pp. 1–175.

Hardy, Alister C., *The Divine Flame*, Collins 1966 (re-issued by the Religious Experience Research Unit, Manchester College, Oxford, 1978).

The Biology of God, Jonathan Cape, 1975.

The Spiritual Nature of Man, Clarendon Press, 1979.

Darwin and the Spirit of Man, Collins, 1984.

Harris, Horton, *David Friedrich Strauss and his Theology*, Cambridge University Press, 1973.

Harris, Marvin, *Cannibals and Kings: The Origins of Cultures*, Fontana, 1978.

Hay, David, 'Religious Experience Amongst a Group of Post-graduate Students: A Qualitative Study', *Journal for the Scientific Study of Religion*, Vol. 18 (2), 1979, pp. 164–82.

'The Taboo on Religion', *The Clergy Review*, Vol. 69, No. 5, 1984, pp. 157–162.

'Religious Experience and its Induction', in, *Recent Advances in the Psychology of Religion*, edited by L. B. Brown, Oxford, Pergamon Press, 1985.

'The Varieties of Religious Experience by William James: A Review', *Modern Churchman*, Vol. 27 (2), 1985, pp. 45–49.

'Religious Experience as Liberation', *Faith and Freedom*, Vol. 39 (3), 1986, pp. 137–150.

Hay, David, and Heald, Gordon, 'Religion is good for you', *New Society* Vol. 80, 17 April, 1987.

Hay, David, and Morisy, Ann, 'Reports on Ecstatic, Paranormal or Religious Experience in Great Britain and the United States – A Comparison of Trends', *Journal for the Scientific Study of Religion*, Vol. 17 (3); 1978, pp. 255–68.

'Secular Society/Religious Meanings: a Contemporary Paradox', *Review of Religious Research*, Vol. 26 (3), 1985, pp. 213–227.

Hayward, John (ed.), *The Penguin Book of English Verse*, Penguin Books, 1956.

Hodgson, P. C. (ed.), *The Life of Jesus Critically Examined*, S.C.M., 1972.

Hood, Ralph, 'The Construction and Preliminary Validation of a Measure of Reported Religious Experience', *Journal for the Scientific Study of Religion*, Vol. 14, 1975, pp. 29–41.

'Conceptual Criticisms of Regressive Explanations of Mysticism', *Review of Religious Research*, Vol. 17, 1976, pp. 179–88.

'The Conceptualisation of Religious Purity in Allport's Typology', *Journal for the Scientific Study of Religion*, Vol. 24 (4), 1985, pp. 413–417.

Hornsby-Smith, Michael P., and Lee, Raymond M., *Roman Catholic Opinion*, University of Surrey, 1979.
Huxley, Aldous, *The Perennial Philosophy*, Chatto & Windus, 1946.
Inglis, K. S., *Churches and the Working Classes in Victorian England*, Routledge & Kegan Paul, 1963.
Jahoda, Gustav, *The Psychology of Superstition*, Penguin Books, 1970.
James, William, *The Will to Believe*, Longmans, Green, 1904.
    The Varieties of Religious Experience, Fontana, 1960; Penguin American Library, 1982.
    Collected Letters, 2 Vols., Atlantic Monthly Press, Boston, 1920.
Jefferies, Richard, *The Story of My Heart*, Eyre & Spottiswoode, 1949.
John of the Cross, St, *Poems* (tr. Roy Campbell), Harvill Press, 1951.
    The Collected Works (tr. Kieran Kavanaugh, O.C.D., and Otilio Rodriguez O.C.D.), Washington D.C.: Institute of Carmelite Studies, 1973.
Johnston, William, *Silent Music*, Fontana, 1976.
Jones, Ernest, *The Life and Works of Sigmund Freud* (3 vols.), Hogarth Press, 1959.
Jungmann, J. A., *The Mass of the Roman Rite: Its Origins and Development* (2 vols.), New York: Benziger Brothers, 1951, 1955.
Kadowaki, J. K., *Zen and the Bible*, Routledge & Kegan Paul, 1980.
Kahoe, Richard D., 'The Development of Intrinsic and Extrinsic Religious Orientations', *Journal for the Scientific Study of Religion*, Vol. 24 (4), 1985, pp. 408–412.
Kaiser, Robert, *Inside the Council*, Burns Oates, 1963.
Kapleau, Philip, *The Three Pillars of Zen*, Boston: Beacon Press, 1967.
Katz, Steven T. (ed.), *Mysticism and Philosophical Analysis*, New York: Oxford University Press, 1978.
King, Richard, 'William James and Max Weber' (unpublished paper).
Kinsey, Alfred C., Pomeroy, W. B., and Martin, C. E. *Sexual Behaviour in the Human Male*, Philadelphia: W. B. Saunders, 1948.
Krummacher, Friedrich Wilhelm, *An Autobiography*, T. & T. Clark, 1869.
Kuhn, Thomas, *The Structure of Scientific Revolutions* (2nd edn) University of Chicago Press, 1970.
Küng, Hans, *Infallible?*, Fontana, 1972.
Kushner, A. W., 'Two Cases of Auto-Castration due to Religious Delusions', *British Journal of Medical Psychology*, Vol. 40, 1967, pp. 293–8.
Ladurie, Emmanuel Le Roy, *Montaillou: Cathars and Catholics in a French Village 1294–1324*, Scolar Press, 1978; Penguin Books, 1980.

Laing, R. D., and Esterson, A., *Sanity, Madness and the Family*, Vol. 1
    Families of Schizophrenics, Tavistock, 1964.
Lang, Andrew, *The Making of Religion*, Longmans, Green, 1898.
Lanternari, V., *The Religions of the Oppressed: A Study of Modern
    Messianic Cults*, New York, Knopf, 1963.
Las Casas, Bartolomé de, *The Tears of the Indians* (tr. J. Phillips) New
    York: Oriole Chapbooks, 18, 1972.
Laski, Marghanita, *Ecstasy*, Cresset Press, 1961.
Lawrence, W. Gordon, *Making Life at Work Have Quality*, Tavistock
    Institute of Human Relations, Document No. 2 T281, 1979.
Lenin, V. I., *On Religion*, Moscow: Progress Publishers, 1969.
Levin, Jeffrey S., and Markides, Kyriakos S., 'Religious Attendance
    and Subjective Health', *Journal for the Scientific Study of Religion*,
    Vol. 25 (1), 1986, pp. 31–39.
Lewis, David, 'All in good faith', *Nursing Times*, March 18–24, 1987,
    pp. 40–43.
León-Portilla, Miguel (ed.), *The Broken Spears*, Constable, 1962.
Leroi-Gourhan, André, *Les Religions de la préhistoire: Paléolithique*,
    Paris: Presses Universitaires de France, 1964.
Leroi-Gourhan, Arlette, 'The Flowers Found with Shanidar IV, a
    Neanderthal Burial in Iraq', *Science*, Vol. 190, 1975, pp. 562–4.
Leuba, James H., 'Recent French Books on Religious Mysticism'
    Psychological Bulletin, Vol. 23, 1926, p. 723.
    The Psychology of Religious Mysticism, Kegan Paul, Trench, Trubner,
    1929.
Lévi-Strauss, Claude, *Totemism* (tr. Rodney Needham, with an intro-
    duction by Roger Poole), Penguin Books, 1969.
Lewis, I. M., *Ecstatic Religion*, Penguin Books, 1971.
Lienhardt, Godfrey, *Divinity and Experience. The Religion of the Dinka*,
    Clarendon Press, 1961.
Lindsay, Peter H., and Norman, Donald A., *Human Information Pro-
    cessing*, New York: Academic Press, 1977.
Ling, Trevor, *A History of Religion East and West*, Macmillan, 1968.
Lubac, Henri de, *The Drama of Atheist Humanism*, Sheed & Ward,
    1949.
Lukes, Steven, *Émile Durkheim: His Life and Work*, Allen Lane, 1973.
McLeod, Hugh, *Class and Religion in the Late Victorian City*, Croom
    Helm, 1974.
Mair, Lucy, *An Introduction to Social Anthropology*, Clarenden Press,
    1965.
Malinowski, Bronislaw, *Magic, Science and Religion and Other Essays*,
    Souvenir Press, 1974.
Maréchal, Joseph, *Studies in the Psychology of the Mystics*, Burns Oates
    & Washbourne, 1927.

Maringer, Johannes, *The Gods of Prehistoric Man*, Weidenfeld & Nicolson, 1960.

Martin, David, *The Religious and the Secular*, Routledge & Kegan Paul, 1969.

A General Theory of Secularisation, Oxford: Blackwell, 1978.

Marx, K., and Engels, F., *On Religion*, Moscow: Progress Publishers, 1957.

Collected Works, Vol. II, Lawrence & Wishart, 1975.

Maslow, Abraham, *Religions, Values and Peak Experiences*, Columbus: Ohio State University Press, 1964.

Max-Müller, F., *Lectures on the Origin and Growth of Religion*, Longmans, Green, 1878.

Merleau-Ponty, Maurice, *Phenomenology of Perception*, Routledge & Kegan Paul, 1962.

Merton, Thomas, *The Sign of Jonas*, Hollis & Carter, 1953.

Michie, James, *The Poems of Catullus*, Rupert Hart-Davis, 1969.

Middleton, Dorothy, *Baker of the Nile*, Falcon Press, 1949.

Midgley, Mary, *Beast and Man*, Hassocks, Sussex: Harvester Press, 1979.

Miller, Perry, 'Jonathan Edwards on the Sense of the Heart', *Harvard Theological Review*, Vol. 41, pp. 122–145.

Munro, N. G., *Ainu Creed and Cult*, New York: Columbia University Press, 1963.

Nuffield Chemistry, *The Basic Course, Stages I and II*, Longmans/Penguin Books, 1966.

Osipov, G. V. (ed.), *Town, Country and People*, Tavistock, 1969.

Otto, Rudolf, *The Idea of the Holy* (tr. John W. Harvey) Oxford University Press (2nd edn), 1950.

Pannikar, Raymond, *The Unknown Christ of Hinduism*, Darton, Longman & Todd, 1965.

Paul, Leslie, *A Church by Daylight*, Geoffrey Chapman, 1973.

Perry, Ralph Barton, *The Thought and Character of William James*, 2 vols, Little, Brown and Co., Boston, 1935.

Pickering, W. S. F., *Durkheim on Religion*, Routledge & Kegan Paul, 1975.

Piggott, Stuart, *The Druids*, Thames & Hudson, 1968.

Plamenatz, John, *Karl Marx's Philosophy of Man*, Oxford, 1975.

Poulain, Auguste, *The Graces of Interior Prayer*, Kegan Paul, Trench, Trubner, 1912.

Powell, David, E., *Anti-Religious Propaganda in the Soviet Union: A Study of Mass Persuasion*, Cambridge, Massachusetts: M.I.T. Press, 1975.

Pratt, J. B., *The Religious Consciousness: A Psychological Study*, New York: Macmillan, 1923.

250 *References Cited*

Princeton Religion Research Center, *The Unchurched American*, Princeton Religion Research Center and the Gallup Organization, 1978.

Proudfoot, Wayne and Shaver, Phillip, 'Attribution Theory and the Psychology of Religion', *Journal for the Scientific Study of Religion*, Vol. 14 (4), 1975, pp. 317–30.

Raine, Kathleen, *The Collected Poems of Kathleen Raine*, Hamish Hamilton, 1965.

Rappaport, Roy A., 'The Sacred in Human Evolution', *Annual Review of Ecology and Systematics*, Vol. 2, 1971, 23–44.

Reik, Theodor, *From Thirty Years with Freud*, New York: Farrar & Rinehart, 1940.

Religious Tract Society, *The Child's Companion and Juvenile Instructor*, London, 1854.

Riley, Carrol L., et al., *Man Across the Sea: Problems of Pre-Columbian Contacts*, Austin, University of Texas Press, 1971.

Robertson, Roland, *The Sociological Interpretation of Religion*, Oxford: Blackwells, 1969.

Robinson, Edward, *The Original Vision*, Religious Experience Research Unit, Manchester College, Oxford, 1977.
    Living the Questions, Religious Experience Research Unit, Manchester College, Oxford, 1978.

Ross, Dorothy, *G. Stanley Hall: The Psychologist as Prophet*, University of Chicago Press, 1972.

Roszak, Theodore, *The Making of a Counterculture*, Faber & Faber, 1970.

Rynne, Xavier, *Letters from Vatican City; The Second Session; The Third Session; The Fourth Session*, Faber & Faber, 1963–6.

Sapp, Gary L., and Jones, Logan, 'Religious Orientation and Moral Judgement', *Journal for the Scientific Study of Religion*, Vol. 25 (2), 1986, pp. 208–214.

Schachter, S., and Singer, J. E., 'Cognitive, Social and Psychological Determinants of Emotional State', *Psychological Review*, Vol. 69, 1962, pp. 379–99.

Schleiermacher, Friedrich, *On Religion: Speeches to its Cultured Despisers* (tr. J. Oman), New York: Harper & Row, 1958.

Schmidt, Wilhelm, *The Origin and Growth of Religion* (tr. H. J. Rose), Methuen, 1931.

Sejourné, Laurette, *Burning Water: Thought and Religion in Ancient Mexico*, Thames & Hudson, 1956.

Sekida, Katsuki, *Zen Training: Methods and Philosophy*, New York: Weatherhill, 1975.

Seligman, C. G., *Races of Africa*, Oxford University Press, 3rd edn, 1957.

Smart, Ninian, *The Religious Experience of Mankind*, Fontana, 1971.
  The Science of Religion and the Sociology of Knowledge, Princeton University Press, 1973.
Smith, Huston, 'Do Drugs Have Religious Import?', *Journal of Philosophy*, Vol. 61 (18) 1964, 517–30.
Solecki, Ralph, *Shanidar. The First Flower People*, New York: Knopf, 1971.
Spilka, Bernard, ' "The Compleat Person": Some Theoretical Views and Research Findings for a Theological Psychology of Religion', *Journal of Psychology and Theology*, Vol. 4 (1), 1976, pp. 15–24.
Spilka, Bernard, Cojetin, Brian and McIntosh, Danny, 'Forms and Measures of Personal Faith: Questions, Correlates and Distinctions', *Journal for the Scientific Study of Religion*, Vol. 24 (4), 1985, pp. 427–442.
Spilka, Bernard, Shaver, Phillip and Kirkpatrick, Lee A., 'A General Attribution Theory for the Psychology of Religion', *Journal for the Scientific Study of Religion*, Vol. 24 (1), 1985, pp. 1–19.
Staal, Frits, *Exploring Mysticism*, Penguin Books, 1975.
Stace, W. T., *Mysticism and Philosophy*, Philadelphia: J. B. Lippincott, 1960.
Starbuck, E. D., *The Psychology of Religion*, New York: Walter Scott, 1899.
Stolz, Anselm, *The Doctrine of Spiritual Perfection*, St. Louis: B. Herder Book Co., 1938.
Strauss, David Friedrich, *The Life of Jesus Critically Examined* (ed. P. C. Hodgson), S.C.M., 1972.
Strommen, Merton P. (ed.), *Research on Religious Development: A Comprehensive Handbook*, New York: Hawthorn Books Inc., 1971.
Strout, Cushing, 'The Pluralistic Identity of William James', *American Quarterly*, Vol. 23, 1971, pp. 135–152.
Suzuki, D. T., *Outlines of Mahayana Buddhism*, New York: Schocken Books, 1963.
Teresa of Avila, St, *Complete Works of St Teresa* (tr. and ed. E. Allison Peers), 3 vols., Sheed & Ward, 1975.
Thomas, Edward, *The Collected Poems of Edward Thomas* (ed. and introduced by R. George Thomas), Clarendon Press, 1978.
Thomas, Keith, *Religion and the Decline of Magic*, Penguin Books, 1973.
Thurstone, L. L., and Chave, E. J., *The Measurement of Attitude*, University of Chicago Press, 1929.
Towler, Robert, *Homo Religiosus*, Constable, 1974.
Tracy, Patricia J., *Jonathan Edwards, Pastor: Religion and Society in Eighteenth Century Northampton*, New York: Hill and Wang, 1980.

Turner, Harold, W., *Rudolf Otto: The Idea of the Holy* (with 'Introduction to the Man' by Peter R. McKenzie), Department of Religious Studies, Aberdeen University, 1974.

Tylor, Edward, *Primitive Culture* (2 vols.), John Murray, 1871.

Unger, Johan, *On Religious Experience: A Psychological Study*, Stockholm: Almquist & Wiksell, 1976.

Vermaseren, Maarten J., *Cybele and Attis: The Myth and the Cult*, Thames & Hudson, 1977.

Wach, Joachim, *The Comparative Study of Religions*, New York: Columbia University Press, 1958.

Sociology of Religion, University of Chicago Press, 1962.

Walters, O. S., 'Religion and Psychopathology', *Comprehensive Psychiatry*, Vol. 101 (5), 1964, pp. 24–35.

Washburn, S. L., and Jay, P. C. (eds.), *Perspectives on Human Evolution*, Holt, Rinehart & Winston, 1968.

Watson, J. B., *Behaviorism* (2nd edn) Kegan Paul, Trench, Trubner, 1931.

Watson, P. J., Morris, Ronald, J., Foster, James E. and Hood, Ralph W., 'Religiosity and Social Desirability', *Journal for the Scientific Study of Religion*, Vol. 25 (2), 1986, pp. 215–232.

Watts, Alan, *The Way of Zen*, Penguin Books, 1962.

Watts, Michael, *The Dissenters*, Vol. I, Oxford, Clarendon Press, 1978.

Wauchope, Robert, *Lost Tribes and Sunken Continents*, University of Chicago Press, 1962.

Weber, Max, *The Protestant Ethic and the Spirit of Capitalism*, (translated by Talcott Parsons), George Allen and Unwin, 1930.

Wilson, Bryan, *Religion in Secular Society*, Watts, 1966.

Winslow, E. O. (ed.), *Jonathan Edwards: Basic Writings*, New York: New American Library, 1966.

Woolf, Stuart, *A History of Italy 1700–1860*, Methuen, 1979.

Worsley, Peter, *The Trumpet Shall Sound*, McGibbon & Kee, 1968.

Wuthnow, Robert, *Peak Experiences: Some Empirical Tests*, mimeographed publication # A161 of the Survey Research Center, University of California, Berkeley, 1976.

Yinger, J. Milton, *The Scientific Study of Religion*, Collier-Macmillan, 1970.

Opening doors to the World of books

Book Tokens

Book Tokens can be bought and exchanged at most bookshops